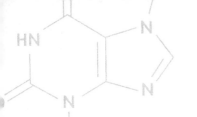

SCIENTIFICALLY
Sweet

A SCIENTIFIC AND DELICIOUS APPROACH
TO ARTISANAL BAKING

written and photographed by

Christina Marsigliese

designed by

Sylvie Gosselin

Written and photographed by Christina Marsigliese
Designed by Sylvie Gosselin
Text © 2012 Christina Marsigliese
Photography © 2012 Christina Marsigliese
www.christinamarsigliese.com

This is me. I am Christina Marsigliese. I am a Food Scientist, a self-taught baker and a never-recovering chocaholic. I was raised in the kitchen between my mom running around with her hands covered in flour and my dad yelling at me to stop making a mess. I cook every day, but mostly I like making and eating things that involve butter, sugar and insurmountable amounts of cocoa. For six years of my sweet life I focused my brain on the glorious science of food in post secondary education. I have worked in the food industry developing products that you buy at the supermarket and I have also worked as a pastry cook at some top fine dining restaurants. My passion (or obsession) with food started at a very young age as I come from a large Italian family where food has always been at the center of attention. I have learned a lot from my mom and Nonna who cooked with so much ease that I'd swear they were born with a wooden spoon in hand. My interest in baking struck me during one high school summer break while my parents were away at work all day. It gave me plenty of time to feed my curiosity (literally) and to clean up the disastrous kitchen before they got home. I dedicated my sunny days to developing my own recipe for the best fudgy brownies after following too many that turned out cakey. This curiosity led me to the University of Guelph where I achieved a Bachelors degree in Food Science. Later, I traveled to Europe where I studied in several countries to obtain my Masters degree in the same field. During this time I wrote a thesis on the sensory profile of Portuguese red wines while living in Porto. I spent most of my afternoons drinking full-bodied reds, eating Magnum ice cream bars and taking in the gorgeous landscape of the Douro Valley. Food Science involves all of the stages in the development of a food product from the farm to your table and how ingredients react under different circumstances. I've learned that any baking-related issue can be resolved or realized using a scientific eye. Hopefully I can rub my nerdy food obsession off on you. I'm sure these recipes will win you over. And hey, if something goes wrong, just think – at least you can eat your experiments.

A BIG

Thank You

Here's a big fat thank you to my very talented friend
Sylvie Gosselin who designed this gorgeous book and made
my concepts come to life on paper. She really let my style and
personality shine through subtle touches on these pages, and this
book would not be possible without her.

Also, to my best friend, true love and fellow Food Scientist – my
husband Jonathan – thank you for your immense support. You
put up with dessert for breakfast for the past year without gaining
an ounce. Not only are you extremely tolerant and kind, but you
have one heck of a metabolism. As sweet as my recipes may be,
you did your best not to sugar-coat your feedback because you
know how I can tell when you're lying. I love you babe.

I dedicate this book to my angel, my Nonno Sam, whose smile was warm enough to melt a pile of chocolate. We would sit for hours talking about food and his eyes would light up as much as mine. He had a true passion for food and was quite an artisan himself. He paid so much respect to his garden and guarded it with his life, tending to it as if it was his first born. He made his own wine and aged his own cheese – something that I will miss with longing taste buds. From his meaty, sweet heirloom beefsteak tomatoes to his stunning egg-plants, Nonno knew what good food should taste like. He supported me so much and loved that I loved to cook and bake. He also had a thing for chocolate and I like to think I get that from him. I love you Nonno.

xo

CONTENTS

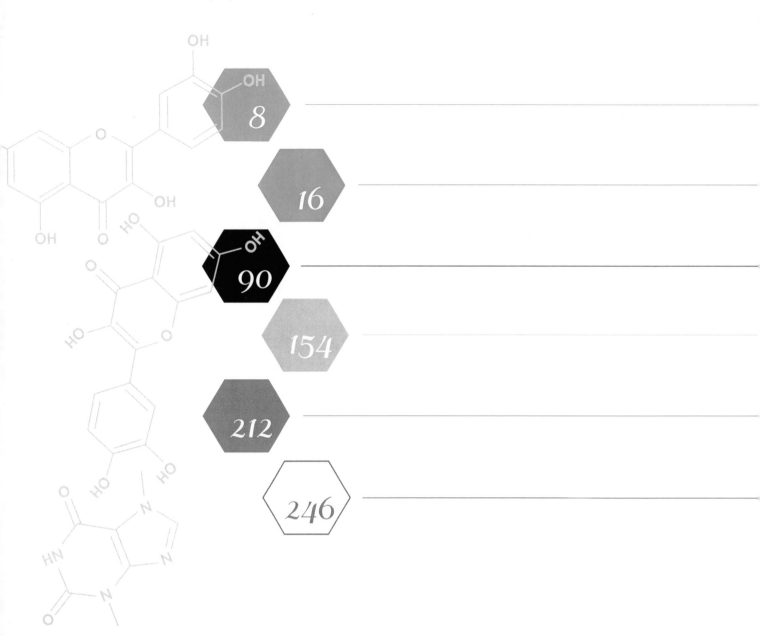

Introduction

I believe that Food Science can make you a better baker whether you're a novice or a top chef. I wrote this book not only to share food knowledge and extraordinary recipes with all of the bakaholics out there, but also because I just really love each of these recipes and I want to make sure I never forget them. I want you to be able to refer to these words any time you have a glitch in the kitchen. If you've ever wondered why that cookie recipe you got from your friend's aunt's mother has never turned out as great as hers, it might be because she didn't tell you that she refrigerates her dough before baking. Something that simple can change things dramatically.

Good food comes from good food, and it also comes from great technique. The recipes in this book use fine ingredients paired with teachings on how to mix them all together for incredible results. Growing up in an Italian family helping my mom prepare effortful three-course meals nearly every day has likely influenced the way I perceive food. Every family event, whether it was a small gathering with my grandparents or a congregation of the whole herd, there was always bountiful food and vast quantities of my Nonno's homemade vino. There was no way to escape it – not that I ever wanted to. The first thing my grandmother would ask the minute after greeting me at her door was "Are you hungry? Do you want a shnap?" (Shnap means "snack" in her wonderfully hilarious Italian accent). And don't even consider saying "No". My friends learned that fast enough, because saying "No" to an offer of food at Nonna's only meant that she would do one of two things:

a) continue asking you every three minutes until you said "Yes", or

b) take food from every storage device in the house and present it in front of you until the sight and smell of her treats caused you to give in.

If you put up too much of a fight she would pull out the extreme card and accuse you of having anorexia. Although, *she* pronounced it "annalessia" and then proceeded to tell you a story about how anorexia was named after a girl called "Anna Lessia" who died because she didn't eat enough. She stood by that story.

So, I think it was inevitable. Food, to be more specific, great food, was born into me the second I was born into my family. Some people call it an obsession and I guess I can't really disagree. I have been given the nickname of 'Food Police' (I think it sounds pretty cool). It came about because I am definitely *that* person. I'm the one who scopes out the pizza before everyone arrives to the dinner table so I can snag the best slice. You know, the one that has the perfect sauce-to-cheese ratio, the crispiest crust, just the right amount of pepperoni and the most mushrooms. Ya, that's me. I do the same thing with cakes, pies, cookies...it can get really annoying.

All of my life's events fueled me to tackle a Masters Degree in Food Science. What is Food Science? Most people immediately think of nutrition or culinary arts; however, it is so much more... Food Science satisfies the curiosity of how food works. It involves chemistry, microbiology, physics, engineering, sensory analysis and nutrition. Baking is a science in itself. It is based on a series of chemical and physical phenomena. Have you ever wondered how eggs can be whipped to such remarkable volumes, and what is the rationale for adding baking powder versus baking soda? Why does over-mixing make a tough cake, and how can I prevent caramel from turning grainy? After almost 6 years of university, I now have thorough answers to these questions. As a Food Scientist, I want to share this knowledge with you in hopes that you will feel empowered and 100% ready to get your bake on.

Baking is very technical and not as easy-going as cooking mainly since baked goods are defined by their texture almost more than their flavour. Most recipes need to be followed with precision because slight modifications can have major influences on texture. One must also grasp the concepts behind different mixing techniques since each step in a recipe has a purpose and serves to aerate, emulsify, homogenize or stabilize.

Baking requires patience and attention. Most people I encounter who say that they "can't bake" or that "nothing ever turns out" later reveal that they never really follow the directions properly. Hmm... Why not? I bet if more people were aware of the importance of certain steps and what would happen if they skipped that step then perhaps they would be less inclined to do so. To have courage to bake successfully means to appreciate the purpose for different instructions in a recipe so that you are less likely to disregard them. The recipes in this book describe the methods in detail to simply outline the functions of critical steps. This keeps you informed so that you understand the necessity behind the directions. After mastering a recipe, you can go back and make it your own because you will learn what can and can't be changed without sacrificing quality.

I am super proud of this book because it showcases great recipes that cover all aspects of baking moods and occasions while explaining techniques and tips to help you achieve the best results. There are elegant and simple recipes that are essential for dinner parties, including a Spiked Silk Chocolate Tart, decadent Raspberry Jewel Devil's Food Cake and Fudge Almond Torte. There are wonderful holiday-inspired desserts and comfort foods, such as Pear Apple & Oat Pie, Mom's Classic Cranberry Almond Biscotti and Sticky Toffee Pudding. There are truly unique recipes, including Goat Cheese Swirl & Strawberry Brownies, Crème Brûlée Cupcakes and Mocha Truffle Hazelnut Cookies. There's a whole chapter dedicated to candy so that you can totally impress your friends by making Salted Honey Butter Caramels for their birthday parties and baby showers, give away Gingerbread Truffles at Christmas and send them Homemade Strawberry Jam in Spring.

The techniques and ingredients required to make the perfect pie crust and tart pastry are explained in detail. You will learn how slight differences in ingredient proportions and mixing styles can change the overall outcome of baked goods. For example, I've included a series of three different styles of chocolate chip cookies, including Chewy, Thick & Chunky and my classic "World Famous" original. I share a few secret ingredients that can significantly alter the texture, appearance and flavour of the cookies. Knowing this, you will be able to tailor a recipe to make a cookie that suits your own desires.

Scientifically Sweet is made with my heart and soul. It is essential for beginner bakers as it provides them with tools to get started and feel confident with step-by-step, easy-to-understand instructions. It is also a must-have for experienced bakers who are interested in learning the science behind baking and improving their technique. The elegant and unique recipes and photography in this book alone are enough to intrigue any cookbook enthusiast. Overall, I believe that the words on these pages will allow you to better interpret the backbone of a recipe and help you to become more fearless. After all, *you can bake*. I know you have it in you.

I suggest and hope that when you pick up this book, you choose the recipe that you are most comfortable with even if it happens to be the simplest one, such as my Perfectly Dark Chocolate Brownies. Having success with this recipe will encourage you to try another and this confidence will help you tackle one of the more complex recipes, such as the Dark Chocolate Truffle Cake. Make sure to read the introductory pages to wrap your head around really important things, like measuring technique and conversions, before you get started. Always read a recipe through before attempting it so that you can get your thoughts organized.

Never forget that as the old saying goes, practice truly does make perfect. So, don't give up if something doesn't turn out flawlessly. After all, there will be other chances and you *will* eat again. And believe me, I tell myself this all the time.

Equipment

THE RIGHT BAKING EQUIPMENT WILL HELP YOU TO ACHIEVE TOP RESULTS IN THE KITCHEN. It is important to always use the baking pan type and size specified in a recipe. The wrong size may cause your dessert to overflow, sink in the middle or burn around the edges. The type of material can also affect the outcome as different pans require different baking times. Generally, I recommend metal bakeware for cakes and brownies, and sometimes nonstick materials are great for cakes that require inverting for presentation. Metal conducts heat more effectively and evenly, and desserts baked in this type of bakeware require the shortest baking times. Ceramics, such as glass and stoneware, are poor conductors of heat but are excellent at retaining heat once heated. So, these dishes require longer baking times. Nevertheless, they will keep your dessert warm longer than metallic pans of comparable shape and size. I prefer to use ceramics when making fruit-based desserts such as pies, crumbles, crisps and cobblers.

Always adjust your oven rack to the center position before preheating unless otherwise specified. Most cakes, cookies and brownies are baked in the center, while pies and some tarts are baked on the bottom rack for all or part of the baking time. This directs heat to the bottom crust and sets the base.

Before you bake a single thing, run out and get yourself an oven thermometer! It is one of the most important tools for successful baking. Since all ovens vary slightly, especially older ones, a thermometer is the only way to know how accurate yours is. If you think you can't bake, think again – it might just be your wonky oven! I find that baking in a still electric oven (without convection) produces the best results in most cases.

Baking temperature varies depending on the type of product and quantity of batter or dough. Generally, if the temperature is too low during baking, the product may not rise properly or dry out by the time it is cooked through. If the temperature is too high, the product may brown too quickly, form a hard crust and have an undercooked interior with dry edges.

Cakes baked in 8 or 9-inch pans usually use 350°F, which allows for even rising and cooking without over-browning. At this temperature, the batter is able to set as air bubbles form and expand to entrap them in a network within the baked cake. At lower temperatures, the air might escape at the surface before the batter has a chance to set, resulting in a dense cake that collapses or shrinks during cooling.

PANS AND TRAYS:

- 1-, 2- and 4-quart heavy-bottomed saucepans
- rectangular (17x11x1-inch and 13x9x1-inch) rimmed metal baking sheets
- standard 12-cup metal muffin pan
- 24-cup mini metal muffin pan
- two 8-inch round metal cake pans
- two 9-inch round metal cake pans
- 8-inch round metal springform pan
- 9-inch round metal springform pan
- 8-inch round glass pie dish
- 10-inch round metal bundt pan
- 9 x 5-inch rectangular metal loaf pan
- 8 x 8-inch metal baking pan
- 8 x 8-inch glass baking dish
- six 4-inch round fluted tart pans with removable bottoms
- 8-inch round fluted metal tart pan with removable bottom
- 9-inch round fluted metal tart pan with removable bottom
- 14 x 5-inch rectangular fluted metal tart pan with removable bottom
- 3-inch round, 4-oz (½ cup) capacity ceramic ramekins

Pies normally use two different cooking temperatures. First they are baked in a hot oven between 400°F and 450°F to seal and cook the crust. This prevents the base from getting soggy and also helps to avoid leakage of fruit juices through the seams. Then, the temperature is reduced to around 350°F to cook the fruit filling evenly without burning the crust.

Most cookies bake at 350°F and are usually very slightly under-baked intentionally to produce a nice brown crust with a chewy and soft center. Brownies can be baked at slightly lower temperatures (325°F-350°F) so that they remain dense and do not dry out around the edges.

TOOLS FOR CUTTING, ROLLING, MOVING AND SCOOPING:

Round cookie cutters of various sizes ranging from 1 ½ to 4 inches are good for cutting out scones, biscuits, pastry dough and cookies.

A durable wooden rolling pin is required for rolled cookies, biscuits and pastries, such as pie and tart doughs. I prefer a French-style rolling pin which is simply a large wooden dowel without handles. It may or may not have tapered ends. To care for it, keep it well oiled (about every two months), and dry it immediately after washing with mildly soapy water.

A pastry bench scraper is useful to help lift, rotate and transfer rolled pastry and cookie dough. A large offset spatula will help to transfer cut-out cookies to baking sheets, and is also vital for frosting cakes.

I like to use an ice cream scoop for drop cookies (such as chocolate chip cookies) and cupcake batters. This provides equal portioning so that everything bakes up evenly. Melon ballers are great for scooping balls of ganache to make chocolate truffles.

TOOLS FOR MIXING:

I prefer stainless steel mixing bowls since they can withstand heat but are light enough to lift and maneuver when pouring out batters. It is important that they are heatproof since several recipes in this book will require a double boiler to melt chocolate or cook custards, which means to place the mixing bowl over a pot that contains simmering water. This provides an indirect heat source for gentle heating/cooking.

A fine mesh sieve is required to sift dry ingredients, such as flour, corn starch, baking powder, baking soda and cocoa powder. It serves to lighten or aerate the ingredients, as well

as remove lumps. I also use sieves to strain custards, curds and sauces for an extra smooth texture.

I recommend wide silicone spatulas and wooden spoons for stirring. Silicone can resist heat when you are stirring hot custard and caramel or making candy over the stove. A wide spatula is great for folding ingredients (such as whipped egg whites) into batters as it covers a large surface area and helps to prevent over-mixing. It is also necessary for making cakes and cookies by hand. The wide surface provides for efficient creaming of fat, such as butter, and sugar during the beginning stages of making batters and doughs.

TOOLS FOR DECORATING:

Piping bags and piping tips are very useful for decorating cakes and cupcakes, and they are the simplest way to make your desserts look professional. You can just as easily use a sturdy resealable plastic bag with one of the corners snipped off, but investing in piping tips will give you more control and more variety in terms of shapes, designs and sizes. A cake turntable is optional but makes frosting and decorating cakes a breeze.

PREPARING YOUR BAKEWARE:

Parchment paper is your best friend. Use this to line cookie sheets and cake pans for a perfectly non-stick surface without using extra fat. The one place where parchment paper is not useful is in bundt pans where the design of the pan is too intricate to properly fit the parchment paper.

When lining round cake pans, trace a circle onto the parchment using the cake pan as a guide and place it pencil-side-down on the base of the pan. To line the sides, cut a strip of parchment paper the length of the circumference of the pan and the width of the pan's height and then wrap it around the inner sides. For most cake recipes in this book, however, I generally line the bottom of the pan with parchment and then coat the sides lightly with butter, followed by a gentle dusting of flour. This provides a slightly abrasive surface for the cake batter to cling onto as it bakes and rises.

Silicone baking mats are great for making French macarons and other delicate cookies, such as tuiles.

Metal cooling racks are necessary for cooling everything from cookies to cakes. They allow for air circulation underneath the baked product for even and rapid cooling.

The Lingo

THERE ARE SEVERAL WAYS TO MIX INGREDIENTS TO FORM A BATTER OR DOUGH. EACH TECHNIQUE CONTRIBUTES DIFFERENTLY TO THE FINAL TEXTURE OF THE BAKED PRODUCT. UNFORTUNATELY, MANY RECIPES USE MIXING TERMS INTERCHANGEABLY, WHICH MAY LEAD TO SOME WONKY RESULTS. HERE ARE SOME DEFINITIONS TO HELP CLEAR THE AIR.

BEAT – to blend or mix vigorously until one ingredient, or a mixture of ingredients, becomes smooth and thoroughly combined. Beating is a method of mixing that can incorporate air into the ingredients and is typically executed using an electric mixer or by hand with a wooden spoon or spatula. It suggests a more vigorous form of stirring.

BLEND – to combine ingredients thoroughly, usually by stirring, so that they become one. This achieves a uniform distribution of ingredients.

BLIND BAKE – to par- or pre-bake an unfilled pastry shell. The pastry should first be pricked with a fork to allow steam to escape during baking and then covered with aluminum foil or parchment paper before filling with dried beans or baking weights to hold its shape.

CARAMELIZE – to heat sugar to high temperatures until it becomes light to dark amber in colour. Caramelization adds complexity and depth of flavour.

CREAM – to beat an ingredient or mixture of ingredients until soft, smooth and airy. Many dessert recipes often require creaming of fat and sugar; this means to aerate and soften room-temperature fat (usually butter) by beating and blending it with sugar until it is smooth, light and fluffy. The sugar crystals cut through the fat globules in the butter, introducing tiny air pocket seeds that will expand further from the leavening gases produced during baking. This technique is usually used for cookies and cakes to create a light texture and fine crumb.

CRIMP – to seal edges of two layers of dough together using fingers or tines of a fork. It is usually applied to filled pastries and pies. For pies, crimping can also be referred to as "fluting".

CUT or RUB IN – to roughly divide cold fat (butter, shortening or lard) into dry ingredients (flour) until the mixture resembles a dry, course/crumbly meal and the cold fat retains some of its solid shape. This can be done using two knives, a pastry cutter, a food processor or your fingertips, although it is important to keep all tools cold (including your fingers) and work quickly as you do not want the fat to melt. If using a food processor, one must be careful not to over-process the mixture, as the friction will create heat and result in a paste-like dough.

DOCK – to lightly pierce or prick (with a fork) to create small holes in pastry for steam to escape during baking. This helps to preserve the flat and uniform shape of the dough so that it does not puff up excessively in the center when heated.

DOT – to scatter bits, usually of butter, over the surface of food before baking. This promotes browning on the surface and is normally done to create a golden, crisp crust or topping. This is often applied to pie fillings and crumble toppings.

DOUBLE BOILER – refers to a method of cooking using indirect heat; a double boiler is used to warm or cook heat-sensitive foods such as custards, curds, delicate sauces and chocolate. A heatproof bowl or pot is set over another pot in a way that it sits partway inside the other. The bottom pot is used to hold simmering water, which gently heats the mixture in the upper pot or bowl.

DUST – to lightly and evenly sprinkle a powdered ingredient, such as flour, icing sugar or cocoa powder, over a flat working surface for rolling out pastry dough to prevent sticking or to delicately decorate the top of a food. For the latter, a fine mesh sieve is often used to gently sprinkle icing sugar or cocoa over a dessert at the end of baking as a finishing touch.

"everything in moderation, including moderation"

– Julia Child

EMULSIFY – this generally refers to combining two ingredients that do not normally combine easily (such as oil and water) until they form a smooth and homogeneous mixture. More specifically it involves fine dispersion of one liquid into another.

FOLD – to gently incorporate one ingredient (or mixture of ingredients) into another without stirring or beating. Folding usually involves the addition of one light, aerated mixture (whipped cream or beaten egg whites) to a more dense/moist base mixture (batter). A wide rubber spatula is often used to cut down through the two mixtures, sliding the spatula across the bottom of the bowl, and then turning the mixtures over one another by bringing the base mixture up from beneath the aerated one. This technique is repeated to gently combine the ingredients. It is done to retain air within the batter and create a very light product, such as sponge cake, soufflé or mousse.

KNEAD – to push, pull, fold and press dough repeatedly until it is smooth and soft. This is typically done to develop a gluten structure, which provides the elastic and chewy texture of baked products, such as bread.

SCALD – to heat a liquid, such as milk or cream, just below boiling point, when bubbles begin to form around the inner edges of the pan and steam forms at the surface.

SIFT – to aerate dry ingredients, such as flour, by passing them through a fine mesh sieve or a sifter. This is achieved by holding the sieve with the intended ingredients at a height over a bowl and tapping the side of the sieve to allow small portions of the ingredients to pass through gently. This helps to ensure a light or soft texture in the end product, and to remove lumps or foreign matter.

SOFT PEAKS – refers to foam edges (of whipped egg whites or whipped cream) that keep some shape but droop once lifted. They are somewhat wobbly before sugar is added.

STIFF PEAKS – refers to foam edges (of whipped egg whites or whipped cream) that hold their shape and have defined edges. When sugar is beaten into whipped egg whites that have reached the stiff peak stage, they are opaque, thick, and shiny or glossy.

STIR – This is the simplest of the mixing techniques as it involves combining ingredients together gently with a utensil, usually a spoon or a spatula, using a circular motion.

TEMPERING – a heating technique used to gently bring up the temperature of one, or a mixture of, cold or room temperature ingredient(s). It involves the gradual addition of a hot liquid into a cool ingredient or mixture of ingredients with constant stirring or whisking so that the two components eventually reach the same temperature and consistency. This is most commonly used to make custards, where cream or milk is scalded and then very slowly added to a mixture of eggs and sugar while whisking constantly. This prevents egg proteins from curdling once the custard is cooked further over the direct heat of the stove. Tempering can also refer to a series of heating and cooling techniques applied to melted chocolate in order for it to set with the most appealing texture and appearance.

WHIP or WHISK – Vigorous mixing of an ingredient or combination of ingredients in a way that incorporates air and creates volume, such as in whipping cream and egg whites. This method typically requires the use of a whisk or electric mixer.

Measuring Technique

Baking is not very forgiving when it comes to estimation, so having a good understanding of measuring technique will guarantee smiles. Small variances in quantities of ingredients can have a major impact on the final texture, structure and overall quality of the desired product. All of the ingredients used in baking (flour, sugar, eggs, butter, leavening agents, etc.) have key functions. So, precision is your friend here!

I feel lost without my scale sometimes. It really is my best friend when I'm baking and I've become very attached to it. Unfortunately, 'eyeballing' measurements doesn't work well when you're baking if your intention is to get good results, which I'm sure it is. A difference of just 1 tablespoon can make drastic changes in a recipe, so it's important to be as accurate as possible. I mainly use it to weigh things that are subjective and bulky, like butter, chocolate, nuts and dried fruit. When a recipe calls for ½ cup of chopped chocolate, it could vary from anywhere between 2 and 4 ounces depending on how coarsely it is chopped. You can find small inexpensive kitchen scales at any hardware store and a maximum capacity of 5 kg is plenty.

Always measure liquid ingredients in glass volumetric measuring cups. Likewise, measure dry ingredients in plastic or metal dry measuring cups. These tools are typically not interchangeable because if you use volumetric measuring cups to measure dry ingredients, such as flour, you will likely need to tap it on the counter to get a level reading. This compacts the ingredient and gives you more than what is actually called for in the recipe.

Using the "spoon and level" method is ideal for measuring dry ingredients because it gives the most accurate quantity by not compacting it. To do this, gently spoon the ingredient into the cup measure so that it is softly piled above the rim. Then, use a straight flat edge to scrape off the excess by dragging it across the top of the measuring cup and creating a level surface, letting the excess fall back into the container. The "scoop, sweep &

level" method is a quicker way to measure but tends to over-estimate. This is done by drawing your measuring cup through the ingredient to gather a heaped amount and then leveling off the surface with a straight edge. The process of "sweeping" when you gather a powdery ingredient like flour tends to pack it into the measuring cup depending on how forceful you are while drawing it through and how dense the ingredient is in its storage container. One cup of flour measured this way can differ by up to 30 grams more than the same amount measured using the "spoon and level" technique, ultimately making your cake drier or your dough stiffer. Also, never tap down the measuring cup because it causes the ingredient to settle.

The exception to these rules is brown sugar since it is moist and not free-flowing. Most, if not all, recipes call for packed brown sugar which means you need to gently press and pack it into the measuring cup until it is level with the rim.

Truly, the most accurate way to measure ingredients is to weigh them using a scale. Although all of the recipes in this book have been tested with imperial measurements using the "spoon & level" method, metric values are provided for ingredients that are difficult to measure such as chopped fresh fruit, chocolate, nuts, coconut and dried fruit. Metric values have also been provided for cocoa powder and icing sugar, which can be difficult to measure accurately since they are quite lumpy. The one thing I must always use my scale for is to weigh butter. Unless it comes in stick form with markings on the wrappers, it is very difficult to measure. For example, it's difficult to estimate ¼ cup of butter from a 1 pound block. The measurement conversion chart lists all of the equivalents that you will need for the recipes in this book.

Since solid ingredients have specific densities, a 'cup' of one ingredient may not weigh the same as a 'cup' of another. Here are some useful measuring equivalents for common baking ingredients:

INGREDIENT	IMPERIAL	METRIC
butter	1 cup/8 oz	227 g
all-purpose flour	1 cup/5 oz	142 g
granulated sugar	1 cup/7 oz	200 g
packed brown sugar	1 cup/7 ¾ oz	220 g
cocoa powder	1 cup/3 oz	85 g
sifted icing sugar	1 cup/4 oz	113 g

Measurement Conversion Chart

U.S. SYSTEM		VOLUME	UNITS OF MASS FOR BUTTER	
		METRIC	IMPERIAL	METRIC
1 tsp	⅓ tbsp	5 ml	——	——
1 ½ tsp	½ tbsp	7 ml	¼ oz	7 g
3 tsp	1 tbsp	15 ml	½ oz	14 g
2 tbsp	⅛ cup	30 ml	1 oz	28 g
4 tbsp	¼ cup	60 ml	2 oz	56 g
5 ½ tbsp	⅓ cup	80 ml	2 ¾ oz	75 g
6 tbsp	——	90 ml	3 oz	85 g
8 tbsp	½ cup	118 ml	4 oz	113 g
10 ½ tbsp	⅔ cup	158 ml	5 ¼ oz	150 g
12 tbsp	¾ cup	178 ml	6 oz	170 g
16 tbsp	1 cup	237 ml	8 oz	227 g

Header spanning: EQUIVALENTS over VOLUME and UNITS OF MASS FOR BUTTER

Creating a general conversion chart for converting solid cup measurements from the U.S. system to imperial or metric units would be useless because the value depends on the density of the ingredient you are measuring. One tablespoon of sugar weighs more than one tablespoon of flour. Use the information from the table on page 14 to determine the weights of corresponding dry cup measurements for most staple baking ingredients. Since butter is a semi-solid at room temperature, one dry cup is roughly equal to a volumetric cup. So, I have laid out all of the cup-to-mass conversions you will need to make the recipes in this book in the above chart.

Although most recipes equate 1 cup with 250 ml, this is not the case. If you look at your volumetric measuring cup, you'll see that the marking for 1 cup does not line up with the metric measure for 250 ml on the other side. It is because the official volumetric cup measure in Canada is based on the American fluid ounce so that 1 cup = 237 ml (8 fl. oz. x 29.57 ml). For ease of measuring, it is usually rounded up to 250 ml. The other measurements that are fractions of 1 cup are also based on 237 ml. For example, ½ cup (0.5 x 237 ml) is actually equal to 118.5 ml, not 125 ml. For convenience, amounts are usually rounded to whole numbers or multiples of 25 since the 250 ml liquid measure is graduated in 25 ml divisions.

This volumetric replacement system is not suitable for large quantities or in cases where exact ingredient proportions are crucial. When doubling or tripling a recipe, too much error can occur if one ingredient is rounded up or down for ease of measuring without considering their relationships with other ingredients. If this is the case, exact conversions are made first and then rounded to the closest convenient measure.

1 Canadian fluid oz. = 28.4 ml (same as mass; 1 oz. = 28.4 g)
1 U.S. fluid oz. = 29.57 ml

Note: ALL INGREDIENTS SHOULD BE AT ROOM TEMPERATURE UNLESS OTHERWISE SPECIFIED.

COOKIES
and
BROWNIES

fig. 1

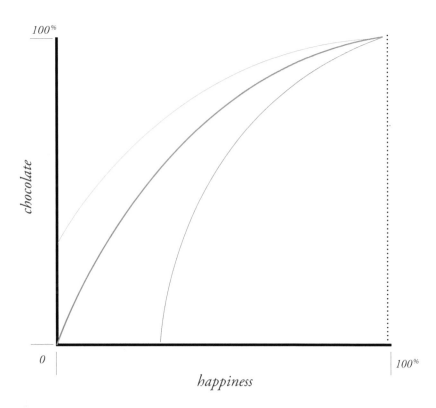

The Secret Life of Cookies

How much will power does it take to refuse a cookie? A lot. It's like ice cream – no matter how old you get, it's still irresistible. Seeing an old couple enjoying ice cream cones or nibbling on cookies brings a huge smile on my face. It just shows that some childhood pleasures are timeless.

Cookies come in so many forms, from drop cookies (most famously the Chocolate Chip Cookie), ice box cookies, rolled cookies and biscotti. They can be crisp, soft, chewy or gooey. They can be big, small, thick or thin. They're very customizable since a basic cookie dough is a canvas for as many mix-ins as you can think of, from chocolate to nuts and dried fruit. This chapter explores all of those options, leaving you with a big selection of cookies to choose from for any occasion.

Most cookie recipes begin with the creaming method, involving vigorous beating of butter and sugar before eggs, flour, leaveners and other ingredients are mixed in. This provides structure and tenderness. The type of sugar influences the final texture of the cookies. Regular white granulated sugar creates a crisp and brittle texture, while brown sugar creates a softer and chewier texture. This is a result of the molasses in brown sugar, which binds water and keeps it moist. Other unrefined brown-coloured sugars, such as muscovado, should not be used interchangeably with regular dark brown sugar since it contains more moisture and can affect the texture of the final cookie dough.

Majority of cookie recipes, and all of the ones in this book, use all-purpose flour to make them toothsome and provide texture. Most of all, it makes them easy to put together since many of us keep all-purpose flour on hand.

AN IN-DEPTH LOOK AT...
THE CHOCOLATE CHIP COOKIE:

At its core, it is a brown sugar dough studded with deep, dark pools of chocolate. It's simple and it's delicious. So, I have included 3 different variations of chocolate chip cookie recipes in this book. Excessive? Maybe. But, considering that it is probably the most popular cookie of all time, I think it is justifiable. Over the years people have developed specific tastes and preferences for this classic cookie. Some like them thick, some like them thin, some like them crispy and some like them soft or chewy. All of these different textures can be achieved using certain ingredients, and by changing their proportions.

First of all, there are a few key elements that I believe must be present in all chocolate chip cookies: chocolate, brown sugar, baking soda and pure vanilla extract. This might seem obvious, but let me explain myself.

CHOCOLATE: I rarely use 'chocolate chips' to make chocolate chip cookies. I use chocolate chunks or chopped chocolate. Since chocolate is one of the main attractions of these cookies, it's only right that you use the best you can find to be respectful. I prefer bittersweet with a minimum of 70% cocoa, but anything over 50% will work great. The dough is already quite sweet, so using dark chocolate complements it wonderfully. For that rustic look, pure chocolate chunks or disks are important because they melt nicely and help the cookie spread, crack and create crevices. My favourite way to achieve these little pools of chocolate is to break up a thin (¼-inch thick) bar with my hands (Lindt's bittersweet is my weapon of choice). Chocolate 'chips' or morsels have a high sugar content and often contain milk solids because they are made to hold their shape during baking.

BROWN SUGAR: The chewy texture and rich butterscotch flavour is due to brown sugar. I always use more brown sugar compared to white sugar for the best flavour and texture. In addition to this, it plays an important role in the spreading and puffing of the dough. Molasses is slightly acidic, allowing it to react with baking soda to promote rising. If the balance of acid and alkaline is off there can be residual soda in the recipe that will leave an undesirable soapy taste. During baking, both white and brown sugars undergo caramelization reactions to produce attractive golden colours and delicious flavours.

BAKING SODA: Sodium bicarbonate is basic or alkaline, meaning that it requires an acidic ingredient to react with in order to release carbon dioxide and help your cookies puff and spread. Too much baking soda will encourage too much spreading, leaving you with limp, pancake-like cookies and an unpleasant soapy aftertaste. On the other hand, not enough soda will result in pale, flavourless dough balls. More acidic batters (those that use baking powder) give the dough a lower setting temperature so that it sets before the butter melts and the resulting cookies are thicker. They also brown less and have a much more subtle caramel or butterscotch-like flavour. This is because special browning reactions that occur between certain sugars and proteins, called 'Maillard Browning', are accelerated in alkaline conditions. This not only makes the cookies look rich and delicious, but it encourages the development of complex caramel and toffee-like flavours.

VANILLA EXTRACT: One of the main elements that makes chocolate chip cookies so comforting and addictive is pure vanilla extract. The aroma fills your house as they bake and has a soothing effect. It also enhances the butterscotch flavours. For the best tasting cookies, use a good quality pure vanilla extract. I prefer Bourbon vanilla, which is made from vanilla beans grown in Madagascar.

LIQUID SUGAR: Corn syrup, molasses and honey act as humectants, which retain moisture and keep cookies soft or even slightly gooey in the middle. They also provide reducing sugars to participate in Maillard reactions for enhanced caramel flavours. Honey and molasses are also quite acidic; hence, they can react with baking soda.

EGGS: I use large size eggs in all of my recipes like most recipes do. One large egg weighs 56-58 grams. This is not a big deal in terms of cooking, but in baking it can make a significant difference as a medium or extra large egg can vary by more than 5 grams, or over a teaspoon of liquid, compared to a large egg. This can add up as the batch size increases and depending on how many eggs a recipe calls for, ultimately changing the final texture of the cookie. Remember to always let the eggs come to room temperature before using them unless otherwise specified.

Troubleshooting: Falling Flat!

Over-spreading is a common problem when it comes to Chocolate Chip Cookies, and it often leads to very brown, overly crisp and flat cookies. It is due to several factors:

1) the dough is too alkaline (i.e. too much baking soda)

2) oven temperature is too low (get an oven thermometer!)

3) the dough is too warm (i.e. the butter is too soft). Room temperature is around 23°C (73°F), so if your kitchen is hotter than this you can refrigerate the butter shortly before using it. Refrigerating the dough (chilling) for several hours before baking makes thicker cookies because it firms up the butter so that the dough sets before the fat melts.

4) there is not enough strength and structure in the dough or the dough is too wet. Be sure to accurately measure the flour because it contributes proteins and starches that play a big role in how your cookies bake. Chilling also serves to thoroughly hydrate the dry ingredients for better flavour development, more even browning and less spreading.

MAILLARD BROWNING:

Maillard Browning is probably the most delicious reaction in the culinary world as it is responsible for the bitter caramel-flavoured crust on seared steak, the golden crust on baked brioche, the rich flavour of toffee sauce and the tasty 'brown bits' that stick to the bottom of a roasting pan and serve as the base for rich sauces. More importantly, products of Maillard browning contribute to the flavour of chocolate. It is a complex reaction between certain sugars (reducing sugars) and proteins (specifically amino acids) under very high temperatures. After a series of rearrangements and degradations, the Maillard reaction ultimately produces potent compounds with nutty, floral, toasted, meaty and caramel-like flavours and aromas. It also creates brown-coloured compounds called melanoidins.

The Secret Life of Brownies

It's amazing how a dessert as humble as the brownie can stimulate so much discussion and ignite passion. Some like it fudgy and some like it cakey – so I've heard. I have yet to meet a person who prefers a cakey brownie. In my opinion, there shouldn't be such a thing. Wouldn't that just be chocolate cake? My perfect brownie is dense and fudge-like with a chewy texture and intense chocolate flavour. They don't all have to be super heavy – I get the appeal of a lighter version but it should still have that chew factor that cake could never have. There are many things that contribute to this, including mixing technique, type of ingredients and their relative proportions.

FAT: In most brownie recipes, fat can come from both butter and chocolate. Aside from adding rich flavour, butter lends tenderness and soft chewiness. Chocolate also contributes fat in the form of cocoa butter that is very hard at room temperature. So, brownies made with chocolate will have a firmer, fudgier texture as opposed to brownies made solely with cocoa powder, which have a softer, chewier texture.

SUGAR: Sugar can be in the form of, well, regular white granulated sugar and brown sugar but also chocolate. Sweet, semisweet, dark and bittersweet chocolate all contain sugar in different proportions with sweet chocolate having the most. The moist, chewy and fudgy texture of brownies is due in large part to a relatively high dose of sugar. Although the ratio of butter to sugar in a brownie is very similar to a cookie or even cake recipe, the main difference lies in its comparison to the dry ingredients. Brownies have a very high ratio of sugar to flour. Sugar is very hygroscopic, meaning that it has a great ability to absorb water, which keeps brownies dense and moist. Less of the sweet stuff creates a lighter and softer texture. It also plays an important role in the development of the much sought-after shiny crust, in which case a very fine granulation, such as in caster/castor, superfine or instant dissolving sugar, is preferred.

SALT: Even the most perfect brownie can be ruined if salt is forgotten. Trust me...I've made that mistake. I ended up sprinkling salt on top of my brownie as if I was seasoning a steak. Salt drastically brings out the richness of butter and cocoa, and helps to offset the intense sweetness. Without it, brownies taste flat and very one-dimensional as with many baked goods.

FLOUR: Brownies do not contain a lot of flour, so there is little structure in the batter which ensures that the result will be dense and chewy rather than dry, airy and cake-like. The little structure that it does contribute, however, is very important as it helps to build and hold a network of tiny air bubbles and provides some emulsification functionalities. The starch in flour also absorbs and holds onto water, preventing it from evaporating too quickly at the surface. Paired with proper baking times, it will help define the line between a sloppy, goopy brownie and a moist fudgy one.

EGGS: Brownies contain a relatively high proportion of eggs compared to other desserts. Their high protein content provides structure without drying out the batter like flour would. This is because flour contains a lot of starch. Proteins also have great water-binding capacity which contributes to the gooey texture of brownies. These egg proteins can interact with sugar to create the thin, tissue paper crust on top of every respectable batch of brownies. It is really important that your eggs are at room temperature when making them so that they incorporate well into the batter and help to dissolve the sugar. Since most of us rightfully store our eggs in the refrigerator, submerge them in a bowl of warm water for 5-10 minutes while you prepare the rest of your ingredients.

CHOCOLATE: The type of chocolate you use can affect the flavour, texture and development of a shiny top on a batch of brownies due to the varying levels of sugar and cocoa solids. I typically use dark chocolate, but that is a very vague statement as there are different types, including semisweet and bittersweet. Dark chocolate generally has between 28% and 50% sugar, or 72% (bittersweet) and 50% (semisweet) cocoa mass or cocoa liquor, respectively. Cocoa mass basically means unsweetened chocolate, which contains cocoa solids (ground defatted cocoa nibs) and cocoa butter. In my recipes that call for semisweet dark chocolate, I specifically use one with 54% cocoa.

THE INFAMOUS CRUST:

The sight of a thin, shiny, wrinkly, paper-like, crispy top on brownies is enough to make me cry. I just adore it and to me, it is the sign of a great brownie. The development of this crust depends on several different factors, including the size of your eggs, the type of chocolate you use and your specific mixing technique. Most of all, it relies heavily on dissolved sugars. So, the granulation of your sugar (powdered, superfine, fine or coarse) plays a major role.

For a while I believed it was magic – with some recipes that shiny crust appeared and sometimes not. Ever wonder why? Well I did and I tested a ridiculous 16 batches of brownies in a matter of a few days to figure it out. There are two main methods for making brownies. There's the 'one bowl method' that involves adding sugar, eggs and dry ingredients respectively to a mixture of melted chocolate and butter. Then there's the 'ribbon stage method' where the sugar and eggs are first beaten until thick and voluminous before melted chocolate, melted butter and dry ingredients are stirred in.

The 'Ribbon Stage' method:

This method involves creating an egg foam in which whole eggs are blended with sugar and beaten until the mixture thickens and doubles in volume. The 'ribbon stage' refers to a phenomenon in which the egg and sugar mixture forms a slowly disappearing ribbon on the surface of itself when some of it is lifted with a utensil and allowed to fall back into the bowl. It is best achieved using an electric hand mixer or stand mixer. Using this method will almost guarantee a shiny crust on your brownies because sugar is able to dissolve in the moisture from the eggs and then re-crystallize at the surface.

In this method, you'll notice that a shiny film develops on the surface of the batter rather quickly, within the first 5 or 10 minutes of baking. It is a result of egg protein and sugar interactions in a saturated sugar solution. During whipping (physical stress), egg proteins are denatured or unraveled while air bubbles are being introduced. These denatured proteins have an affinity for air and become spread out thinly along the surfaces of air bubbles, which increases their surface area. Dissolved sugar forms a viscous, syrupy liquid that surrounds egg proteins and stabilizes them. It's similar to meringue where sugar is added to stiffen beaten egg whites. A shiny crust develops quickly because egg proteins are very sensitive to heat. When spread so thin, they are able to cook readily at temperatures much lower than required to bake brownies and the finely dissolved sugar crystallizes in a very organized fashion. These crystals reflect light and appear shiny, similar to the film that forms on breads and pastries after they've been brushed with an egg wash or milk.

The batter at the surface of a batch of brownies cooks and dries out so quickly that it can literally separate from the rest of the batter, leaving a dull sugary crust beneath it. For some people (including me) this is a good thing, but for others it is a pain because the crust crumbles and flakes off when you slice the brownies.

This ribbon stage method produces a very dense but soft brownie due to many small air bubbles. I personally love this texture, but brownies made this way are very susceptible to over-baking. Keep an eye on them as they can become dry if over-baked. The extent of whipping of the eggs and sugar will determine the thinness and brittleness of the crust as well as the fudge factor. Over-whipping can lead to a very light and mousse-like texture, which isn't such a bad thing if you like mousse.

The 'One Bowl' Method:

This method is fast and simple but a little more stubborn. You'll find that achieving a shiny crust is hit or miss mainly because of the lack of dissolved sugars. A higher quantity and/or finer granulation of sugar is required to create this appearance for recipes that use this method since it is more difficult for the sugar to dissolve. If you value a shiny top as much as I do, seek out superfine or instant dissolving sugar for these recipes. In some countries, it is also referred to as caster or castor sugar.

In some cases, more flour may also be required to bind water and prevent it from evaporating before the batter sets. If there is not enough dissolved sugar or other water-binding ingredients in the recipe, such as flour or starch, you may notice that the surface of your brownies is covered in small holes or craters as a result of steam escaping. This is mostly aesthetic, though, and the texture is usually always a win as long as you don't over-mix once the flour is added. Brownies made using this method are more likely to develop a wrinkly crust if a high quantity of melted chocolate (especially semisweet chocolate) is used in the recipe rather than cocoa powder because chocolate contains very finely ground sugar that dissolves readily in the batter.

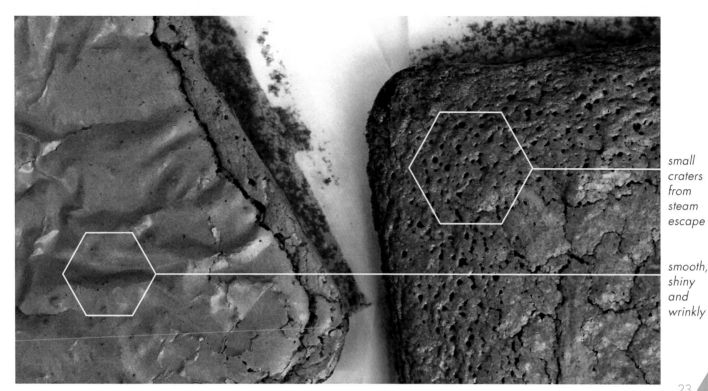

small craters from steam escape

smooth, shiny and wrinkly

BAKING TIME:

An important challenge with all brownies is how long they should be baked. Even the slightest minute or two can turn a moist, dense brownie into one that is dry and cake-like. Most brownies baked in an 8 x 8-inch metal pan will require between 20 and 25 minutes in a moderate oven, depending on the quantity of batter. I recommend testing with a toothpick after 20 minutes and then keeping a close eye on it afterwards.

Despite most recipes that instruct you to bake until a tooth-pick inserted into the center comes out clean, I'm afraid that brownies will be over-cooked at this point. I suggest to bake until a toothpick inserted someplace between the center and edge of the brownies comes out with a few moist crumbs. This ensures that the edges won't be dry and over-baked. A toothpick inserted into the center should have a tiny bit of sticky batter clinging to it or a few moist and sticky clumps. You do not want the toothpick to be clean. Another important factor when it comes to baking time is your baking vessel – I almost always use metal pans which conduct heat very efficiently. If using ceramic, you will have to increase your baking time by 10-15 minutes.

COOLING:

Letting brownies cool completely and even refrigerating them for a couple of hours before slicing is crucial to the develop-ment of their richness and chewy texture. During cooling, the eggs, which have puffed up or souffléd while baking, will fall as the air bubbles deflate. There is not enough structure-providing gluten protein from the flour to reinforce the batter. Also, brownies that are baked correctly (i.e. not over-baked) will indeed fall slightly because the batter shouldn't set so strongly. Most importantly, the chocolately flavours intensify as they cool.

Due to their fairly high fat content, brownies tend to have a greasy texture when warm, specifically for those made with a combination of cocoa powder and butter instead of chocolate. This is a result of the lack of an emulsifier called lecithin, which is an important ingredient that chocolate manufacturers use to prevent the separation of cocoa butter. Cooling baked brownies diminishes the greasy feeling by allowing the fat to firm up and the starches to set.

The Facts

raw *vs* toasted

The high oil content of nuts makes them suitable to dry cooking methods, such as toasting or roasting, which brings out their flavours and promotes Maillard browning (a really delicious reaction between proteins and sugars). Toast your nuts for recipes like drop cookies, biscotti & brownies to add complexity and richness. Be careful not to take them too far though, because they can give your dessert an almost savoury flavour when used in high amounts.

natural *vs* Dutched cocoa

Cocoa powder is typically available in two forms: natural and Dutch-processed. Natural cocoa is made from roasted, defatted cocoa nibs, and has a pronounced bitterness and complex chocolate flavour. Dutch-processed cocoa is made from defatted chocolate liquor (ground cocoa nibs) that has been treated with an alkali salt solution, such as potassium carbonate, in order to increase its pH value (percent hydrogen ions). This neutralizes its acidity to give it a more mellow flavour and also functions to improve its suspension in water and enhance colour. Most cocoa powders on the market today are at least mildly processed, but this designation may or may not appear on the label. Due to different acidity levels, Dutched cocoa cannot always be used interchangeably with natural cocoa in recipes that use baking soda. Natural cocoa is acidic and so it is often paired with baking soda (basic) to react and produce carbon dioxide gas to leaven the batter. If the recipe includes other acidic ingredients, such as sour cream, brown sugar or vinegar, then the result will be less noticeable if Dutched cocoa is used in its place. However, if the recipe relies solely on natural cocoa for its acidity, then using the Dutched variety can result in a soapy flavour from unreacted baking soda and a flat baked good due to lack of leavening. Most recipes that use Dutched cocoa include baking powder for all or some of its leavening power. Generally, you can substitute natural cocoa for Dutch-processed in most recipes with slight differences in flavour but not the other way around.

stand *vs* hand mixer

Although many bakers can't live without their stand mixers, it is important to realize that they require a minimum volume to perform properly. So, they are not ideal for small batches. To make batter for a dozen cupcakes or a small batch of cookie dough, I prefer to use my electric hand mixer or my wonderfully seasoned hands. Creaming fat and sugar by hand using a wide rubber spatula can actually be more efficient than a stand mixer for recipes that generally require less than ½ cup of butter. If the volume of ingredients is too little, then it will simply rest in the small space between the beater and the bowl of an electric stand mixer and remain untouched. This neglect will prevent you from achieving optimal volume in your batter which can have a detrimental effect on the texture of the finished product. Either way, always take care to scrape down the sides and bottom of the bowl as often as necessary.

brown *vs* white sugar

Brown sugar, when referred to as "raw sugar", can be partially refined white sugar that contains some residual molasses (aka. it is not completely refined). Nowadays, it is typically produced by adding some molasses back to completely refined white sugar crystals. This allows the manufacturers to control the colour, such as in the production of light and dark brown sugars, and to make more consistent products. Molasses is a natural by-product of making sugar. During the refinement process, it is separated and removed to make table sugar from the juice of sugar cane plants. Due to the trace mineral content of molasses, brown sugar has some nutritional benefits when compared to white sugar, but the amounts are so small that it is nothing to write home about. The main difference between the two, aside from flavour, is their effects on baking. Molasses adds moisture and acidity to brown sugar, which is required in certain recipes to react with baking soda and help your baked good rise. In addition, dark brown sugar contains more molasses than light brown sugar. So, it is important to follow these recipes accurately.

"World Famous" Chipped Chocolate Cookies

Makes about 24 cookies

Ingredients:

2 ¼ cups all-purpose flour

¾ tsp baking soda

¾ tsp fine sea salt

¾ cup unsalted cultured butter, ❓ at room temperature

1 vanilla bean pod, seeds scraped

1 cup packed dark brown sugar

½ cup granulated sugar

2 large eggs, at room temperature

1 tsp pure Bourbon vanilla extract

3 oz/85 g bittersweet chocolate (72% cocoa), finely chopped

6 oz/170 g dark chocolate (64% cocoa), coarsely chopped

In a medium bowl, whisk together flour, baking soda and salt; set aside.

In the bowl of an electric stand mixer fitted with the flat beater/paddle attachment, beat butter with vanilla bean seeds on medium speed for 30 seconds. Add both sugars and beat on medium speed until the mixture looks somewhat light and fluffy but still grainy, 1 ½ to 2 minutes. Add eggs one at a time and beat until incorporated after each addition, about 20 seconds per egg. Mix in vanilla extract until evenly blended.

Gradually add flour mixture in two additions, mixing on low speed for no more than 10 seconds after each addition. Some flour should still be visible since you will continue to mix the dough when you add the chocolate. Now, add finely chopped chocolate and mix on low speed just until evenly distributed. Fold in coarsely chopped chocolate by hand until well combined. The dough will be moist.

Turn dough out onto a large piece of plastic wrap and wrap well without pressing it down or compacting it. Refrigerate for 24-36 hours. Do not skip this step – it's worth the wait.

When you are ready to bake, preheat your oven to 350°F. Line two large baking sheets with parchment paper. Remove dough from fridge about 10 minutes before baking so it is easier to work with.

Roll 1 ½ to 2-oz mounds of dough into balls and place on prepared trays, spacing them about 2 ½ inches apart. Flatten each dough ball slightly with the palm of your hand and bake until golden around the edges, 10-12 minutes. Let cookies sit for a minute on the tray before transferring to a wire rack to cool.

✪ The 'Classic' Chocolate Chip Cookie

This is a classic chocolate chip cookie recipe made better with the addition of vanilla bean to intensify the comforting aroma that makes these cookies so distinct and desirable.

With whole eggs and a combination of white and brown sugar, they bake up with crisp edges and tender interiors. The shards of chipped bittersweet chocolate guarantee chocolate flavour in every bite and help to balance out the sweetness of the dough. Just the right amount of baking soda promotes the development of delicious caramel flavours and a hefty dose of sea salt complements them perfectly.

Chilling the dough for so long lets the flour and baking soda hydrate for more even browning and a richer flavour. You'll notice that the dough will feel drier after refrigeration. Keep a close eye on the mixing time during creaming because over-mixing will incorporate so much air that these cookies won't spread very much and develop a more cakey texture.

❓ Cultured butter has bacterial cultures added to it (the same cultures used to make cheese), giving the dough a richer flavour. It is also slightly acidic, which allows it to react more thoroughly with baking soda. If you only have regular unsalted butter on hand though, it will do just fine.

Thick & Chunky Chocolate Macadamia Nut Cookies

Makes 18-20 cookies

Ingredients:

1 ½ cups all-purpose flour

½ tsp baking powder

¼ tsp plus ⅛ tsp baking soda ❷

pinch of freshly grated nutmeg

½ cup unsalted butter, at room temperature

¾ cup packed dark brown sugar

¼ cup granulated sugar

½ tsp coarse sea salt

1 large chilled egg

1 tsp pure vanilla extract

3 oz/85 g semisweet chocolate (54% cocoa), chopped into small chunks

3 oz/85 g pure milk chocolate, chopped into small chunks

2 oz/56 g whole roasted & salted macadamia nuts (about ½ cup), coarsely chopped

First place room temperature butter in the refrigerator until slightly firm, about 15 minutes.

Meanwhile, whisk together flour, baking powder, baking soda and nutmeg in a medium bowl; set aside.

Combine butter, both sugars and salt in the bowl of a stand mixer fitted with the flat beater/paddle attachment and beat on medium to medium-high speed until light and fluffy, about 3 minutes. Scrape down the bottom and sides of the bowl several times during creaming.

Once fully creamed, scrape down the bowl once more, add egg and vanilla extract and beat on medium speed until well incorporated, about 30-40 seconds. The mixture may look slightly curdled at this point – that's OK. Add the flour mixture all at once and mix on low until mostly combined, about 25 seconds. Add chocolate and macadamia nuts and mix just until evenly distributed, about 10 seconds. Remove bowl from the mixer and fold the dough several times by hand using a wide rubber spatula to make sure everything is evenly incorporated.

Preheat your oven to 350°F. Line two large baking sheets with parchment paper and set aside.

Loosely grab 1 ½-oz portions of dough (do not pack down) and place on prepared baking sheets, spreading them 2 inches apart. Cover the baking sheet loosely with plastic wrap and refrigerate for 20-30 minutes.

Bake until golden brown, about 10-12 minutes. Let cookies sit on the baking sheet for 1 minute before transferring to a wire rack to cool.

❖ The secrets to being 'Thick and Chunky':

A high flour-to-fat ratio keeps this dough drier than most chocolate chip cookie doughs, giving it more structure and strength. The addition of baking powder keeps the batter more acidic thanks to its cream of tartar or sodium acid pyrophosphate content so that the dough sets at a lower temperature. Since baking soda promotes spreading, the balance of soda and baking powder in this recipe helps to prevent them from lying too flat.

Lastly, for thick cookies I've used a combination of semisweet and milk chocolate for their higher sugar content and hence,

lower cocoa butter content, compared to bittersweet chocolate. This will help the chocolate chunks hold their shape better in the dough so that they don't melt as readily and cause the cookies to spread out. Chilling the dough before baking keeps the butter cold and firm so that it doesn't melt instantly with the heat of the oven – a trick my Zia taught me many years ago when I was just a little cookie monster.

❷ Make sure to measure your baking soda very accurately because any more that this will trigger spreadation (yes, I said spreadation).

Chewy Chocolate Chunk Cookies

Makes about 22 cookies

Ingredients:

1 ¾ cups plus 2 tbsp all-purpose flour

½ tsp baking soda

½ tsp salt

⅔ cup unsalted butter, at room temperature

1 cup packed dark brown sugar

¼ cup granulated sugar

1 large egg, at room temperature

1 large egg yolk, at room temperature

1 tsp golden corn syrup

1 ½ tsp pure vanilla extract

7 oz/200 g bittersweet chocolate (72% cocoa), chopped into chunks or broken into pieces

In a medium bowl, whisk together flour, baking soda and salt; set aside.

In a large bowl, cream together butter and both sugars by hand using a wide rubber spatula or wooden spoon until somewhat fluffy and smooth. Add whole egg and stir until well incorporated (do not beat). Stir in egg yolk. Add corn syrup and vanilla extract and stir until blended and smooth.

Add flour mixture to the butter mixture all at once and stir until most of the flour is absorbed but a few streaks remain. Add chocolate chunks and fold them into the dough until evenly incorporated. Do not over-mix. You should end up with a soft, somewhat moist dough. Place a piece of plastic wrap directly over the surface of the dough in the bowl and refrigerate for 3 to 4 hours. Do not skip this step. Chilling mainly allows the butter to firm up so that it doesn't melt too quickly in the oven, letting the dough set before the butter melts. This way the cookies don't spread flat like pancakes and remain a bit gooey in the middle even once the tops are nicely golden.

Preheat your oven to 350°F.

Line two large baking sheets with parchment paper. Roll 1 ½-oz mounds of chilled dough into roughly-shaped balls and place them onto prepared baking sheets, spacing them 2 ½ inches apart. You can also use a 1 ½-oz trigger/quick-release ice cream scoop to portion the dough. Bake until golden brown but still soft in the middle, about 10 minutes. Do not over-bake because these cookies will set as they cool.

Let cookies settle on the baking sheet for about 30 seconds before carefully transferring them to a wire rack to cool.

✪ The 'Chew' Factor:

These cookies have a crisp shell with a gooey center when eaten fresh and they maintain their toothsome texture even after 3 days. This is due to a high ratio of total sugar (more sugar than flour by weight) as well as a high brown-to-white sugar ratio. The addition of corn syrup helps to keep these cookies soft and chewy by retaining moisture so that they don't dry out. The extra egg yolk provides dense protein and adds depth of flavour by promoting more browning through the Maillard reaction.

Above all, I encourage you to make the dough by hand. This actually contributes greatly to the moist, dense and chewy texture since manual labour works less air into the dough (mainly during the creaming of butter and sugar).

Chilling the dough before baking benefits the flavour and texture of these cookies by allowing the flour in the dough to hydrate evenly. It also firms up the butter to reduce spreading for slightly thicker cookies.

Orange Rosemary Shortbread

Makes 24 cookies

....

Shortbread gets its name from its main ingredient – lots of butter. That's because fat has the remarkable ability to shorten the texture of baked goods, making them more tender and crumbly. On a food chemistry level, fat coats gluten-forming protein molecules in flour (glutenin and gliadin) and prevents them from linking together and forming a network of long stretchy gluten strands. This process is referred to as shortening since the fat essentially shortens the protein strands, and ultimately provides insurance that the cookies won't develop a tough, elastic texture. The combination of orange and rosemary will knock your boots off so make sure you're not wearing any boots. It's a sophisticated sweet and savoury combo that makes these little darlings perfect appetizers for a swanky Saturday night dinner. Did I mention they're easy as heck to make?

....

Ingredients:

1 cup all-purpose flour

1 tbsp corn starch

¼ tsp salt

½ cup unsalted butter, at room temperature

⅓ cup granulated sugar

½ tsp pure vanilla extract

2 tsp finely grated orange zest

¾ tsp finely chopped fresh rosemary

1 stem fresh rosemary, leaves plucked for topping

¼ cup finely chopped candied orange peel (optional)

Preheat your oven to 325°F.

Have ready a 24-cup mini muffin pan and set aside.

In a medium bowl, whisk together flour, corn starch and salt; set aside.

In a large bowl, cream together butter and sugar using a wooden spoon or rubber spatula until somewhat light and fluffy. Stir in vanilla extract, orange zest and chopped rosemary until well blended. Add flour mixture and candied orange peel (if using) and stir until a soft dough forms.

Divide the dough into 24 portions, squeezing it slightly in your hand so that the dough holds together. Place each portion in the base of each cup of the prepared muffin pan. Gently press the dough into the cup to fill the base using your fingertips. Do not pack it too tightly or the cookies will be less tender.

Gently press one or two small leaves of rosemary over the surface of each cookie and bake until golden brown around the edges, about 12-13 minutes.

Let cookies cool in pan for about 10 minutes before transferring individually to a wire rack to cool completely (use a small offset spatula or butter knife to help release the cookies from the sides of the pan).

Mom's Classic Cranberry Almond Biscotti

Makes about 24 cookies

....

These classic biscotti are based on my Mom's recipe. She bakes loads of them every year during the holidays and we never get tired of them. "Biscotti" are named after their method of baking as it means "twice cooked" in Italian. First, the dough is formed into logs and baked until golden. After cooling slightly, the logs are sliced and baked once more until crisp. The traditional dry texture of biscotti make them a perfect complement to a cup of hot coffee or espresso; however, I find this recipe holds its own.

....

Ingredients:

2 cups all-purpose flour

2 tsp baking powder

¼ tsp salt

3 ½ oz/100 g whole almonds (about ⅔ cup)

⅓ cup unsalted butter

1 tbsp finely grated orange zest, (the zest of about one orange)

2 large eggs, at room temperature

¾ cup granulated sugar

1 tsp pure vanilla extract

½ tsp pure almond extract

2 oz/56 g dried cranberries (about ½ cup)

1 large egg, well beaten

Preheat your oven to 350°F.

Line a large baking sheet with parchment paper and set aside.

In a large bowl, whisk together flour, baking powder and salt. Stir in almonds and set aside.

In a small saucepan over low heat, melt butter with orange zest to infuse it with the citrus flavour and set aside to cool slightly.

In a medium bowl, whisk eggs to blend evenly. Gradually add sugar while whisking until smooth and lightened in colour by just a shade. Whisk in melted butter, vanilla extract and almond extract until well incorporated. Pour this mixture into the bowl with the flour mixture and stir gently until most of the flour is absorbed. Add dried cranberries and fold them through until a soft, slightly sticky dough forms.

Transfer dough to a lightly floured work surface, divide it in half and roll each portion into an 11-inch long log. Transfer logs to prepared baking sheet making sure to leave space between them. Flatten and form logs with your hands so that they become 12 inches long and about 3 inches wide. Brush tops and sides with beaten egg and bake until golden brown and slightly cracked at the surface, 20-25 minutes.

Transfer baking sheet to a wire rack and let biscotti logs cool on pan for about 20 minutes, or until cool enough to handle. Reduce oven temperature to 300°F.

Transfer each log to a cutting board and use a serrated knife to slice it diagonally into ¾-inch-thick pieces with a gentle sawing motion. Place biscotti back on the baking sheet with the cut side facing down and bake until very lightly golden, dry and crisp, about 7 minutes per side.

Transfer cookies to a wire rack to cool completely. These are tender enough to eat on their own, yet still crunchy enough to dip in your coffee. Either way, I know you'll make my Mama proud.

Peanut Butter Deluxe Oatmeal Cookies

Makes about 20 cookies

Ingredients:

¾ cup all-purpose flour

½ tsp baking soda

¼ tsp baking powder

½ tsp ground cinnamon

¼ tsp ground nutmeg

¼ tsp salt

½ cup quick-cooking or minute oats

6 tbsp unsalted butter, at room temperature

⅔ cup packed dark brown sugar

⅓ cup granulated sugar

¼ cup smooth, all natural peanut butter ❓

1 large egg, at room temperature

½ tsp pure vanilla extract

1 cup old-fashioned large flake rolled oats

3 oz/85 g best quality semisweet or dark chocolate chips (about ½ cup)

2 oz/56 g dried cranberries (about ½ cup)

1 ½ oz/42 g sultana raisins (about ⅓ cup)

In a medium bowl, whisk together flour, baking soda, baking powder, ground cinnamon, ground nutmeg and salt. Stir in quick-cooking or minute oats and set aside.

In a large bowl, cream together butter with both sugars by hand using a wide rubber spatula or wooden spoon until well blended and the mixture looks like wet sand. This will take 1 or 2 minutes. Stir in peanut butter until smooth. Stir in egg and vanilla extract until well incorporated. Mix in the rolled oats so they are well coated with the wet mixture and let stand for a couple of minutes to soften them. Add the flour mixture and stir it in gently until it is mostly incorporated but a few streaks of flour remain. Add chocolate chips, dried cranberries and raisins and fold them into the dough until evenly distributed.

Place a piece of plastic wrap directly on the surface of the dough in the bowl and refrigerate for 30 minutes. This lets the oats hydrate and soften up a bit, and also promotes even browning during baking.

Preheat your oven to 350°F. Line two large baking sheets with parchment paper and set aside.

Roll 1 ½-oz portions of dough into balls and place them on prepared baking sheets, spacing them 2 inches apart. Flatten dough balls with the palm of your hand and form round disks with about ½-inch thickness (this is necessary as these cookies don't spread much on their own from all the oats jam packed in the dough). Bake until lightly golden but still slightly gooey in the center, about 10-12 minutes (they will set up as they cool). Let cookies cool for 1 minute on the baking sheet. At this point I like to press on them gently with the back of a spatula while still hot so that they stay dense and chewy. Transfer cookies individually to a wire rack to cool completely before storing in an airtight container.

❓ All natural peanut butter is made from 100% ground peanuts. It has an intense peanut flavour and stick-to-the-roof-of-your-mouth texture without the added salt, sugar and hydrogenated vegetable fats. Oil separation is a natural occurrence, so when you open the jar for the first time, stir it in with a spoon and store in the refrigerator. Do not pour off the oil because it will change the consistency and fat composition of the peanut butter, ultimately changing the texture of these cookies.

Orange Molasses Cream Cookies

Makes 20-22 cookies

....

A change from your typical chewy molasses cookies (which are divine nonetheless) these cookies have a light and delicate, almost cake-like texture with a crunchy sugar crust. They get this way from the addition of whipping cream which creates a moist, soft dough and coarse sanding sugar that makes them sparkle.

....

Ingredients:

1 ¾ cups plus 2 tbsp all-purpose flour

½ tsp baking soda

1 tsp ground cinnamon

½ tsp ground ginger

¼ tsp ground clove

¼ tsp ground nutmeg

¼ tsp ground allspice

¼ tsp salt

½ cup packed light brown sugar

¼ cup unsalted butter

2 tsp finely grated orange zest

½ cup 35% whipping cream

¼ cup dark cooking molasses

1 large egg white

½ cup coarse sanding sugar for rolling

Preheat your oven to 350°F.

Line a large baking sheet with parchment paper; set aside.

In the bowl of stand mixer fitted with the flat beater/paddle attachment, sift together flour, baking soda, ground cinnamon, ground ginger, ground clove, ground nutmeg and salt. Whisk in brown sugar. Mix on low speed until brown sugar is well blended and there are no lumps, about 2 minutes.

In a small saucepan over low heat, stir together butter and orange zest just until butter is melted and the orange scent has infused it. Stir in cream and molasses. Let cool slightly – it should be around room temperature.

In a medium bowl, whisk egg white just enough to break it up and then whisk in cooled cream mixture until well blended. Pour this mixture into the bowl with the flour mixture and beat on low speed until it forms a soft dough, about 20 seconds. Take the bowl off of the mixer and mix it by hand using a rubber spatula until all of the flour is incorporated. The dough will be soft and sticky. Place a piece of plastic wrap directly against the dough in the bowl and refrigerate for 30 minutes. It will firm up as it hydrates during the chilling period.

Form heaped tablespoons of dough (about 1 ounce portions) into balls and roll in sanding sugar. Place them on prepared baking sheet, spacing them 2 inches apart, and refrigerate for 15 minutes.

Flatten each ball slightly with the bottom of a glass and bake until lightly browned on the bottom, 12-13 minutes. Transfer cookies to a wire rack to cool completely.

❂ NOTE: Fat acts as a flavour carrier in most cases. Infusing flavours into butter is a great way to extract the most potential from them since many flavour compounds are fat-soluble, such as those found in vanilla and essential oils from citrus peel, herbs and spices.

Whole Wheat Chocolate Chunk Cookies with Toasted Coconut

Makes about 16 cookies

....

A healthy chocolate chip cookie – dare I say it? Too late, because I just did. Don't let the extra fiber scare you. The nuttiness of whole wheat flour plays off the nuttiness of the toasted coconut so you almost can't even notice it. It adds complexity, making it a mature yet fun way to switch up your chocolate chip cookie routine.

....

Ingredients:

¼ cup sweetened flaked coconut

¾ cup whole wheat flour

¾ cup all-purpose flour

½ tsp baking soda

½ tsp salt

½ cup unsalted butter, at room temperature

½ cup packed dark brown sugar

½ cup granulated sugar

1 large egg, at room temperature

1 tbsp 2% milk

1 tsp pure vanilla extract

5 oz/142 g bittersweet chocolate (72% cocoa), coarsely chopped

To toast the coconut, pour it in a single layer in a dry frying pan over medium-low heat. Cook until it turns golden brown and smells nutty, shaking the pan frequently for even browning. This will take about 6 minutes. Transfer toasted coconut to a small bowl to cool.

In a medium bowl, whisk together both flours, baking soda and salt; set aside.

In a large bowl, cream together butter and both sugars until light and fluffy using a wide rubber spatula. Stir in egg until well blended and smooth. Add milk and vanilla and stir to incorporate. Add the dry ingredients all at once and stir until mostly combined but a few streaks of flour remain. Add chopped chocolate and toasted coconut and fold it into the dough until evenly distributed.

Turn dough out onto a large piece of plastic wrap and wrap well. Refrigerate for 10-12 hours – this is important to allow the whole wheat flour to hydrate so that these cookies won't be dry.

Remove dough from the refrigerator and let it rest at room temperature for about 10 minutes before baking so that it is easier to work with.

Preheat your oven to 350°F.

Line two large baking sheets with parchment paper and set aside.

Roll 1 ¾-oz portions of dough into balls and place on prepared baking sheets, spacing them 3 inches apart. Flatten each dough ball into a disk using the palm of your hand or the bottom of a measuring cup and bake until golden brown around the edges but still slightly soft in the middle, 10-11 minutes. Transfer cookies to a wire rack to cool completely.

Iced Italian Lemon Cookies

Makes about 36 cookies

My mom makes these cookies every Christmas in ridiculous quantities. I guess that's her way of making up for only making them once a year. They're simple and light with a tender crumb – not what you'd expect from a typical cookie. Italians really don't do anything extravagant with dessert, but they have a way of making simple flavours feel satisfying and comforting. Whatever you do, make sure you do not disregard the glaze because its sweet and sour intensity really makes these little guys memorable.

For the cookie dough:

2 ¾ - 3 cups all-purpose flour

1 tbsp baking powder

¼ tsp salt

1 ½ tbsp finely grated lemon zest (zest of about 2 lemons)

1 cup granulated sugar

2 large eggs, at room temperature

2 large egg yolks

2 tbsp freshly squeezed lemon juice

½ cup unsalted butter, melted and cooled

¼ tsp pure almond extract (optional)

For the lemon glaze:

6 oz/170 g sifted icing sugar (about 1 ½ cups)

2-3 tbsp freshly squeezed lemon juice

⅓ cup finely chopped roasted and salted pistachios

Preheat your oven to 325°F.

Line two large baking sheets with parchment paper and set aside.

In a medium bowl, whisk together 2 ¾ cups flour, baking powder and salt.

In a large bowl, combine lemon zest and sugar and rub it together until the sugar takes on a faint yellow colour and becomes very fragrant. Add whole eggs and yolks and beat on medium-high speed using an electric hand mixer until pale and thick, about 1 ½ - 2 minutes. Beat in lemon juice, cooled melted butter and almond extract (if desired) until well blended.

Add about one-third of the flour mixture and beat on the lowest speed until combined. Add half of the remaining flour mixture and beat just until incorporated. Finally, fold in remaining flour by hand until blended, being careful not to over-mix. The dough should be soft and moist, but not too sticky. If it feels wet and sticky, fold in up to ¼ cup more flour. You will know that the dough is the right texture if it begins to pull away from the sides of the bowl, but still feels very soft. Resist the temptation to add any more flour than this or the cookies will be dry.

Place a piece of plastic wrap directly over the surface of the dough in the bowl and refrigerate for 30 minutes. It will firm up and become easier to handle once rested and chilled.

Roll 1-oz portions of dough into smooth balls and place on prepared baking sheets, spacing them 1 ½ inches apart. Bake until the bottoms are golden but the tops have barely taken on any colour, 14-16 minutes. Transfer cookies to a wire rack to cool completely.

To make the glaze, whisk together icing sugar and 2 tablespoons of lemon juice in a small bowl until smooth. Add more lemon juice, ½ teaspoon at a time, until it reaches drizzling consistency but is still rather thick. Glaze the cookies by either dipping the tops into the icing or spooning it over the top, allowing it to drip down the sides. Let the icing set for just a few seconds before sprinkling chopped pistachios over top.

Soft Chocolate Gingerbread Cookies

Makes about 20 cookies

Ingredients:

1 ½ cups all-purpose flour

1 tsp baking soda

¼ tsp salt

2 tbsp unsweetened cocoa powder

½ cup unsalted butter, at room temperature

¾ cup packed dark brown sugar

1 tsp ground ginger

¾ tsp ground cinnamon

⅛ tsp ground clove

⅛ tsp ground nutmeg

2 tbsp dark cooking molasses

1 large egg, at room temperature

5 oz/142 g semisweet chocolate (54% cocoa), chopped into chunks

granulated sugar for sprinkling

In a medium bowl, combine flour, baking soda and salt. Sift in cocoa powder and whisk to blend evenly; set aside.

In a large bowl, beat butter until creamy using a wide rubber spatula. Add brown sugar, ground ginger, ground cinnamon, ground clove and ground nutmeg and cream together with the butter until somewhat light and fluffy. Stir in molasses until well blended. Add egg and stir until well incorporated. Add flour mixture all at once and fold it in until just combined and flour is mostly absorbed. Finally, fold in chocolate chunks until evenly distributed and no streaks of flour remain, but do not over-mix.

Turn dough out onto a piece of plastic wrap and wrap well. Refrigerate for 30 to 45 minutes.

Preheat your oven to 350°F.

Line two large baking sheets with parchment paper and set aside.

Roll 1 to 1 ½-oz mounds of dough into balls (about 1 ¼-inch balls) and place them on prepared baking sheets, spacing them 2 ½ inches apart. Flatten very slightly with your palms, sprinkle with a bit of granulated sugar and bake until cracked at the surface and still a bit soft in the middle, about 9-10 minutes. Do not over-bake or they will be dry, not soft.

Let cool 1 minute on baking sheet before transferring to a wire rack to cool completely.

Brown Butter Pecan Cookies

Makes about 20 cookies

....

These cookies will make you think of butter in a whole new way. The recipe is simple to let the complex nutty flavours of brown butter shine. If you've never browned butter before, give it a shot and you'll find yourself putting it on everything. Pecans add even more richness while brown sugar contributes butterscotch undertones. If you are a fan of chewy cookies, then you'll love the texture of these babies thanks to the high milkfat content of brown butter and the moisture-retaining properties of light brown sugar.

....

Ingredients:

3 oz/85 g whole pecans (about ¾ cup)

½ cup unsalted butter

1 ¼ cups all-purpose flour

¼ tsp baking soda

heaped ¼ tsp salt

1 cup packed light brown sugar

1 large egg, at room temperature

1 tsp pure vanilla extract

To toast pecans, place them in a single layer in a dry frying pan over medium-low heat, shaking the pan frequently until they are toasted and fragrant, 6-8 minutes. Let cool completely, chop coarsely and set aside.

To brown the butter, place it in a small saucepan over medium-low heat and stir until completely melted. Allow butter to come to a boil, stirring constantly. It will bubble and crackle as its water content evaporates. Continue to cook, stirring frequently, until the crackling noises begin to fade and the bubbles subside. A dense foam will form at the surface as the last bit of water squeezes out, and the colour will progress from golden yellow to tan and finally, brown.

This takes around 8 to 10 minutes. Keep a close eye on it as butter can turn from brown to burnt within a matter of seconds. Once you smell that nutty aroma and begin to see little brown bits as you stir, take the pan off the heat and immediately pour the brown butter into a medium heatproof bowl. *(If you happen to cook it too far and the brown bits are now (burnt) black bits, you can strain the butter through a fine mesh sieve or a cheese cloth to remove them, as they can impart a bitter flavour to your dessert).* Let it cool to room temperature and then place it in the refrigerator, stirring every 3 to 5 minutes until it firms up but still feels pliable.

Preheat your oven to 350°F. Line two baking sheets with parchment paper and set aside.

In a small bowl, whisk together flour, baking soda and salt; set aside.

Add brown sugar to the bowl with the brown butter and cream together until light and fluffy using a spatula. Stir in egg and vanilla extract until well combined and smooth. Add flour mixture and stir until well incorporated. The dough will be stiff. Fold in chopped pecans.

Roll 1-oz portions of dough into balls and place on prepared baking sheets, spacing them about 2 inches apart. Flatten dough balls slightly with the bottom of a dry measuring cup and place the baking sheets in the fridge until the dough is firm, about 25 minutes. Bake until golden brown, about 10-12 minutes. Transfer cookies to a wire rack to cool completely.

Since brown butter has all of its water removed, it essentially becomes pure milkfat and it is no longer an emulsion. As a result, the cookies will feel slightly greasy when warm but will handle just fine once cooled.

....

✪ Brown Butter:

The "brown" part in brown butter is caused by a complex reaction between lactose and amino acids from milk proteins, called Maillard browning, which ultimately produces a nutty, toffee-like flavour that is completely unlike the creamy nature of fresh butter. It imparts richness to just about anything it is added to. When making brown butter, use a light-coloured pan so you can keep track of the colour transformations as it cooks. Stir or swirl the pan occasionally for even browning.

Apricot & Walnut Olive Oil Biscotti

Makes about 24 cookies

Ingredients:

2 cups <u>minus</u> 2 tbsp all-purpose flour

1 ¼ tsp baking powder

¼ tsp salt

¼ tsp freshly cracked black pepper

1 large egg, at room temperature

1 large egg yolk

⅓ cup granulated sugar

⅓ cup packed dark brown sugar

2 tbsp freshly squeezed orange juice

1 tbsp finely grated orange zest

¼ cup extra virgin olive oil

2 oz/56 g coarsely chopped walnuts (about ½ cup)

3 oz/85 g coarsely chopped dried apricots (about ½ cup)

1 large egg, well beaten, for brushing the top

Preheat your oven to 350°F.

Line a large baking sheet with parchment paper and set aside.

In a medium bowl, sift together flour, baking powder, salt and pepper; set aside.

In a large bowl, combine egg, yolk and both sugars and whisk vigorously by hand until it becomes pale and thick, about 1 minute.

Add orange juice and orange zest and whisk until the mixture is frothy, about 30 seconds longer. Using a large rubber spatula, stir in olive oil and then fold in dry ingredients all at once until almost completely incorporated but a few streaks of flour remain.

Gently fold in walnuts and apricots until evenly blended and flour is absorbed. The dough will be slightly stiff.

Divide dough into two equal portions and roll each half into a 10-inch log on a very lightly floured work surface. Transfer logs to prepared baking sheet, spacing them 3 inches apart. Flatten each log with your hands so that they are about 2 ½ inches wide. Brush them evenly with beaten egg and bake until golden brown and slightly cracked at the surface, about 23-25 minutes. Transfer baking tray to a wire rack and let biscotti logs cool on tray for about 20 minutes. Reduce oven temperature to 300°F.

Once slightly cooled, use a serrated knife to slice logs on a bias to form ¾-inch-thick pieces. Place cookies back on your parchment-lined baking sheet, laying them cut-side-down, and bake until dry and very slightly golden, 7-8 minutes per side. Transfer cookies to a wire rack to cool completely before storing in an airtight container.

⭐ Storing Nuts:

The high oil content of nuts that makes them so tasty also makes them susceptible to staling due to rancidity, which is caused by oxidation of fats that produces off-flavours in the presence of heat, light and moisture. So, it's best to store nuts (without the shells) in an airtight container in the fridge or freezer. I usually keep mine in the freezer if I've stocked up for a few months. Nuts lend well to freezing due to their low water content, so there's less risk of damage due to ice crystal formation. The oils, however, also have a tendency to absorb surrounding flavours so it really is important to make sure your container is airtight.

Choc-A-Lot Cookies

Makes 16-18 cookies

....

Salted butter combined with a hefty dose of dark brown sugar gives these cookies a rich toffee flavour. A bit of instant coffee simply enhances the roasted bitter notes of the cocoa, making the flavour more robust as opposed to contributing a pronounced coffee flavour. Basically, toffee, cocoa, vanilla, dark chocolate, coffee and salt make for one heck of a cookie.

....

Ingredients:

1 cup plus 3 tbsp all-purpose flour

½ tsp baking soda

½ tsp fine sea salt

1 oz/28 g unsweetened Dutch-processed cocoa powder (about ⅓ cup)

½ cup salted butter, at room temperature

⅔ cup packed dark brown sugar

⅓ cup granulated sugar

1 tsp golden honey

1 large egg, at room temperature

1 tsp pure vanilla extract

¼ tsp espresso coffee grounds or finely ground instant coffee granules

6 oz/170 g bittersweet chocolate (72% cocoa), chopped into chunks

In a medium bowl, combine flour, baking soda and salt. Sift in cocoa powder to remove any lumps and then stir the ingredients together to blend evenly; set aside.

In a large bowl, cream together butter and both sugars using a wide rubber spatula until light, fluffy and smooth. This will take 1 or 2 minutes. Mix in honey. Add the egg, vanilla extract and espresso coffee grounds and stir until well incorporated. The batter will look somewhat fluffy and should not look curdled.

Add flour mixture to the butter mixture all at once and stir until most of the flour is absorbed but a few streaks remain. Add chocolate chunks and fold them into the dough until evenly incorporated. Do not over-mix. You should end up with a soft and somewhat moist dough. Place a piece of plastic wrap directly over the surface of the dough in the bowl and refrigerate for 30 to 45 minutes.

Preheat your oven to 350°F.

Line two large baking sheets with parchment paper and use a 1 ½-oz quick-release ice cream scoop to portion mounds of dough, spacing them 2 inches apart. Alternatively, loosely drop 1 ½-oz mounds of dough (about two tablespoons) onto prepared baking sheets. If you like the bumpy rustic look of these cookies, do not roll the dough into smooth balls. Cover the trays loosely with plastic wrap and refrigerate until the dough is firm, about 15 minutes.

Bake until the surfaces look slightly dry and cracked, but the dough still a bit soft and gooey in the middle, about 9-10 minutes. Let cookies cool for 30 seconds on the baking sheet before transferring to a wire rack to cool completely. Do not over-bake these because they will set up further as they cool.

Caramel Shortbread

Makes about 12 wedges

....

*Shortbread differs from sugar cookie dough in that it contains
no eggs and it is unleavened, meaning that it does not contain
baking powder or baking soda.*

....

Ingredients:

1 cup all-purpose flour

2 tbsp potato starch

½ cup unsalted butter, at room temperature

¼ cup granulated sugar

¼ tsp salt

¼ cup Salted Caramel Sauce (page 231)

½ tsp pure vanilla extract

Preheat your oven to 300°F. In a medium bowl, whisk together flour and potato starch; set aside.

In a large bowl, cream together butter, sugar and salt using a wide rubber spatula until light and fluffy. Stir in salted caramel sauce and vanilla extract until well blended. Add flour mixture and stir until a soft dough forms.

Use an offset spatula to spread dough evenly into an 8-inch round fluted tart pan with removable bottom. Smooth the top with the spatula. Refrigerate 10 minutes.

Prick dough all over with a fork in an even pattern and use a knife to score it into 12 equal wedges. Scoring means to make shallow cuts to mark 12 wedges.

Bake until the top is evenly golden, about 30 minutes. Let cool completely in the pan on a wire rack. Remove sides of pan and slice into 12 wedges, using the marks as a guideline.

Black & White Meringue Kisses

Makes about 48 meringues

Ingredients:

3 large egg whites, at room temperature

pinch of salt

¼ tsp plus ⅛ tsp cream of tartar

⅔ cup granulated sugar

½ tsp pure vanilla extract

2 tsp unsweetened cocoa powder

Preheat your oven to 175°F. Line two baking sheets with parchment paper or silicone mats. Fit two pastry bags with large (1 cm) open star or round tips and set aside.

Combine egg whites, salt and cream of tartar in the bowl of a stand mixer fitted with the whisk attachment. Beat on medium-high speed until foamy, about 30 seconds. With mixer running, slowly add sugar, one tablespoon at a time.

After you've added about half of the sugar, stop the mixer, scrape down the sides of the bowl to incorporate any stray sugar granules. Secure bowl to the mixer, increase speed to high and continue adding remaining sugar, one tablespoon at a time. Beat until stiff peaks form and mixture is very thick and creamy. It should resemble shaving cream and feel quite smooth when you rub a bit of it between your thumb and forefinger. This can take up to 4 minutes.

Divide beaten egg whites in half between two clean bowls. Fold vanilla extract into one bowl and set aside. In the other bowl, sift cocoa powder over egg whites and fold it in until well incorporated. Fill each pastry bag with separate meringue flavours and pipe small (1-inch wide, 1-inch-high) round or star shapes onto prepared baking sheets.

Bake until crisp but not brown, about 1 hour 45 minutes to 2 hours. Turn the oven off and let the meringues cool in the oven with the door ajar. Once cool, transfer to an airtight container.

The Breakfast Cookie

Makes about 16 large cookies

....

Imagine trail mix all stirred up to make the perfect chewy Breakfast cookie. The dough is made with both white and whole wheat flour, sweetened with brown sugar and honey, and flavoured with a generous teaspoon of ground cinnamon. Whole almonds add great crunch and toasty flavour, since they roast up slightly as the cookies bake. Eating one of these creates a bit of a sensory overload, making it perfect for waking you up in the morning! How about fiber? Got it! Almonds, wheat bran, dried fruit, flax seeds and sunflower seeds...they're all a source of fiber. Flax and sunflower seeds contain essential fatty acids that help our brains function more efficiently – I could definitely use that in the morning. This is totally legitimate.

....

Ingredients:

1 cup all-purpose flour

¼ cup whole wheat flour

¾ cup old-fashioned large flake rolled oats

1 tsp ground cinnamon

½ tsp baking soda

½ tsp baking powder

¼ tsp salt

6 tbsp unsalted butter, at room temperature

¾ cup packed light brown sugar

2 tbsp golden honey

1 large egg, at room temperature

1 tsp pure vanilla extract

2 ½ oz/70 g whole almonds (about ½ cup)

1 ½ oz/42 g sunflower seeds (about ⅓ cup)

2 tbsp flax seeds

1 ½ oz/42 g golden raisins (about ⅓ cup)

1 ½ oz/42 g dried cranberries (about ⅓ cup)

Preheat your oven to 350°F.

Line two baking sheets with parchment paper and set aside.

In a medium bowl, whisk together both flours, oats, ground cinnamon, baking soda, baking powder and salt until evenly blended; set aside.

In a large bowl, beat together butter, sugar and golden honey until smooth and creamy using an electric hand mixer on high speed, about 1 minute. Beat in egg and vanilla extract until smooth.

Add flour mixture all at once to the butter mixture and beat on low speed until it is mostly combined, about 10 to 15 seconds.

Use a rubber spatula to fold in almonds, sunflower seeds, flax seeds, raisins and dried cranberries all at once.

Use a 1 ½-oz ice cream scoop to drop mounds of dough onto the prepared baking sheets, spacing them 3 inches apart. Flatten each cookie slightly using the bottom of a drinking glass or dry measuring cup and bake until golden brown around the edges, about 10-12 minutes.

Let cookies cool on the pan for about 1 minute before transferring them individually to a wire rack to cool completely.

These stay soft and chewy for days in an airtight container!

Mocha Truffle Hazelnut Cookies

Makes about 24 cookies

For the truffle filling:

4 oz/113 g semisweet chocolate (54% cocoa), finely chopped

¼ cup 35% whipping cream

¾ tsp instant coffee granules

For the cookie dough:

1 ½ cups all-purpose flour

½ tsp baking powder

3 ½ oz/100 g ground roasted hazelnuts❓ (about ¾ cup whole hazelnuts), divided

½ cup unsalted butter, at room temperature

¾ cup granulated sugar

¼ tsp salt

1 large egg, at room temperature

1 tbsp hazelnut or coffee liquor

½ tsp pure vanilla extract

To make the truffle filling, place chocolate in a heatproof bowl. Combine cream and instant coffee in a very small saucepan over medium-low heat and scald it so that it just barely comes to a boil. Immediately pour it over chopped chocolate and stir it around gently using a silicone spatula just to bring majority of the chocolate in contact with the hot cream. Let the mixture stand for 2 minutes and then stir slowly starting in the center and working your way out to the sides of the bowl in a spiral pattern until the mixture is smooth and glossy. Let mixture cool to room temperature and then refrigerate until firm, about 2 hours or overnight.

Line a small baking sheet with waxed paper. Using a melon baller or a small spoon, roll teaspoons of truffle filling into balls and then place them on the lined baking sheet. Refrigerate until firm while you make the cookie dough.

Preheat your oven to 350°F and line two baking sheets with parchment paper.

In a medium bowl, whisk together flour, baking powder and ½ cup of ground hazelnuts; set aside.

In the bowl of a stand mixer fitted with the flat beater/paddle attachment, beat butter with sugar and salt on medium-high speed until lightened, about 30 seconds. Scrape down the bowl and beat until fluffy, about 15 seconds more. Add egg, hazelnut or coffee liquor and vanilla extract and beat on medium speed until well blended and smooth. Add flour mixture and beat on low speed until just incorporated, about 15 seconds.

To assemble the cookies, grab a 1-oz portion of dough, flatten it a bit in your hand and place a truffle in the center. Gently wrap the dough around the truffle and pinch it together at the seam to seal it completely. Roll the cookie in your hand gently to make it smooth and then roll it around in the remaining chopped hazelnuts, applying some pressure to make sure they adhere. Place the cookies on the prepared baking sheet, spacing them 1 ½ inches apart and bake until slightly golden and cracked at the surface, about 15 minutes. Transfer cookies to a wire rack to cool.

❓ To make ground roasted hazelnuts, spread whole nuts on a dry baking tray and roast at 350°F until lightly browned and fragrant, about 6-8 minutes. Keep an eye on them and shake the tray frequently to prevent burning. While warm, place hazelnuts in the center of a clean dish cloth, fold the cloth over them like you are tucking them in to bed and rub or massage them around to release their bitter skins. Transfer skinned hazelnuts to a food processor and pulse until they resemble fine bread crumbs.

Extra Large, Extra Spicy Molasses Crinkle Cookies

Makes 15 large cookies

Ingredients:

2 ¼ cups all-purpose flour

1 ½ tsp baking soda

1 ½ tsp ground ginger

1 ½ tsp ground cinnamon

1 tsp ground mustard

½ tsp salt

½ tsp finely ground freshly cracked black pepper

⅔ cup unsalted butter, at room temperature

1 cup packed dark brown sugar

¼ cup dark cooking molasses

1 large egg, at room temperature

1 tbsp 2% milk

½ cup granulated sugar for rolling

In a medium bowl, whisk together flour, baking soda, ground ginger, ground cinnamon, ground mustard, salt and pepper; set aside.

In the bowl of an electric stand mixer fitted with the flat beater/paddle attachment, cream together butter and brown sugar on medium speed until somewhat light and fluffy but still grainy, 1 ½ to 2 minutes. Beat in molasses until well incorporated, about 10 seconds. Add egg and beat until smooth and the mixture no longer looks curdled, about 25 seconds. Beat in milk until well combined. Scrape down the sides of the bowl with a rubber spatula several times during mixing.

Add half of the flour mixture and beat on low speed until mostly combined, about 15 seconds. Add remaining dry ingredients and beat just until evenly blended. Do not over-mix. The dough will be slightly stiff but still soft and smooth. Place a piece of plastic wrap directly over the surface of the dough to cover it and refrigerate for about 2 hours. Chilling will allow the dry ingredients to hydrate thoroughly so that the cookies colour evenly and develop a rich brown tone.

Remove dough from the refrigerator and let it stand at room temperature for about 15 minutes before rolling to make it easier to work with.

Preheat your oven to 375°F.

Line two large baking sheets with parchment paper and set aside.

Place granulated sugar in a small bowl. Roll 2-oz mounds of dough (about ¼ cup) into balls and then roll them around in sugar to coat. Transfer dough balls to baking sheets, spacing them 2 to 3 inches apart, and flatten slightly with the bottom of a dry measuring cup.

Bake until cracked on the surface and lightly browned around the edges, 10-11 minutes. Let cool for 30 seconds on baking sheet before transferring individually to a wire rack to cool completely.

Double Chocolate Coconut French Macarons

Makes 30-35 sandwich cookies

....

Not unlike most fine French foods, macarons can be finicky! Use a scale for this recipe to weigh out the major ingredients, especially if this is your first time making them. It's really not as daunting as some make it out to be – just follow the directions vigilantly and measure your ingredients accurately as always.

....

For the macarons:

1 oz/28 g unsweetened desiccated coconut

3 oz/85 g blanched ground almonds (almond meal)

6 ½ oz/185 g icing sugar

15 g (2 ½ tbsp) unsweetened cocoa powder

3 ½ oz/100 g egg whites (about 3), at room temperature

⅛ tsp salt

¼ tsp cream of tartar

45 g (3 tbsp) granulated sugar

For the filling:

⅓ cup plus 1 tbsp 35% whipping cream

pinch of salt

4 oz/113 g dark chocolate (64% cocoa), finely chopped

Line two large baking sheets with silicone mats or parchment paper; set aside.

Place coconut in the bowl of a food processor and process until very fine. Add ground almonds, icing sugar and cocoa powder and process until evenly blended and very fine-textured, 1-2 minutes. Scrape around the bowl to make sure everything is evenly combined. Pass the mixture through a sieve and set aside. You can use whole blanched almonds, but be sure to process them until they are very, very fine (a coffee grinder works well for this).

Combine egg whites, salt and cream of tartar in a medium bowl. Beat with a hand mixer on medium speed until they appear foamy, like bubble bath, 25-30 seconds. While the mixer is running, carefully pour in the granulated sugar in a slow steady stream while continuing to beat on medium-high until the egg whites reach a consistency similar to that of shaving cream or mousse (the hair product). This will take about 3 minutes. Adding the sugar this early in the beating process will promote the incorporation of tiny air bubbles and ensure that the egg whites create a stable foam. Do not over-beat or the whites will become dry.

Add almond mixture to the meringue all at once and gently fold/stir it in until it resembles thick pancake batter but not more than 45 strokes. Immediately scoop the batter into a large pastry bag fitted with an open round tip (Ateco #803). Standing the bag in a tall glass can help stabilize it. It is important to work quickly at this point because the batter will get runny as it sits.

Pipe small 1-inch rounds onto prepared baking sheets, spacing them 2 inches apart (they will spread slightly). Let the piped rounds stand at room temperature for 25-30 minutes to allow their outer surfaces to dry out and harden a bit. They are ready when you can touch the surface and your finger remains clean, with no batter sticking to it.

Preheat your oven to 300°F. When ready, bake for about 16-17 minutes. Transfer baking sheet to a wire rack and let macarons cool on the tray for 15 minutes before transferring them individually to a wire rack to cool completely.

To make the filling, heat cream with salt in a small saucepan over medium-low heat until bubbles begin to form around the edges. Remove from heat and add chocolate. Let stand for 3 minutes before stirring gently with a spatula until smooth and glossy. Transfer to a clean bowl and cool at room temperature without stirring until thick and spreadable, about 30 minutes.

Spoon or spread the frosting on the flat side of one macaron, and then place another one on top to form a sandwich. Repeat with the remaining macarons and store in an airtight container.

....

✪ NOTE: Adding sugar to the egg whites near the beginning of the whipping stage is important to create a stable, fine-textured foam that holds up well to mixing and piping. It also helps to create a moist, spongy and marshmallow-like texture in the baked macarons.

Dark Chocolate-Dipped Fennel Biscotti

Makes about 24 cookies

....

I first tried the combination of dark chocolate and fennel at my Nonna's house when I was about 12 years old. It was incredible and it stuck with me. Now it's stuck in this book so you can enjoy it too.

....

Ingredients:

1 ⅔ cups plus all-purpose flour

2 ½ oz/70 g ground almonds (about ⅔ cup)

1 tbsp fennel seeds, lightly crushed in a mortar and pestle

1 tsp baking powder

¼ tsp salt

2 large eggs, at room temperature

⅔ cup granulated sugar, plus extra for sprinkling

2 tbsp unsalted butter

2 tsp finely grated lemon zest

1 tsp pure vanilla extract

½ tsp pure almond extract

2 tbsp 35% whipping cream for brushing

6 oz/170 g dark couverture chocolate (64% cocoa), finely chopped

Preheat your oven to 350°F. Line a large baking sheet with parchment paper and set aside.

In a medium bowl, whisk together flour, ground almonds, fennel seeds, baking powder and salt.

In the bowl of a stand mixer fitted with the flat beater/paddle attachment, beat eggs on medium speed until blended, about 15 seconds. With mixer running, gradually add sugar and then beat on medium-high speed until pale and thick, 2-3 minutes.

Meanwhile, in a small saucepan over low heat, combine butter with lemon zest until melted. Stir in vanilla extract and almond extract and set aside to cool slightly. This helps to infuse the butter with the citrus flavours. Gradually add this mixture to the whipped eggs and beat until well combined. Add the flour mixture all at once and beat on low speed until blended. The dough will be sticky. Cover the bowl with a tea towel and let the dough rest for 5 minutes.

Turn dough out onto a lightly floured work surface and bring it together to form a smooth mass, folding it over itself and kneading it very gently a couple of times. Add a tablespoon or so more flour if necessary to prevent sticking. The dough will be soft. Roll it out into a 12-inch log and transfer to prepared baking sheet. Flatten the log so that it is about 13 inches long and 3 inches wide. Brush the top and sides with cream and sprinkle generously with granulated sugar. Bake until golden brown and slightly puffed, 23-25 minutes.

Transfer baking sheet to a wire rack and let biscotti log cool on pan for 15 minutes. Reduce oven temperature to 300°F. Transfer log to a cutting board and use a serrated knife to slice it diagonally into about ½-inch-thick slices with a gentle sawing motion. Place cookies back on the baking sheet so that they are sitting upright and bake until dry and crisp, 10-15 minutes. Let biscotti cool completely before dipping.

Place 5 oz of finely chopped chocolate in a heatproof bowl set over a pot with ½-inch of barely simmering water. Stir constantly until almost completely melted (some small pieces of solid chocolate should remain). Remove bowl from over pot and stir until smooth, allowing the residual heat to melt the rest of the chocolate. Add remaining ounce of chopped chocolate and stir until smooth and melted, placing bowl over hot water for a few seconds if necessary. Do not over-heat the chocolate (it should not exceed 90°F). Dip the tips, or entire length, of each biscotti in melted chocolate and then place on a piece of wax paper until completely set.

Cardamom Spice Wafers

Makes about 36 cookies

Ingredients:

1 ⅔ cups all-purpose flour

1 tbsp corn starch ❓

½ tsp baking powder

¼ tsp salt

¾ tsp ground cardamom

¼ tsp ground allspice

⅛ tsp ground cinnamon

½ cup unsalted butter, at room temperature

⅔ cup granulated sugar

1 large egg, at room temperature

1 tsp pure vanilla extract

In a medium bowl, whisk together flour, corn starch, baking powder, salt, ground cardamom, ground allspice and ground cinnamon and set it aside.

In the bowl of a stand mixer fitted with the flat beater/paddle attachment, beat butter on medium speed until smooth and creamy, about 20 seconds. Add sugar and beat on medium speed until pale and fluffy, about 1 ½ to 2 minutes. Scrape down the sides and bottom of the bowl, add egg and vanilla extract and beat on medium speed until well incorporated, 30-45 seconds. If the mixture still looks a tad bit curdled, it's OK.

Add flour mixture in two batches and mix on low speed until it becomes moistened and forms a crumbly dough, about 15 seconds between additions. Remove the bowl from the mixer and finish mixing by hand using a rubber spatula until a soft dough forms.

Turn dough out onto a large piece of plastic wrap and use your hands to form it into a 9 to 10-inch long log (1 ½ inches wide). Use the plastic wrap and a ruler to roll, press, smooth and square off the sides of the log to essentially create a square log (if that makes any sense). Place the log on a baking sheet to keep the edges flat and refrigerate until firm, about 2 hours. Rotate it every 15 minutes to make sure all four sides stay flat and the log keeps its square shape.

Preheat your oven to 350°F. Line two baking sheets with parchment paper and set aside.

Use a sharp knife to slice the log into squares between ⅛ and ¼-inch thickness and arrange slices on prepared baking sheets. These don't spread much so you can fit quite a few on one tray. Poke cookies with a fork four consecutive times down the center of each one. This helps to let steam escape so that the cookies bake up evenly and stay crisp.

Bake until edges are lightly golden, 10-12 minutes. Immediately transfer cookies to a wire rack to cool completely. Serve with a tall glass of cold milk!

❓ Corn starch keeps these cookies tender and crisp by diluting the flour and reducing the total percentage of protein in the dry ingredients.

Dark Chocolate Pecan & Date Rugelach Pinwheels

Makes about 24 cookies

For the dough:

4 oz/113 g brick cream cheese, at room temperature

½ cup unsalted butter, at room temperature

2 ½ tbsp golden honey

¼ tsp salt

1 ¼ cups all-purpose flour

For the filling:

3 oz/85 g finely chopped pitted dried dates (about ⅔ cup)

2 oz/56 g finely chopped pecans (about ½ cup)

2 oz/56 g bittersweet chocolate (72% cocoa), chopped into small pieces

⅓ cup packed dark brown sugar

¼ tsp freshly grated nutmeg

2 tbsp 35% whipping cream

In a large bowl, beat cream cheese with a wooden spoon until creamy. Add butter and beat together with the cream cheese until smooth. Stir in honey and salt until well combined. Add flour and stir until well incorporated. Dough will be smooth and soft but not sticky. Turn dough out onto a piece of plastic wrap, flatten into a rectangle and wrap well. Refrigerate at least 2 hours.

Remove dough from fridge about 15 minutes prior to rolling so that it is easier to work with. Line two large baking sheets with parchment paper and set aside.

In a small bowl, stir together chopped dates, pecans, chocolate, brown sugar, nutmeg and cream until evenly combined and set aside.

Divide dough in half. On a lightly floured work surface, roll out one half into a 12x7-inch rectangle, arranging it so that the lengths are facing north and south. Sprinkle half of date/nut mixture in an even layer over the rectangle leaving a ½-inch border. Starting with the length furthest from you, roll it up towards yourself into a snug log. As you reach the end, brush the edge closest to you lightly with cold water to help seal it. Pinch the seam together to seal the log nicely. Repeat with second half of dough. Place logs, seam-side-down, on prepared baking sheets, cover loosely with plastic wrap and refrigerate until firm, about 15 minutes.

Preheat your oven to 350°F.

Slice logs into ½ to ¾-inch rounds and lay them cut-side-down on lined baking sheets, spacing them about 1 ½ inches apart. Flatten them slightly with the bottom of a measuring cup (I like to do this to give them a more rounded shape but it is totally optional). Bake until lightly browned, 16-18 minutes, and then transfer to a wire rack to cool completely.

Sparkly Ginger Cookies

Makes about 20 cookies

Ingredients:

1 ½ cups plus 1 tbsp all-purpose flour

1 ¼ tsp ground ginger

¾ tsp baking soda

½ cup unsalted butter, at room temperature

½ cup packed light brown sugar

½ cup granulated sugar plus ½ cup extra for rolling

¼ tsp salt

2 tsp dark cooking molasses

1 large egg, at room temperature

½ tsp pure vanilla extract

¼ tsp pure cinnamon extract ❷

Preheat your oven to 350°F.

Line two large baking sheets with parchment paper and set aside.

In a medium bowl, whisk together flour, ground ginger and baking soda; set aside.

In a large bowl, cream together butter, brown sugar, ½ cup of granulated sugar and salt using a wide rubber spatula until somewhat light and fluffy. This will take about 1 minute. Stir in molasses until evenly blended.

Add egg, vanilla extract and cinnamon extract and stir until well incorporated and the mixture no longer appears curdled. Add dry ingredients to butter mixture all at once and fold it in gently until evenly incorporated and no streaks of flour remain. The dough will be soft. Place a piece of plastic wrap directly against the surface of the dough in the bowl and refrigerate for 20 minutes.

Place remaining ½ cup of sugar in a bowl. Roll 1 to 1 ¼-oz portions of dough into balls and then roll them around in sugar so that they are evenly coated. Place them on prepared baking sheets, spacing them 2 inches apart and bake until golden and cracked at the surface, 9-10 minutes. Let cookies cool for 30 seconds on the baking sheet before transferring them individually to a wire rack to cool completely.

✱ Ground Ginger:

Powdered ginger is the dried and ground version of fresh ginger. It has an earthy flavour and is less pungent compared to its fresh counterpart, which has more of a medicinal character. It pairs naturally with other baking spices, including cinnamon, clove and nutmeg, such as in gingerbread cookies.

❷ You can find cinnamon extract in the baking aisle of your grocery store, in the same place where you find vanilla, peppermint and almond extracts. It contains pure cinnamaldehyde, which is the organic phenolic compound responsible for the characteristic flavour and aroma of cinnamon, and is used to give red cinnamon heart candies their spicy punch.

Cinnamon Toffee Icebox Sandwich Cookies

Makes about 30 cookies

For the dough:

1 ½ cups all-purpose flour

1 tsp ground cinnamon

½ tsp baking powder

¼ tsp salt

½ cup unsalted butter, at room temperature

½ cup granulated sugar

¼ cup packed light brown sugar

1 large egg, at room temperature

1 tsp pure vanilla extract

For the filling:

1 recipe Toffee Sauce (page 230)

In a medium bowl, whisk together flour, cinnamon, baking powder and salt; set aside.

In a bowl of an electric stand mixer fitted with the flat beater/paddle attachment beat butter with both sugars on medium speed until pale and fluffy, about 1 ½ minutes. Add egg and vanilla and mix on medium speed until smooth, about 30 seconds. With mixer on low speed, slowly add flour about ½ cup at a time and mix just until a soft dough forms. Do not over-beat. This should only take about 10 seconds.

Turn the dough out onto a piece of plastic wrap, wrap well and refrigerate until firm, 1 to 2 hours.

Preheat your oven to 325°F. Line two large baking sheets with parchment paper and set aside.

Roll dough out to ⅛-inch thickness and cut out as many 2-inch rounds as you can (I like to use a size just barely smaller than 2 inches). Carefully transfer cookies to prepared baking sheets using a large offset spatula. Refrigerate cookies on the trays for about 10 minutes and then bake until golden around the edges, 8-10 minutes. Transfer cookies to a wire rack to cool completely.

Spread about ¾ teaspoon of toffee sauce on the bottom sides of half of the cookies and make little sandwiches by placing the remaining cookies on top. Keep refrigerated in an airtight container to prevent the filling from oozing out. I love to eat these right from the fridge because when they're cold, the filling is nice and chewy.

✪ NOTE: If you don't have time to make the toffee sauce, a great alternative is to spread some creamy natural peanut butter between these cookies instead and they will be incredible. I find the combination of peanuts and cinnamon to be rather comforting.

Crisp & Spicy
Mayan Cocoa Thins

Makes about 3 dozen cookies

For the dough:

1 cup all-purpose flour

1 oz/28 g unsweetened Dutch-processed cocoa powder (about ⅓ cup)

¼ cup granulated sugar

¼ tsp salt

¼ tsp ground clove

6 tbsp very cold butter, cut into ½-inch pieces

1 large egg yolk

1 ½ tbsp ice cold water

1 tsp pure vanilla extract

For the topping:

2 tbsp granulated sugar

¾ tsp ground cinnamon

¼ tsp cayenne pepper

1-2 tbsp 35% whipping cream

In a large bowl, whisk together flour, cocoa powder, sugar, salt and ground clove until evenly blended. Using a pastry blender or your fingertips, cut or rub butter into flour until it resembles coarse bread crumbs. The butter should be well dispersed with some oat flake-sized pieces remaining, but there should be no dusty flour left in the bowl. Use a fork to beat egg yolk well with water and vanilla extract in a small bowl until very fluid and drizzle into flour mixture while gently stirring with the fork. Continue to mix dough until dry ingredients are moistened and it holds together in clumps. Turn dough out onto a clean work surface and bring it together to form a mass.

Now apply the fraisage technique to form a cohesive dough. Use the heel of your hand to push portions of dough away from you, smearing it along the work surface to distribute fat into the flour. Repeat this process up to 5 times total, but only go over each portion of dough once or the pastry will become tough. You should be able to see faint streaks of butter marbled throughout the dough, which will give it a slightly flaky texture. Gather dough into a ball using a bench scraper, flatten into a disk, wrap tightly with plastic wrap and refrigerate until firm, about 2 hours.

Preheat your oven to 350°F.

Line two baking sheets with parchment paper and set aside.

On a lightly floured work surface roll dough out to ⅛-inch thickness. Use a 2 to 2 ½-inch round to cut out as many circles as you can and carefully transfer them to prepared baking sheet using a large off-set spatula. Gather scraps of pastry, re-roll it and cut out more circles until most of the dough is used up. Place the trays in the refrigerator to let the dough rounds chill for 10 minutes.

In a small bowl, stir together sugar, cinnamon and cayenne pepper until evenly combined. Brush each cookie lightly with cream and generously (and I mean generously) sprinkle sugar mixture evenly over the cookies. Be sure to use up all, or at least most, of this sugar mixture because it gives the cookies a lovely crunch and sparkle.

Bake until crisp and slightly puffed, 9-10 minutes. Transfer cookies to a wire rack to cool completely.

Wrinkly

Whispy

Dull

Matte

Shiny

Brownie Crust
Personality

Burnt Sugar Banana Brownies

Makes 16 servings

For the caramelized bananas:

3 tbsp granulated sugar

1 tbsp light corn syrup

1 tbsp water

1 large ripe banana, peeled, halved crosswise and sliced lengthwise into ¼-inch-thick strips

For the brownie batter:

4 oz/113 g bittersweet chocolate (72% cocoa), coarsely chopped

6 tbsp unsalted butter

⅓ cup all-purpose flour

¼ tsp salt

2 tbsp unsweetened cocoa powder

2 large eggs, at room temperature

½ cup granulated sugar

⅓ cup packed light brown sugar

½ tsp pure vanilla extract

Preheat your oven to 325°F. Line an 8 x 8-inch baking pan with parchment paper, leaving a 2-inch overhang on each side; set aside.

To caramelize the bananas, first make sure you have them sliced and ready to go. You will need a speckled, ripe but firm banana. At the right stage of ripeness, they will be more delicate and a bit trickier to handle, but their sugar content will help the caramel stick to them nicely.

Sprinkle sugar in an even layer in a shallow 1-quart sauce-pan over medium-low heat. Add corn syrup and drizzle water around the outside edges of the sugar and continue to cook without stirring until amber in colour, about 8 minutes. Begin swirling the pan periodically to colour evenly once the syrup turns golden. Wash down the sides of pan with a pastry brush dipped in water to dissolve any crystals that may form. Watch closely because once the sugar begins to change from colourless to brownish-yellow, the reaction will proceed very quickly. When the caramel is almost ready, the large bubbles will subside and a golden foam will appear at the surface. Turn off the heat but keep the pan over the heat source and carefully add bananas. Very gently turn them to coat in caramel and let them cook for 20-30 seconds so that some moisture is released and the hard caramel liquefies to form a bit of a sauce. If you don't cook them long enough, the caramel syrup will turn into hard candy and form a crust around the bananas, but if you cook them for too long the bananas will get mushy and fall apart. Slide them off of the pan and onto a plate; set aside for later.

In a large heatproof bowl set over a pot with ½-inch of barely simmering water, stir together chocolate and butter until completely melted, smooth and glossy; set aside to cool slightly, about 5 minutes. In separate small bowl, add flour and salt. Sift in cocoa powder, whisk to blend evenly and set aside.

In a medium bowl, beat eggs with both sugars using an electric hand mixer on high speed until pale, thick and fluffy, about 3 minutes. When you lift up the beaters, the egg mixture will form a slowly disappearing ribbon on the surface of itself when it falls back into the bowl. Beat in vanilla extract. Stir in warm chocolate mixture until well blended. Add flour mixture and fold it in using a rubber spatula until well incorporated and smooth. Pour batter into prepared pan and use the back of the spatula to smooth out the surface. Carefully transfer bananas over the brownie batter in a single layer, spacing them about 1 inch apart. Spoon some of the residual caramel sauce over the bananas.

Bake until slightly puffed and a toothpick inserted into the center comes out with a few bits of sticky batter, 20-25 minutes. Transfer pan to a wire rack to cool completely before cutting into squares.

....

✪ NOTE: if you bake these brownies in a ceramic baking dish, increase the baking time by about 10-15 minutes as ceramic does not transfer heat as efficiently as metal.

Gianduja Chocolate Brownies

Makes 12-16 brownies

....

Box mixes? What the heck are those? Throw them out. These brownies have all the softness and chewiness of a boxed mix without the box. Icing or confectioner's sugar is the secret ingredient in this recipe to lend a tender yet decadent texture, while also creating a shiny and crackly top due to its instant-dissolving properties. The use of cocoa powder and butter as opposed to melted chocolate also keeps them soft, making them the perfect vehicle to drive around some hazelnut studded chocolate chunks. "Gianduja" refers to this very Italian combination of hazelnut and chocolate. At first glance, 2 ¼ cups of icing sugar may sound like a lot, but by weight it's the typical amount used in most brownie recipes.

....

For the gianduja chocolate:

2 oz/56 g raw hazelnuts

5 oz/142 g pure milk chocolate

For the brownie batter:

9 oz/255 g sifted icing sugar (about 2 ¼ cups)

½ cup all-purpose flour

½ cup salted butter

½ tsp instant coffee granules

1 ¾ oz/50 g unsweetened cocoa powder (about ½ cup plus 1 tbsp)

½ tsp salt

2 large eggs, lightly beaten

1 tsp pure vanilla extract

1 tbsp hot water

Line a baking sheet with parchment paper and set aside.

To make gianduja chocolate, toast hazelnuts by placing them in a single layer in a dry frying pan over medium heat. Keep an eye on them, shaking the pan frequently, until fragrant and lightly browned, 6-7 minutes. Transfer nuts to a dry dish towel and rub off the skins while warm. Place them in the bowl of a food processor and pulse 10-15 times until they resemble coarse crumbs; set aside.

Place milk chocolate in a medium heatproof bowl set over a pot with ½-inch of barely simmering water. Stir frequently until completely melted and smooth. Stir in ground hazelnuts until evenly blended and then spread this mixture in a layer about ¼-inch thick over the parchment-lined baking sheet. Refrigerate until firm and then chop into chunks; set aside.

Preheat your oven to 350°F. Line an 8 x 8-inch metal baking pan with a strip of parchment paper, leaving a 2-inch overhang on opposite ends and butter the exposed sides.

In a small bowl, whisk together icing sugar and flour until evenly blended and set aside. Place butter in a small 1-quart saucepan over medium-low heat and stir until completely melted. Whisk in instant coffee granules, cocoa powder and salt until blended and smooth. Set aside to cool slightly.

Add beaten eggs, vanilla extract, hot water and cocoa mixture to the bowl with the icing sugar and beat for 1 minute on medium speed using an electric hand mixer. The batter will be smooth. Fold in chopped hazelnut chocolate. Pour batter into your prepared pan, spreading it into the corners. Bake until slightly puffed and the top is shiny, wrinkly and cracked, about 25 minutes. A toothpick inserted someplace between the center and the edge of the pan should come out with a few moist crumbs. Make sure you do not over-bake these! Once cooled, run a knife along the bare sides of the pan and use the overhanging parchment to lift brownies out and onto a work surface. Slice brownies into 12 or 16 squares using a hot dry knife and serve.

....

✪ Toasting Nuts:

The high oil content of nuts makes them suitable to dry cooking methods, such as toasting or roasting, which brings out their flavours. It adds complexity and richness to baked good by promoting Maillard browning (a really delicious reaction between proteins and sugars).

Espresso Brownies

Makes 12-16 brownies

....

These brownies are for true coffee and dark chocolate lovers. The use of bittersweet chocolate with the addition of cocoa powder and espresso coffee grounds creates a robust flavour. Combined with the slightly lower amount of sugar compared to most brownies, these are rich and dark and highlight the bitter roasted notes of both coffee and chocolate.

....

Ingredients:

6 oz/170 g bittersweet chocolate (72% cocoa), coarsely chopped

⅓ cup unsalted butter

2 tsp espresso coffee grounds

½ cup <u>minus</u> 1 tbsp all-purpose flour

¼ tsp salt

1 tbsp unsweetened cocoa powder

2 large eggs, at room temperature

¾ cup plus 2 tbsp granulated sugar

1 tsp pure vanilla extract

Preheat your oven to 350°F.

Line an 8 x 8-inch baking pan with parchment paper, leaving a 2-inch overhang on opposite ends and butter exposed sides.

In a large bowl set over a pot with ½-inch of barely simmering water, stir together chocolate, butter and espresso grounds until completely melted, smooth and glossy; set aside to cool about 5 minutes.

Meanwhile, in a separate small bowl, add flour and salt. Sift in cocoa powder to remove lumps and whisk to blend evenly; set aside.

In the bowl of a stand mixer fitted with the whisk attachment, beat eggs with sugar and vanilla extract on high speed until pale, thick and fluffy, 3-5 minutes. When you lift up the beaters, the egg mixture will form a slowly disappearing ribbon on the surface of the mixture when it falls back into the bowl.

Remove bowl from mixer and gently stir in slightly cooled chocolate mixture until evenly blended. Fold in flour mixture until well incorporated and smooth. Pour batter into prepared pan and use the back of the spatula to smooth out the surface.

Bake until slightly puffed and a toothpick inserted someplace between the edge and the center comes out with a few moist crumbs, about 20 minutes. The top should be shiny, wrinkly and cracked.

Transfer pan to a wire rack and let cool completely. Once cooled, run a knife along the bare sides of the pan and use the overhanging parchment to lift brownies out and onto a work surface. Slice brownies into 12 or 16 squares using a hot dry knife and serve.

....

✪ NOTE: As for most recipes, it is important to have your eggs at room temperature in order for them to whip up properly, dissolve the sugars, and for the warm melted chocolate to become evenly blended into the batter. Since most of us store our eggs in the fridge, simply submerge them in a bowl of warm water for about 10 minutes before using them.

Goat Cheese Swirl & Strawberry Brownies

Makes 12 brownies

I know I can ramble on and on about the importance of letting brownies cool completely before eating them, but I'll spare you the lecture just this once. Eating these brownies slightly warm reminds of strawberry pie. The strawberries roast in the oven and their flavour permeates the entire batch. In turn, the batter lends some of its sweetness making the berries taste like candy! Now, I realize that I shoved whole fresh strawberries right into my brownie batter. It's madness. I strongly encourage you to try it or I wouldn't have thrown it in your face like this, but I also understand that this is a big step out of the box. If you prefer to leave them out, reduce the baking time by 3-5 minutes and your chocolate goat cheese dreams will come true.

For the brownie batter:

12 small strawberries, washed and dried

3 ½ oz/100 g bittersweet chocolate (72% cocoa), coarsely chopped

⅓ cup unsalted butter

¾ cup plus 2 tbsp superfine sugar (caster or instant dissolving sugar)

¼ tsp salt

½ tsp pure vanilla extract

1 large egg, at room temperature

1 large egg white (reserve the yolk for the swirl)

⅓ cup plus 1 tbsp all-purpose flour

For the cheese swirl:

3 ½ oz/100 g brick cream cheese, at room temperature

2 oz/56 g goat cheese, at room temperature

2 tbsp superfine sugar

1 large egg yolk

Preheat your oven to 325°F. Line an 8 x 8-inch baking pan with parchment paper, leaving a 2-inch overhang on each side.

To prepare the strawberries, use a paring knife to slice off the tip of any over-sized ones if necessary so that each one is about 1-inch long; set them aside. Try to use local, seasonal strawberries not only for their superior flavour but for their vibrant redness that permeates throughout because some of their colour will leach out into the batter during baking and you don't want to be left with anemic-looking berries.

Place chocolate and butter in a large heatproof bowl set over a pot with ½-inch of barely simmering water. Stir constantly using a rubber spatula until completely melted and smooth. Gradually stir in sugar and salt over the heat until evenly blended and then set aside to cool slightly for 1 minute. Add vanilla extract and whole egg and whisk until well incorporated and batter is smooth. Whisk in egg white until well combined and batter appears glossy. Add flour and stir it in gently until you can no longer see it.

Pour batter into prepared pan, reserving about ½ cup, and place it in the freezer to firm up as you prepare the cheese swirl.

To make the cheese swirl, combine cream cheese with goat cheese in a medium bowl and beat with an electric hand mixer on medium speed until smooth. Beat in sugar until glossy and then beat in egg yolk just until combined. Spread cream cheese mixture evenly over the chilled brownie batter. Dollop reserved brownie batter over the surface and use the blunt edge of a knife to swirl the two batters into each other. Stick the prepared strawberries into the batter, spacing them evenly apart, and bake until slightly puffed and still a bit soft in the middle, 28-30 minutes. Let them cool for about 30 minutes before slicing and serve warm.

Due to the high moisture content of the strawberries, these brownies don't keep for more than two or three days in the refrigerator, but after you discover how incredible these are, I'm sure storing them won't be an issue.

Perfectly Dark Chocolate Brownies

Makes 12-16 brownies

....

This is my classic go-to brownie recipe. These beautiful chocolate squares are dense and fudgy without being gooey due to the decent amount of flour in the batter. They're the kind that leave teeth marks when you bite into them. Make sure your eggs are at room temperature to help dissolve the granulated sugar and achieve that lovely and irresistible shiny crust.

....

Ingredients:

3 oz/85 g bittersweet chocolate (72% cocoa), coarsely chopped

2 oz/56 g unsweetened chocolate, coarsely chopped

6 tbsp unsalted butter

½ tsp fine sea salt

2 large eggs, at room temperature

½ tsp pure vanilla extract

1 cup granulated sugar

½ cup all-purpose flour

Preheat your oven to 350°F. Line an 8x8-inch metal baking pan with parchment paper leaving a 2-inch overhang at each side.

In a medium heatproof bowl set over a pot with ½-inch of barely simmering water, stir together bittersweet chocolate, unsweetened chocolate and butter using a spatula until completely melted, smooth and glossy. Stir in sea salt and set aside to cool slightly, about 3 minutes.

Meanwhile, whisk eggs and vanilla extract in a medium bowl just enough to blend and break up the yolks. Gradually add sugar in a steady stream while whisking constantly. Once combined, whisk vigorously by hand until slightly thickened and lightened by a shade. This will take about 30 seconds. Add warm chocolate mixture and whisk until evenly blended.

Sprinkle flour over the mixture and stir it in gently using a rubber spatula until well incorporated and batter is smooth. Pour batter into prepared pan, spread it out into the corners and bake until the top is shiny and a toothpick inserted into the center of the brownies comes out with a few moist sticky bits, 18-20 minutes.

Transfer pan to a wire rack and let cool completely before unmolding. Once cooled, use the overhanging parchment to lift brownies out and onto a work surface. Slice them into 12 or 16 squares using a hot dry knife and serve!

For an even more fudge-like texture, refrigerate for 1 to 2 hours before serving.

Chocolatte Brownies

Makes 12-16 brownies

Ingredients:

4 oz/113 g semisweet chocolate (54% cocoa), coarsely chopped

⅓ cup unsalted butter

1 ½ tsp espresso coffee grounds

¼ tsp salt

¾ cup superfine sugar, such as caster or instant dissolving sugar

2 tsp 2% milk

1 tbsp unsweetened cocoa powder

½ tsp pure vanilla extract

2 large eggs, at room temperature

½ cup all-purpose flour

⅓ cup sweetened condensed milk

Preheat your oven to 325°F. Line an 8 x 8-inch metal baking pan all the way around with aluminum foil leaving a 2-inch overhang at each side. Lightly butter the foil and set aside.

In a medium heatproof bowl set over a pot with ½-inch of barely simmering water, stir together chocolate, butter, coffee grounds and salt with a rubber spatula until completely melted, smooth and glossy. Gradually pour in sugar in a steady stream while whisking until completely blended. Remove bowl from the heat and whisk in milk, cocoa powder and vanilla extract.

Whisk in eggs, one at a time, until well incorporated, about 30-40 strokes per egg. The batter will change from dull and broken-looking to smooth and glossy.

Scatter flour over the batter and stir gently until well combined and batter is smooth.

Drizzle condensed milk over the batter in a zig-zag pattern and use the blunt edge of a knife to gently swirl it in. Try to swirl at the surface, being careful not to get too much condensed milk deep within the batter.

Bake until a toothpick inserted into the center comes out with some bits of sticky batter, 20-25 minutes. Transfer to a wire rack and let cool completely.

Once cooled, use the overhanging foil to lift brownies out and onto a work surface. Slice brownies into 12 or 16 squares using a hot dry knife and serve.

Roasted Cherry Fudge Brownies

Makes 16 brownies

For the roasted cherries

1 cup pitted and halved sweet cherries

1 tbsp granulated sugar

For the brownie batter:

5 oz/142 g bittersweet chocolate (72% cocoa), coarsely chopped

6 tbsp unsalted butter

¾ cup superfine sugar, such as caster or instant dissolving sugar

¼ cup packed dark brown sugar

¼ tsp salt

2 large eggs, at room temperature

⅓ cup all-purpose flour

16 pitted sweet cherry halves for topping

½ tsp flaked sea salt for topping

Preheat your oven to 425°F.

In a small roasting pan, combine the fresh cherries and 1 tablespoon of sugar. Roast for 8 minutes, or until the cherries start releasing their juices. Use a slotted spoon to transfer cherries to a bowl and let cool completely.

Reduce oven temperature to 350°F.

Line an 8 x 8-inch metal baking pan with parchment paper, leaving a 2-inch overhang at each side.

Place chocolate and butter in a large heatproof bowl set over a pot with ½-inch of barely simmering water over medium-low heat. Stir using a spatula until completely melted, smooth and glossy. While still over the heat, gradually stir in both sugars and salt. Turn off the heat, but continue to stir the mixture over the pot of hot water for a full minute.

Remove the bowl from the heat and let cool slightly, about 5 minutes.

Whisk the eggs into the chocolate mixture, one at a time, mixing vigorously for 10 seconds to incorporate each before adding the next. The batter should be smooth and shiny. Finally, add flour and gently fold it into the batter until blended and smooth.

Fold in roasted cherries. Scrape the batter into the prepared pan and spread it out evenly. Place 16 cherry halves evenly spaced across the top of the batter and sprinkle flaked sea salt evenly over top. Bake until the surface is bumpy and shiny, 23-25 minutes. A skewer inserted into the center of the brownies should come out with a few moist and sticky bits clinging to it.

Transfer to a wire rack to cool completely. Once cooled, use the overhanging parchment to lift brownies out and onto a work surface. Slice brownies into 16 squares using a hot dry knife and serve.

✪ NOTE: Brownies are one of those recipes that I feel salted butter makes no harm and can actually enhance the flavours by bringing out the rich chocolate intensity. If all you have is salted butter at home, feel free to use it in place of unsalted butter in any of these brownie recipes. In this case, reduce the added salt by about half.

Coconut Praline Brownies

Makes 16 brownies

For the topping:

¼ cup granulated sugar

1 tbsp water

1 ¼ oz/35 g whole almonds (about ¼ cup)

2 oz/56 g sweetened shredded coconut (about ½ cup)

¼ cup sweetened condensed milk

For the brownie batter:

4 oz/113 g bittersweet chocolate (72% cocoa), coarsely chopped

⅓ cup unsalted butter, at room temperature

¾ cup granulated sugar

¼ tsp salt

½ tsp pure vanilla extract

2 large eggs, at room temperature

⅓ cup all-purpose flour

Line a baking sheet with parchment paper or a silicone baking mat and set aside.

To make the praline, spread sugar in a single layer in a small 1-quart stainless steel saucepan over medium heat. Drizzle water around the edges of the sugar and cook without stirring until it begins to bubble and turn a golden colour, about 5 minutes. Begin swirling pan periodically for even colouring. Continue to cook until sugar liquefies and turns golden amber. The large bubbles will subside and a golden foam will form at the surface when the caramel is nearly ready.

Remove from heat, stir in almonds and immediately pour onto prepared baking sheet and flatten with a silicone spatula. Let cool at room temperature until hardened, break into small pieces and then pulse in a food processor until it resembles coarse crumbs.

Preheat your oven to 325°F.

Line an 8 x 8-inch metal baking pan with parchment paper, leaving a 2-inch overhang on each side.

Place chocolate and butter in a large heatproof bowl set over a pot with ½-inch of barely simmering water. Stir constantly until completely melted, smooth and glossy. Remove bowl from heat, gradually stir in sugar and salt. Stir in vanilla extract and let stand 2-3 minutes to cool slightly. Add eggs, one at a time, stirring until well incorporated after each addition. This will take 30-40 strokes per egg. Sprinkle flour over the batter and gently fold it in until smooth.

Pour batter into prepared pan and refrigerate 15 minutes to let it firm up slightly. Retrieve pan from fridge and sprinkle half of praline mixture evenly in one layer over batter. Do not pack it down. Sprinkle coconut in a single layer over praline and then sprinkle half of remaining praline over top. Drizzle condensed milk all over the surface in a zig-zag pattern and then sprinkle remaining praline over top. Bake until slightly puffed, golden and bubbling around the edges, about 20-25 minutes. A toothpick inserted into the center should come out with some bits of sticky batter. Transfer pan to a wire rack and let cool at least 2 hours before cutting into squares using a hot dry knife.

CAKES
and
CUPCAKES

fig. 2

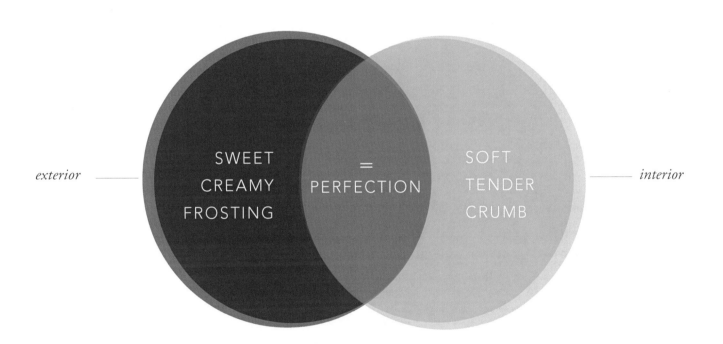

exterior — SWEET CREAMY FROSTING = PERFECTION SOFT TENDER CRUMB — interior

The Secret Life of Cake

Whether it's light and airy or heavy and dense, cake is always a treat. It is typically defined by its tender, fine-textured crumb and sweet flavour. Above all, I find it amazing how heat can transform batter into cake. As amazing as it may be, it can also be scary waiting and watching through the oven window with hopes that all of your hard work and precision will reward you with a tall, moist, evenly browned cake. Sometimes, no matter how lovely or tasty your batter appears, there's no way of knowing what will happen in the oven. That is, unless you know the facts! The exact ingredients, their proportions and the mixing techniques used to make cake batter all produce different results. Having said this, cake styles generally fall into two main categories: shortened cakes and foam cakes.

SHORTENED CAKES: Shortened cakes, also known as butter cakes, are typically made with butter as the primary fat. They are given this name due to their relatively high fat content compared to foam cakes, which 'shortens' the texture by weakening the gluten protein network. This gives them a soft, delicate melt-in-your mouth texture, moist crumb and rich flavour. Butter cakes are probably the most popular owing to their role as the traditional birthday cake. They are generally layered with a sweet and creamy frosting which is slathered both between the layers and then all around them to envelop the entire cake. Most shortened cakes depend mainly on chemical leavening agents, such as baking powder and baking soda, for their height and lightness.

FOAM CAKES: Foam cakes tend to have fewer ingredients and steps than shortened cakes, as well as a high proportion of eggs to flour. The texture of these light and simple cakes is more open, spongy and dry compared to butter cakes since they are generally leaner, containing little or no fat. The terms foam cake and sponge cake are sometimes used interchangeably for this reason. They depend almost entirely on the air beaten into fully whipped eggs for their structure and lightness. The high proportion of eggs also makes them sturdy. Whole eggs, or separated yolks and whites, are beaten vigorously with sugar for several minutes to create a foam through the incorporation of many tiny air bubbles that will expand and make the cake rise during baking. Some foam cakes use chemical leaveners for extra lift and always require gentle folding to combine the ingredients to help retain an airy texture.

Ingredient Functions

THE BASIC INGREDIENTS AND HOW THEY ARE COMBINED TO MAKE A BATTER PLAY KEY ROLES IN CAKE-MAKING.

FATS: Creaming is the first structure-building step in most butter cake recipes, serving to lighten the batter and create an even crumb. It involves thorough and vigorous blending of room temperature fat and sugar until the mixture becomes pale in colour or almost white due to the incorporation of many tiny air cells that scatter light. Whipping introduces air while crystalline sugar granules pierce through fat globules in butter, which helps to distribute fat around air to form stable pockets. In being hydrophobic, or repelled by water, fat is more attracted to air and the solid state of butter allows it to retain a network of air cells. These entrapped bubbles further expand during baking with the help of chemical leavening agents and make the cake rise. Some cake recipes skip the creaming step all together and use a method that blends all of the dry ingredients with the butter to coat the flour with fat before beating in the wet ingredients and creating a smooth batter. These types depend entirely on chemical leaveners for their height and are very tender, yet lack the structure of a traditional cake. For this reason, I prefer to use this method mainly for small cakes and cupcakes.

In addition to developing structure, butter tenderizes by coating flour proteins and preventing the formation of long, elastic gluten strands. It then melts during baking and moisturizes the coagulated and stiffened structure of the cake. Too much fat, however, can lead to a dense and heavy cake, like pound cake. Low fat cakes have a more open and airy texture because the air bubbles are able to expand more in the oven.

Vegetable oil helps to produce a much softer and more moist crumb due to its unsaturated fatty acid content which keeps it liquid at room temperature. The downside to using these plant-derived oils in baking is that they lack body and mouthfeel compared to butter. With the exception of olive oil, they also have little to offer when it comes to flavour. I prefer to use a mix of half and half or 2 parts butter to 1 part oil for most recipes. Strictly oil based batters are best when dealing with strong-flavoured cakes or ones where you won't miss the flavor of butter, like chocolate, spice or carrot.

SUGAR: Aside from adding sweetness and body, sugar helps cake retain moisture. It also plays an indirect role in tenderizing as it competes with flour for available water, preventing the potential formation of elastic gluten proteins. For majority of the recipes in this book, I use regular fine granulated sugar; however, superfine sugar technically achieves better aeration during creaming since there are more sharp edges available to pierce through the fat and create a higher number of tiny air bubbles for a finer texture. Both granulated and dissolved milk sugars undergo a series of complex browning reactions with proteins, called Maillard reactions, which cause the cake's surface to brown and create multiple rich flavour compounds.

EGGS: Eggs have powerful emulsification properties due to a compound called lecithin found in the yolks and their naturally high protein content. They are also critical foaming and structure-building ingredients. I feel that eggs can be disregarded in butter cake recipes and usually don't get the attention they deserve. Once the butter and sugar are creamed sufficiently, the eggs should be beaten in one at a time for at least 30 seconds. This not only serves to emulsify the fat and create a smooth batter, but it also builds volume. After the eggs are blended, the mixture should resemble softly whipped cream. I find that electric hand mixers with their inward spinning wire beaters can create the fluffiest butter cake batters. Egg whites can also be beaten separately to medium-stiff peaks before being folded into a butter cake batter to add lightness.

WHEAT FLOUR: Cake recipes are most commonly based on wheat flour, referring to the powdery white substance made from finely ground or milled cereal grains. Like most flours, wheat flour is composed mainly of starch and protein, yet it is distinguished by its high levels of a class of proteins known as gluten. Once hydrated, through the addition of eggs, water, milk or cream in a cake recipe, gluten develops into a thick, cohesive, elastic mass that becomes more pronounced with prolonged mixing.

When exposed to heat during baking, water vapour and gas bubbles expand, allowing the batter to puff. The network of proteins from flour and eggs coagulates around these air bubbles to provide structure and hold the foam together. Starch granules (rigid cells containing starch molecules) from flour and other sources become embedded in this network and absorb moisture from liquid in the batter. In doing so,

the granules soften and swell. Absorbed water disrupts the organized configuration of the granules, causing them to release starch into the surrounding batter in a process known as gelatinization. This starch solution becomes very thick, traps the swollen granules, and then sets upon cooling to form a gel which ultimately creates a firm foam that we call cake.

Majority of the recipes in this book use all-purpose flour mainly for convenience. And, it's called all-purpose for a reason – it works well in many applications. Cake and pastry flours are also used in special circumstances when an especially tender and delicate crumb is desired. Most layer cakes require a more sturdy structure so that they can be manipulated, handled and sliced horizontally for layering without falling apart. I find that butter cakes made with 100% cake or pastry flour can be very wet, gummy and dense since there is not enough structure-building protein to support the weight and density of the batter.

Cake flour is defined by a low protein content and it generally contains 6% to 8% protein, compared to all-purpose flour which consists of 10% to 12% protein. For best results, look for all-purpose flour that has around 10% protein (you can find this information on the nutrition facts panel). Pastry flour, sometimes called 'cake and pastry flour', falls somewhere in the middle with about 9% protein. These low protein flours are made from soft wheat and are typically milled more finely, making them feel softer to produce lighter cakes and delicate pastries.

TUNNELING:

Tunneling is a common defect of shortened cakes and is caused mainly by over-developed gluten as a result of over-mixing the batter. Strong elastic gluten proteins will do a good job of trapping air, as in bread dough, and create a large open network of air cells since it makes it more difficult for air bubbles to break through the structure. On the other hand, tunneling can also occur if there is a lack of structure built into the cake batter to entrap expanding air cells. Too much leavening agent and high baking temperatures can also promote this defect. High heat will cause the surface of the cake to set before gas bubbles can escape. As a result, the bubbles coalesce or merge to form large holes within the crumb.

CHEMICAL LEAVENING: Baking soda is pure sodium bicarbonate and it has the property of releasing carbon dioxide when heated. Since it is strongly alkaline (or basic), it should always be used in recipes that include acidic ingredients (such as brown sugar, honey, molasses, sour cream, buttermilk, natural cocoa or vinegar) in order to get the full gas production potential. If there is an imbalance between the acidic and basic ingredients, there can be too much residual unreacted sodium carbonate which gives the baked product a bitter, "soapy" taste. Generally, cakes, cupcakes and cookies made with baking soda will spread and brown more than those made with baking powder.

Baking powder has everything it needs to produce carbon dioxide gas, including both basic and acidic components. It is typically a mixture of sodium bicarbonate, an acid salt and corn starch. It will begin to react when dissolved in water, and continue to release gas at a faster rate when heated. It is important that cake batters are baked as soon as possible once they are prepared, otherwise the quality of the product can suffer. If the batter is left to sit before it is baked, the leavening agents have time to react, meaning that a lot of gas forms initially. If they have been almost completely depleted or fully reacted, there will be little gas formation during baking and the bubbles will escape the batter before it sets. As a result, the cake collapses once it is removed from the oven.

COCOA: Due to its carbohydrate and protein content, cocoa powder assumes some of the role of flour in cake batters, contributing water-binding and structure-building properties. Cocoa powder generally comes in two forms: natural and Dutch-processed. Natural cocoa is slightly acidic with a pronounced bitterness and a strong chocolatey flavour. Dutch-processed cocoa is made from defatted chocolate liquor (ground cocoa nibs) that has been treated with an alkali salt solution (potassium carbonate) to neutralize its acidity. This mellows out the flavour by reducing the intensity of astringent and bitter compounds, and adds a slight smokiness.

Most notably, Dutching enhances the colour of cocoa by causing its phenolic colour pigments to change and become darker. The extent of colouration depends on several factors including the length of the alkalizing process, temperature, humidity and pressure conditions. Nowadays, most manufacturers process cocoa to achieve a more appealing colour and neutral flavour, although I prefer the complex flavour of natural cocoa. It is crucial that you consider the type of cocoa used in a recipe as some batters and cookie doughs can rely mainly on natural cocoa for its acidity to react with baking soda and provide leavening. If there is no other acidic ingredient in the recipe, much of the baking soda will remain unreacted when Dutched cocoa is used and result in a flat product that has a soapy, bitter taste.

When melted chocolate is used in a recipe, the type of chocolate is important and you should avoid making substitutions. Depending on the manufacturer, chocolate is made in many different forms with varying proportions of cocoa butter, cocoa solids and sugar. So, always use a high quality brand and make sure to match the cocoa solids content on the label with the amount stated in the recipe (sometimes it is mentioned on the ingredient list if not on the front label). A recipe could turn out dry if 70% bittersweet chocolate is substituted for the intended semisweet chocolate. Unless specified, I do not recommend using chocolate chips as these are typically made with a very high sugar content and sometimes contain milk powders. They also have poorer melting properties because of their lower cocoa butter content compared to baking chocolate.

WHAT TYPE OF COCOA POWDER DO I USE?

Most of my recipes have been tested with Fry's cocoa. It has a rich, chocolatey flavour with a tan/camel brown colour similar to natural cocoa. Although it is not labeled as 'Dutched', I know that it is at least mildly processed because of the potassium/sodium carbonate on the ingredient list.

HOW TO COMBINE WET AND DRY INGREDIENTS:

Alternating the dry ingredients with the liquid ingredients once the eggs have been beaten into the creamed fat and sugar helps to create a smooth and homogeneous batter without over-mixing. Some of the dry ingredients are added first since there is enough moisture in the butter/egg mixture to hydrate the flour. This also serves to coat some of the flour with fat and prevent toughening that comes from over-worked gluten proteins. Gently folding in the final fraction of dry ingredients also helps to create a light and tender cake by incorporating it only until it is moistened and helps to control over-mixing.

BAKING & COOLING:

So the batter might look great, but who knows what the oven has in store. A perfectly mixed batter can suffer if the baking conditions are not right. In the oven, gas bubbles whipped into the batter will expand as the cake's structure sets around them to create a firm foam upon cooling. If the temperature is too low, the batter heats too slowly and the gas bubbles over-expand before the cake sets, creating an open, coarse texture in the finished cake. The leavening gases will be released before the other elements in the batter set, preventing the cake from rising and resulting in a dense crumb. If the temperature is too high, a crust forms before the center cooks through, creating a soggy middle or dry edges. The cake will also rise too quickly and unevenly. I always keep an oven thermometer in my oven for accurate temperature readings.

Cakes need to cool to allow the flour's gelatinized starch to gel and firm up. If released too soon, the cake may stick to the pan. If left in the pan too long, the cake can become soggy. Shortened cakes should be cooled in the pan on a wire rack for at least 20 minutes to allow cool air to circulate beneath it and speed cooling. Then remove the cake from the pan and let it cool completely on a wire rack to allow excess steam to escape into the air. Cakes keep well at room temperature for a few days because of their fat and sugar content, which retain moisture. Refrigerating cakes tends to dry them out, but they do freeze well. Wrap completely cooled cakes tightly with several layers of plastic wrap to protect them from freezer burn and other odours.

There are several different types of foam cakes, many of which are used in this book. However, hybrids have been created that use techniques from different styles of cake.

SPONGE CAKE: this can encompass a category of cakes, including génoise and chiffon, as well as refer to a specific style of cake. A sponge cake is typically made without chemical leaveners, relying solely on beaten separated eggs for its lift, and uses egg yolks as its only source of fat. The egg yolks are beaten with some sugar until pale and thick (to the ribbon stage) before stiffly beaten (sweetened) egg whites and flour are gently folded in. Sponge cakes are most often used to make jelly rolls our roulades since their spongy and springy texture is flexible while warm and easily rolled.

GÉNOISE: a type of European sponge cake that uses whipped whole eggs for its structure and leavening. A mixture of whole eggs and sugar are gently warmed over a pot of simmering water (a double boiler) before being beaten very vigorously for nearly 10 minutes until very thick. The eggs take on so much air that they triple in volume and resemble softly whipped cream. The gentle heating relaxes the egg proteins and promotes foaming. Adding the sugar at the beginning stages creates a very fine-textured foam. Génoise uses warm melted butter, which is gently folded into the batter after the foam has formed. It has wonderful flavour but can often be quite dry, which is why it is sometimes brushed with sugar syrup for added moisture. Cornstarch is used in place of some flour to make an even more tender cake with a fine texture and crumb.

CHIFFON: a type of sponge cake that is extremely light, fluffy, soft and moist. Chiffon cake batter makes the most airy cupcakes you will ever have. It is made similar to a classic sponge cake where the eggs are separated and the egg whites are beaten to almost stiff peaks. The difference is that it uses a bit of vegetable oil to give it a moist and tender crumb, as well as baking powder for added aeration. The flour and baking powder is simply stirred into a mixture of egg yolks, sugar, oil and liquid (water, milk or fruit juice) to create a rather sticky batter before the beaten egg whites are gently folded in to lighten it.   .

MERINGUE: a fat-free, sweetened foam that is leavened only with aerated egg whites and does not contain any flour. Meringue is baked slowly in a low oven to produce a delicate, crisp and crunchy dessert that disappears on the tongue.

Dacquoise is a type of meringue cake made with ground nuts and little or no flour that is layered with whipped cream or buttercream.

ANGEL FOOD CAKE: a very light, sweet and fat-free cake that is leavened solely with stiffly beaten egg whites. It is essentially a meringue with flour gently folded in to create a batter.

> **ALL DRIED OUT:**
>
> A dry chiffon cake can be a result of over-beaten egg whites. Be sure to begin adding sugar once the whites reach soft peaks and then continue beating with caution just until stiff peaks form. Do not let them become dry or lose their sheen. Be patient and use medium speed to create uniform-sized air bubbles which will expand evenly in the oven and to control the extent of whipping so that you do not go too far. Over-baking is another common reason for dryness. Bake at 325°F and watch it carefully to ensure the sides do not over-brown or develop crisp edges. When ready, the top will brown slightly and the cake will spring back when pressed gently in the center. Baking at 325°F also ensures that the cake is baked evenly so that it has a uniformly open texture.

Problem Solving:

Collapsing or shrinking is common in sponge cakes. Even a perfectly baked sponge can shrink just slightly, but too much will cause the cake to sink in the middle or collapse. This is due to the high proportion of egg whites compared to flour and it is often a sign that the eggs were not beaten sufficiently to support the structure. So, make sure to take the time to beat them to their utmost volume without becoming dry.

Cakes that are under-baked will collapse or sink significantly due to the lack of structural support in the center, which is the last part to get heated through. Resist the temptation to open the oven too early and make sure to wait until the minimum time stated in the recipe before checking for doneness. The delicate structure that supports the rising of foam cakes can be compromised when baking temperatures fluctuate dramatically. If the cake still leaves a deep indention when pressed gently in the center, then it requires longer baking. Inverting the pan while cooling will ensure the cake does not shrink drastically.

Know your Foam:

Foams are very important in the world of baking. They are usually made from whipped eggs, either whole eggs or egg whites, to give lightness, stability and lift to a variety of desserts, from cakes to silky smooth buttercream frostings. Foams come about from the incredible properties of proteins. They essentially consist of an air phase of tiny bubbles dispersed throughout a continuous water phase. Proteins are the miraculous molecules in egg whites that create a foam structure by forming a thin film or network around air bubbles. Upon physical stress, such as whipping or beating, proteins undergo transformations that expose their hydrophobic (water-repelling) surfaces to allow them to bind together and arrange themselves around air cells.

When you beat raw egg whites to make a foam, you incorporate air bubbles into the water-protein solution, which denatures or unfolds those egg proteins just as heating them would do. This occurs because egg proteins are made up of individual amino acids that have different properties. Some are attracted to water (hydrophilic) while others are repelled by water (hydrophobic). When the protein is curled up in its native state, the hydrophobic amino acids are arranged in the center where they can hide away from the water (called the hydrophobic core), whereas the hydrophilic ones are on the outside surface to be closer to the water.

When an egg protein meets an air bubble, it unfolds so that its hydrophilic parts can be in contact with water and its hydrophobic parts can be exposed to air. Once the proteins unfold, they bond with each other to create a foam – a network that holds the air bubbles in place. During baking, air bubbles expand as the gas inside them heats up and the proteins set them in place so that the structure doesn't collapse once the bubbles burst.

There are three main culinary terms that are used to describe stages of foam development:

SOFT PEAKS – refers to foam edges that keep some shape but droop once lifted. They are somewhat wobbly before sugar is added.

STIFF PEAKS – refers to defined foam edges that hold their shape. Peaks stand up straight once lifted. At (or sometimes just before) this stage is ideal for making soufflés and sponge cakes, where further expansion occurs during baking. It is also perfect for shaping, decorating and piping.

Soft and stiff peaks appear glossy and hold their shape better when sugar is beaten in.

DRY PEAKS – refers to a dull and firm foam that appears lumpy and crumbly. This is commonly used to make very soft-textured frothy meringue, such as floating islands.

There are three important ingredients that can help stabilize egg white foams and prevent weeping of liquid. Recipes that call for beaten egg whites normally involve a pinch of salt, a dash of cream of tartar and/or a few tablespoons of sugar. You may have realized that it is quite tricky to get perfectly whipped egg whites that hold their shape without these ingredients. Fortunately, their proteins have many functional properties that can be manipulated. Salt and acid change the ionic charges of the proteins and cause them to denature or unfold, which helps them to entrap air more readily. When you beat egg whites you are essentially denaturing the proteins mechanically. So, the addition of salt or acid simply facilitates this process and makes it easier to obtain good results.

ACID: Adding some form of acid, such as vinegar, cream of tartar or lemon juice, to egg whites before or during beating improves foamability. Firstly, acid helps to denature or unfold proteins to expose hydrophobic (air-loving) areas that tend to arrange themselves around air bubbles. Acid also neutralizes the charges on these proteins, which makes them less repulsive (I don't mean less ugly, just less hateful of each other and more friendly I suppose) and more likely to come together and form a network around these bubbles. The stabilizing function of acid may be due to an increased concentration of hydrogen ions ($H+$) which hinders the formation of strong sulphur bonds (S–S) between proteins. These sulphur bonds can be so strong that they squeeze water from between protein networks surrounding bubble walls.

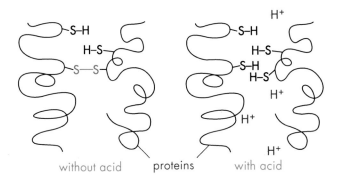

without acid   proteins   with acid

If using only egg whites (versus whole eggs), the foam should be made in a grease-free glass, stainless steel, or, more preferably, copper bowl to ensure maximum aeration.

SALT: Salt has a neutralizing effect on egg white proteins which increases their foamability and foam stability. When salt dissolves into the water of the egg whites, it dissociates into sodium (positive) and chloride (negative) ions which neutralize the charges on proteins and increase their attraction to air bubbles.

If you've ever whipped egg whites without any acid or salt, you might have noticed that shortly after you've put all your heart and soul into achieving perfect peaks, a puddle of water has developed in the bottom of the bowl underneath all the frothiness. So, next time you're whipping up a batch of chocolate soufflés or a meringue pie, remember that those tiny amounts of what seem like minor ingredients will greatly increase your chance for success! A good rule of thumb is to add ⅛ teaspoon of cream of tartar or ¼ teaspoon of vinegar or lemon juice per egg white before beginning to whip or beat.

SUGAR: Sugar is hygroscopic, which means that it readily takes up water. When added to whipped egg whites, it holds onto water between air bubbles in the foam and increases its viscosity. This creates a thick syrup that improves foam stability and prevents liquid from leaking out or separating (a defect known as 'weeping'). Of all the foams used in baking, meringue might be the most famous. To make meringue, sugar is added to beaten egg whites at different stages to stabilize the foam. Basically, the earlier the sugar is added, the denser the meringue and the longer it will take to reach optimal volume. This is because as sugar binds the available water in the egg whites, it leaves the proteins with less of a medium to move around in. This slows them down and hinders their transformations so that they can't arrange themselves at the interface between air and water as easily to form large air bubbles. So, instead they end up forming very tiny air cells to create a very stable, white, thick foam that resembles shaving cream. This technique is used to make French macarons.

Another key point to remember when making meringue is to add sugar very gradually and in a slow stream if adding them to already softly whipped egg whites. If the sugar is added too quickly, it hinders the production of foam and the mixture will be soupy. In this case, it would take a lot of beating and a very long time to reach stiff peaks. Once again, this happens because sugar increases the viscosity of egg whites and makes it more difficult for air bubbles to form.

FAT AND FOAMS:

Fat will depress foam development but it will not completely prevent it. This happens mainly due to fat's greater affinity for the air-water interface. It will compete and interfere with the adhesion of proteins to the air bubble surfaces. Egg yolks are especially naughty as they are high in phospholipids which are great emulsifiers and love to sit on the edge of air bubbles. The problem is that fats lack the elastic properties of proteins and are unable to endure the air pressure of bubbles. As a result, the foam collapses during whipping or beating.

Buttery Vanilla Bean Birthday Cake

Makes 8-10 servings

Having a fluffy and delicious cake recipe that uses all-purpose flour and no exclusive ingredients means it can be your birthday everyday! Cheers to turning 21...again!

For the cake batter:

2 ¼ cups all-purpose flour

2 ½ tsp baking powder

½ tsp salt

⅔ cup unsalted butter, at room temperature

1 vanilla bean pod, seeds scraped

1 ¼ cups granulated sugar

1 tsp pure vanilla extract

2 large eggs, at room temperature

1 cup 2% milk, at room temperature

2 tbsp pure sunflower oil

For the Dark Chocolate Frosting:

6 oz/170 g semisweet chocolate (54% cocoa), chopped into small pieces

4 oz/113 g bittersweet chocolate (72% cocoa), chopped into small pieces

1 tbsp unsalted butter, at room temperature

1 ⅔ cups 35% whipping cream

2 tbsp light corn syrup

pinch of salt

½ tsp pure vanilla extract

Preheat your oven to 350°F. Lightly butter two 8-inch round cake pans and dust lightly with flour, tapping out excess. Line the bottoms with a round of parchment paper and set aside.

In a medium bowl, sift together flour, baking powder and salt; set aside. In the bowl of an electric stand mixer fitted with the flat beater/paddle attachment, beat butter with vanilla bean seeds (reserve pods for the frosting) on medium speed for 30 seconds. With mixer running, gradually add sugar in a steady stream and beat on medium-high until light and fluffy, about 3 minutes. Beat in vanilla extract. Add eggs one at a time and beat on medium speed until well incorporated after each addition. Then, beat on high speed for 20 seconds to whip the eggs and make the batter a bit fluffy.

In a volumetric measuring cup, whisk together milk and oil with a fork. Add one-third of the flour mixture to the butter mixture and beat on medium-low speed until mostly incorporated. Add half of the milk mixture and beat until well blended, about 15 seconds. Beat in half of the remaining flour mixture followed by the last of the milk mixture on medium speed until combined. Increase speed to medium-high and beat for 5-10 seconds to aerate and create a smooth batter. Fold in the rest of the flour mixture by hand until incorporated.

Divide batter evenly among prepared pans and bake until a toothpick inserted into the center comes out clean, 30-35 minutes. Transfer cakes to a wire rack to cool for about 20 minutes. Run a knife around the edges of the cakes, invert pans to release them and let cool completely, upside down, before removing parchment.

To make the frosting, place chopped chocolate and butter in a medium heatproof bowl; set aside. In a small saucepan over medium-low heat, combine cream, corn syrup, salt and vanilla bean pods and bring to a gentle boil. Watch carefully so that it doesn't foam up and bubble over. Reduce heat and simmer very gently for 30 seconds. Remove from heat and let stand for 20 seconds before pouring through a fine mesh sieve and over chopped chocolate. Let stand without stirring for 5 minutes. Using a rubber spatula, gently stir mixture starting from the center and working your way toward the edges until smooth and glossy. If there are still some pieces of solid chocolate, place the bowl over a pot with ½-inch of barely simmering water and heat gently while stirring until completely smooth. Stir in vanilla. Let cool at room temperature until thick and spreadable, 2-3 hours, without stirring. To speed this up, you can refrigerate the frosting until it reaches spreading consistency, about 1 hour, stirring very gently every 10-15 minutes. Even if it appears too thin after 1 hour of chilling, remove it from the fridge because it can set up very quickly at this point and become firm. Avoid stirring too much as this will incorporate air and make it stiff.

To assemble, trim the tops of the cakes if necessary using a serrated knife to make them level. Place one layer on a turn-table or a serving plate. Spread about one-third of frosting evenly over the top. Place the other layer precisely over the frosted layer and top it with remaining frosting. Using a large offset spatula, spread it out to the edges and bring it down to cover the sides until it is evenly coated. Try to avoid over-working the frosting as you decorate the cake, because this will cause it to firm up quite hard once set. The less you work it, the creamier it will be.

Dark Chocolate Truffle Cake

Makes 8-10 servings

For the batter:

1 ¾ cups all-purpose flour

2 tbsp unsweetened cocoa powder

1 ½ tsp baking powder

¾ tsp baking soda

½ tsp salt

½ cup unsalted butter, at room temperature

1 cup granulated sugar

⅓ cup packed light brown sugar

2 oz/56 g unsweet-ened chocolate, melted and cooled

2 large eggs, at room temperature

¼ cup full fat (14%) sour cream, at room temperature

1 tsp pure vanilla extract

1 cup 2% milk, at room temperature

For the Whipped Ganache Frosting:

7 oz/200 g semisweet chocolate (54% cocoa), finely chopped

1 cup 35% whipping cream

1 tbsp light corn syrup

1 tbsp unsalted butter

For the cocoa cream filling:

1 ⅓ cups 35% whipping cream

2 tbsp unsweetened Dutch-processed cocoa powder, sifted

¼ tsp pure vanilla extract

2 tbsp granulated sugar

For the glaze:

2 oz/56 g bittersweet chocolate (72% cocoa), very finely chopped

1 tbsp unsalted butter

1 tbsp 35% whipping cream

2 tbsp 2% milk

1 tbsp light corn syrup

Preheat your oven to 350°F. Lightly butter two 8-inch round cake pans and dust lightly with flour, tapping out the excess. Line the bottoms with a round of parchment paper and set aside.

Sift flour, cocoa powder, baking powder, baking soda and salt into a medium bowl and whisk to blend evenly; set aside.

In a large bowl, beat butter on medium-high speed until creamy using an electric hand mixer, about 10 seconds. Add both sugars and beat until light and fluffy, about 3 minutes. Add melted, cooled chocolate and beat on medium speed until well combined. Beat in eggs, one at a time, mixing until each one is well incorporated. Then, beat on high speed for 10 seconds to whip the eggs and make the batter a bit fluffy. Add sour cream and vanilla extract and beat on high speed until the batter is voluminous, 20-30 seconds.

With mixer on medium-low speed, add one-third of the flour mixture. Once mostly blended, gradually add half of the milk and beat until almost completely incorporated. Repeat this step by adding half of remaining flour mixture followed by the rest of the milk. Do not beat more than 15 seconds between additions. Finally, add the last of the flour mixture and beat until well incorporated. Scrape down the sides and bottom of the bowl and then beat on high speed for just 5 seconds to aerate the batter. Do not over-beat to ensure a tender crumb.

Divide batter evenly among prepared cake pans and smooth the surface. Rap pans on your countertop to let out any large air bubbles. Bake until a toothpick inserted into the center of the cakes comes out clean, about 30 minutes. Transfer cakes to a wire rack to cool for about 30 minutes. Run a butter knife around the outside edges of the cakes, invert pans to release them and let cool completely before removing the parchment, 1-2 hours.

To make the frosting, place chopped chocolate in a medium heatproof bowl. In a small saucepan, combine cream and corn syrup over medium-low heat until you see bubbles forming around the edges and steam coming off of the surface. Immediately pour hot cream over chopped chocolate and let stand for 3 minutes at room temperature. Using a spatula or wooden spoon, stir gently until chocolate is completely melted and mixture is smooth and glossy. Stir in butter until well incorporated. Refrigerate until thick and spreadable but not firm, about 1 hour. Stir every 15 minutes. Transfer ganache to the bowl of a stand mixer fitted with the flat beater/paddle attachment and beat on medium speed until lightened in colour and

fluffy, about 1 ½ - 2 minutes. Alternatively, whip the mixture by hand using a rubber spatula. Do not over-beat or the mixture will become too stiff and grainy, and you won't be able to spread it.

To make the filling, whisk together cream, cocoa powder and vanilla extract in a medium bowl until well blended. Refrigerate about 15 minutes and then beat on medium-high speed using an electric hand mixer until soft peaks form, about 2 minutes. Gradually add sugar and beat until stiff peaks form.

To assemble, trim the tops of the cake layers if necessary using a serrated knife so that they are level. Cut them in half horizontally to create 4 separate layers. Place one bottom layer cut-side-up on a turn-table or a serving plate. Spread one-third of the whipped cream filling over top, leaving about ½-inch border since it will spread slightly with the weight of the above layers. Place the corresponding top layer precisely over the filling and top it with half of the remaining filling. Repeat this step with the other top cake layer and the rest of the filling. Place the final bottom cake layer, cut-side-down, over the top so that the crumbs are facing down. Using a large offset spatula, place about 1 cup of the frosting over the cake, spread it out to the edges and bring it down to cover the sides. Continue applying frosting to the cake until all sides are covered evenly. Refrigerate for about 15 minutes before applying the glaze.

To make the glaze, combine chocolate, butter, cream, milk and corn syrup in a small saucepan over low heat and stir constantly until smooth and glossy. Set aside to cool slightly, about 2 minutes. Pour slightly cooled glaze over top of the cake and spread it out to the edges using an offset spatula, letting it drip over the edges. Place large chocolate curls in a mound in the center of the cake if desired.

✪ Chocolate Curls

To make chocolate curls, place 5 oz of finely chopped semi-sweet dark chocolate (54% cocoa) in a heatproof bowl set over a pot with ½-inch of barely simmering water. Stir constantly until completely melted and smooth. Pour melted chocolate onto the back of a 13x9-inch baking sheet and spread it out in a thin layer, about 1/16-inch thick, using an offset spatula. Let set until firm but still pliable. Score the sheet of melted chocolate into 2x3-inch rectangles. Using a pastry bench scraper, scrape against the edge of one of the rectangles and push towards the opposite end. The chocolate should curl over itself and finish where it has been scored on the other end. Repeat this with the remaining rectangles.

Lemon Layer Cake with Almond Cream Cheese Frosting

Makes 8-10 servings

For the cake batter:

¾ cup cake & pastry flour

¾ cup all-purpose flour

1 tsp baking powder

½ tsp baking soda

¼ tsp salt

3 large eggs

1 tbsp finely grated lemon zest

1 cup granulated sugar

½ cup buttermilk, at room temperature

¼ cup plus 1 tbsp pure sunflower oil

For the lemon filling:

⅓ cup granulated sugar

1 tsp corn starch

pinch of salt

1 large egg

3 large egg yolks

¼ cup freshly squeezed lemon juice

1 tbsp unsalted butter

For the Cream Cheese Frosting:

4 oz/113 g brick cream cheese, at room temperature

⅓ cup unsalted butter, at room temperature

6 oz/170 g sifted icing sugar (1 ½ cups)

⅛ tsp pure almond extract

pinch of salt

1 tbsp 35% whipping cream

Preheat your oven to 350°F.

Line the bottoms of two 8-inch round cake pans with a round of parchment paper but do not grease the sides. Not greasing allows the sponge cake to stick to the sides of the pan to help it rise and prevent it from shrinking as it cools.

Sift both flours, baking powder, baking soda and salt into a medium bowl and whisk together to blend evenly; set aside.

In the bowl of a stand mixer fitted with the whisk attachment, combine eggs and lemon zest and beat on medium-high speed until frothy, about 30 seconds. With mixer running, gradually add sugar in a steady stream and beat on high speed until very pale yellow and voluminous, 3-4 minutes. The eggs should reach the ribbon stage. Beat in buttermilk until well blended. With mixer running, slowly pour in ¼ cup of oil in a thin stream until well incorporated.

Now blend in the flour mixture in four parts to ensure that you do not have any lumps. Sift one-fourth of the flour mixture over the batter and beat on low speed until combined. Sift one-third of the remaining flour mixture over the batter and beat on low speed until incorporated. Repeat this step once more so that three-quarters of the flour mixture has been incorporated. Finally, fold in the remaining flour by hand until the batter is smooth. Fold in remaining 1 tablespoon of sunflower oil.

Divide batter evenly between prepared pans and bake until golden brown on top and it springs back when pressed gently with your finger. A toothpick inserted into the center should come out clean, 26-30 minutes. Turn off the oven, crack open the door and let the cakes cool for 5 minutes in the oven. Transfer cakes to a wire rack and let them cool inverted (this will prevent them from sinking in the middle).

To make the filling, whisk sugar, salt and corn starch in a medium heatproof bowl. Add egg and egg yolks and whisk until blended and smooth. Whisk in lemon juice and set the bowl over a pot with ½-inch of simmering water over medium to medium-low heat. Whisk over the heat for 2 minutes. Switch to a silicone spatula and stir constantly until very thick, like the consistency of pudding. This takes another 5-10 minutes. The mixture will begin to smell very citrusy. Remove lemon curd from heat and pass through a fine mesh sieve and into a small bowl. Immediately stir in butter until completely melted and smooth. Place a piece of plastic wrap directly in contact with the surface of the curd to prevent a skin from forming and refrigerate until thoroughly chilled, about 1 hour.

To make the frosting, beat cream cheese in a medium bowl with an electric hand mixer on medium-high speed until creamy and light, about 1 minute. Add butter and beat until well blended. Gradually add icing sugar about ½ cup at a time while mixing on medium-low speed until well combined and smooth. Add almond extract and salt and beat until smooth and creamy, about 30 seconds. Slowly add cream to adjust the consistency (you may not need a full tablespoon) and beat on high speed for one minute to thoroughly dissolve the sugar, whip the frosting and whiten the colour. If the frosting is too loose, refrigerate it for a few minutes until it reaches spreading consistency.

To assemble the cake, place one layer on a turn table or your serving plate. Fill a pastry bag with about ¾ cup of frosting and cut the tip about ½-inch wide. Pipe around the outside edge of the cake to make a 1-inch border that will hold in the filling (think of a moat around a castle). Pour the chilled lemon curd filling into the center and spread it around to fill within the border. Place the other cake layer over the filling. Using a large offset spatula, cover the entire cake with a thin layer of frosting, called a crumb coat, and refrigerate for 20 minutes. Spread the remaining frosting evenly over the cake, taking care to smooth out the sides. Use the spatula to create a spiral pattern over the surface of the cake. For clean slices, use a very sharp knife, or even a slightly serrated knife – a dull knife will smush and compress the delicate sponge.

Raspberry Jewel Devil's Food Cake

Makes 10-12 servings

For the batter:

2 ¼ cups all-purpose flour

1 ½ tsp baking powder

1 tsp baking soda

½ tsp salt

2 ¼ oz/65 g natural unsweetened cocoa powder (about ¾ cup)

¾ cup boiling water

¾ cup unsalted butter, at room temperature

1 cup granulated sugar

½ cup packed dark brown sugar

2 tsp pure vanilla extract

3 large eggs, at room temperature

½ cup buttermilk, at room temperature

For the Blackout Frosting:

½ cup water

2 tbsp packed dark brown sugar

1 tbsp light corn syrup

1 tbsp unsweetened Dutch-processed cocoa powder

pinch of salt

⅔ cup unsalted butter, cut into ¾-inch cubes

10 oz/284 g dark chocolate (64% cocoa), finely chopped and divided

For the Blackout Filling:

½ cup packed dark brown sugar

1 ½ oz/42 g unsweetened Dutch-processed cocoa powder (about ½ cup)

2 tsp golden corn syrup

½ cup plus 4 tbsp water

pinch of salt

2 ½ tbsp unsalted butter, at room temperature and divided

2 tbsp corn starch

8 oz/227 g fresh raspberries, rinsed and dried (about 2 cups)

Preheat your oven to 350°F. Lightly butter two 9-inch round cake pans and dust lightly with flour, tapping out the excess. Line the bottoms with a round of parchment paper and set aside.

Sift flour, baking powder, baking soda and salt into a large bowl and whisk together to blend evenly; set aside.

In a small bowl, whisk together cocoa powder and boiling water until smooth. Set aside to cool while you make the batter.

In the bowl of an electric stand mixer fitted with the flat beater/paddle attachment, beat butter on medium speed until creamy, about 20 seconds. Add both sugars and vanilla extract and beat on medium-high until pale and fluffy, about 3 minutes. Scrape down the sides and bottom of the bowl several times during mixing. Beat in eggs one at a time so that each one is well incorporated, about 30 seconds on medium speed after each addition. Scrape down the bowl and then beat on medium-high speed for about 20 seconds to whip the eggs and make the batter a bit fluffy. The batter will change from looking curdled to smooth and homogenous.

With the mixer on medium-low speed, add one-third of flour mixture. Once it is mostly blended, slowly pour in the buttermilk and beat until well incorporated. With the mixer on low speed, add half of the remaining flour mixture followed by the cooled cocoa mixture and then beat on medium speed until combined. Scrape down the bowl and then add the last of the flour mixture and beat until evenly blended and the batter is smooth, but be sure not to over-beat or the cake will be tough and dry. Remove the bowl from the mixer and fold the batter a few times using a wide rubber spatula, reaching down to the bottom of the bowl to ensure that everything is evenly blended.

Divide batter evenly among prepared cake pans and smooth the surface. Rap the pans on your countertop to let any large air bubbles escape. Bake until a toothpick or wooden skewer inserted into the center of the cakes comes out clean, 25-30 minutes. Transfer pans to a wire rack to cool for about 20 minutes. Run a butter knife around the outside edges of the cakes, invert the pans to release them and let cool completely before removing the parchment paper.

To make the frosting, whisk together water, brown sugar, corn syrup, cocoa powder and salt until smooth in a medium saucepan. Place the pan over medium-low heat, add half of the butter and cook until the butter is melted and the mixture comes

to a boil, whisking constantly. Once it comes to a boil, remove pan from the heat and add the chopped chocolate, swirling the pan so that all the chocolate comes in contact with the hot liquid. Let stand for 3-5 minutes to gently melt and then whisk until smooth and glossy. Whisk in the remaining butter, one tablespoon at a time, until evenly blended and smooth. Set the frosting aside to cool at room temperature until it is thick and spreadable, about 1-2 hours, stirring every 10 minutes. By this time, the cakes should be cool enough for frosting.

To make the filling, whisk together brown sugar, cocoa powder, corn syrup, ½ cup of water and salt in a 1-quart saucepan over medium heat. Add 2 tablespoons of butter and bring to a boil, whisking very frequently to prevent scorching. In a separate small bowl, whisk cornstarch with 4 tablespoons of water until dispersed. Once boiling, remove cocoa mixture from heat and gradually pour in cornstarch mixture while whisking constantly. Return saucepan to heat, and bring to a boil over medium heat, whisking constantly. Boil about 1 minute, until corn starch is cooked and mixture is very thick, like the consistency of pudding.

Remove from heat and pour into a heatproof metal bowl. Stir in remaining ½ tablespoon of butter until smooth and immediately place a piece of plastic wrap directly in contact with the filling to cover the surface and prevent a film from forming. Cool completely, and refrigerate until firm.

To assemble the cake, first trim the tops of the cake layers if necessary using a serrated knife so that they have an even, flat (not domed) surface. Place one layer on a turn-table or a serving plate. Spread the filling over the top, leaving about ½-inch border around the edges since it will spread slightly with the weight of the top layer. Scatter fresh raspberries over the filling in a single layer. Place the top cake layer precisely over the filling. Using a large offset spatula, place about 1 cup of frosting over the cake, spread it out to the edges and bring it down to cover the sides. Continue applying frosting to the cake until all sides are covered evenly.

....

✪ NOTE: Unless you are planning to keep this cake for more than a couple of days, I would try to avoid refrigerating it as this frosting will harden when chilled.

Chocolate Blueberry Génoise Layer Cake

Makes 8-10 servings

For the cake batter:

⅓ cup all-purpose flour

1 oz/28 g unsweetened cocoa powder (about ⅓ cup)

4 large eggs

⅓ cup granulated sugar

⅓ cup packed light brown sugar

¼ tsp salt

3 tbsp unsalted butter

1 tsp pure vanilla extract

For the blueberry filling:

8 oz/227 g fresh blueberries (about 1 ½ cups)

¼ cup granulated sugar

2 tbsp freshly squeezed lemon juice

1 tbsp water

1 tsp corn starch

For the topping:

¾ cup 35% whipping cream

1 tbsp granulated sugar

1 tbsp unsweetened cocoa powder

2 oz/56 g dark chocolate (64% cocoa), very finely chopped, shaved or grated ❓

½ cup fresh blueberries

Preheat your oven to 350°F. Line a 13x9-inch baking sheet all around with parchment paper so that there is 1-inch overhang along each side.

Sift flour and cocoa powder into a small bowl and whisk to blend evenly; set aside.

In the heatproof bowl of an electric stand mixer, whisk together eggs, both sugars and salt and set over a pot with ½-inch of simmering water. Whisk constantly until sugar is almost completely dissolved and the mixture feels warm to the touch (it should register 110-120°F on an instant read thermometer), about 5 minutes. Remove bowl from over water and attach to a stand mixer fitted with a whisk attachment. Beat on high speed until pale, thick, fluffy and tripled in volume, 6-7 minutes. The mixture will resemble softly whipped cream and fall back into the bowl in ribbons that rest gently on the surface of the batter without disappearing too quickly. You can also do this in a large mixing bowl and use an electric hand mixer, but it will take closer to 10 minutes to reach the same volume.

In a small saucepan, melt butter over low heat with vanilla extract; set aside but keep warm.

Sift about one-third of the flour mixture over the whipped eggs and use a wide rubber spatula to quickly but gently fold it in until mostly combined. Fold in the remaining flour mixture in two parts. Scoop about ¾ cup of the batter into a small bowl with the warm melted butter mixture and stir together gently until well blended. Fold this butter mixture completely into the remaining batter being careful not to deflate it. Pour batter into prepared baking sheet and spread it out evenly into the corners using a large offset spatula. Bake until the top of the cake springs back when pressed with your finger, 12-13 minutes.

Transfer cake to a wire rack and let cool completely in pan. Once cool, invert the cake onto a clean work surface and carefully peel off the parchment. Cut the cake into three equal rectangular pieces (9x4-inch rectangles) and prick them several times with a fork (this will allow the blueberry syrup to soak into it slightly). Cover loosely with plastic wrap so that they don't dry out while you make the filling.

To make the filling, combine blueberries and sugar in a small 1-quart saucepan over medium-low heat and cook, stirring often, until the berries begin to burst and release most of their juices, about 10 minutes. The mixture will look soupy. Do not let the mixture come to a boil or the blueberries will break down into nothing. At this point, brush the cakes evenly with some of this hot blueberry syrup and keep the pot off the heat for a moment. In a small bowl, whisk together lemon juice, water and corn starch until well blended. Stir this mixture into the pan with the blueberries off the heat. Return pan to medium heat and bring to a gentle boil, stirring constantly. Once boiling, continue to cook for another 2-3 minutes until thickened slightly and then set aside to cool while you make the topping.

In a medium bowl, whisk together cream, sugar and cocoa powder. Place the bowl in the refrigerator and chill for 10 minutes. Use an electric hand mixer or a whisk to beat the cream until it reaches soft (almost stiff) peaks. Refrigerate this while you assemble the cake.

To assemble the cake, place one layer with syrup side facing up on your serving platter. Spread half of the slightly cooled blueberry mixture over it (by this time the blueberry filling should be still a bit warm but not hot). Place another cake layer with syrup side facing up over the blueberries. Spread the remaining blueberry mixture evenly over top and then place the final cake layer with syrup side facing down over it. Use a small offset spatula to spread whipped cream all over the cake, coating the sides evenly.

Decorate the top of cake with blueberries and sprinkle chocolate shavings all over it. To cover the sides, put a pile of chocolate shavings in the palm of your hand and carefully push it up against the sides of the cake, starting at the bottom and slowly moving up. Your hand will catch any chocolate that does not adhere at the bottom and bring it up to cover the top sides and edges.

 ❓ To make chocolate shavings, use a sharp heavy knife to finely slice chocolate. This will create shards. Alternatively, you can use a vegetable peeler to shave chocolate as though you were peeling a potato. A stand up cheese grater also works well but creates smaller pieces. Placing a 2-oz piece of chocolate in the microwave for 15-20 seconds at 50% power can help to soften it ever so slightly for easy shaving, grating or peeling.

Raspberry Lemonade Roulade

Makes 8-10 servings

For the filling:

¾ cup granulated sugar

pinch of salt

1 tbsp freshly grated lemon zest

4 large eggs

½ cup freshly squeezed lemon juice

½ cup 35% whipping cream

4 oz/113 g fresh raspberries, rinsed and dried (about 1 cup)

For the cake:

¾ cup cake & pastry flour

½ tsp baking powder

¼ tsp salt

3 large eggs

½ cup granulated sugar

1 tbsp freshly squeezed lemon juice

1 tbsp 2% milk

1 tbsp extra virgin olive oil

½ tsp pure vanilla extract

1 tsp finely grated lemon zest

¼ cup icing sugar for dusting

Preheat your oven to 350°F. Line a 13x9-inch baking sheet with parchment paper leaving a 2-inch overhang around all sides and being sure to fit it well into the corners.

To make the filling, combine sugar, salt and lemon zest in a large heatproof bowl. Rub it all together with your fingers or use a wide rubber spatula to blend as if you were creaming butter with sugar. This will coat the sugar crystals with fragrant oils from the lemon zest. Continue to do this until the sugar takes on a slight hint of yellow and it becomes fragrant. Add the eggs and whisk until smooth. Whisk in lemon juice.

In a separate small bowl, whisk cream until thick and a bit frothy, about 30 seconds. Add it to the egg mixture and stir it in until well incorporated and smooth. Place the bowl over a pot with ½-inch of simmering water and cook, stirring constantly, until the mixture thickens considerably, like pouring custard. It should reach 84°C (183°F) on an instant-read thermometer. Pass the lemon curd through a fine mesh sieve and into a clean bowl to remove any pieces of cooked egg. Let cool slightly at room temperature, place a piece of plastic wrap directly over the surface of the curd and then refrigerate until thoroughly chilled and completely set, about 2 hours.

To make the cake, sift flour, baking powder and salt into a medium bowl and set aside.

In the bowl of an electric stand mixer fitted with the whisk attachment, beat eggs on medium-high speed for 2-3 minutes. The whipped eggs will lighten in color considerably and have the appearance of yellow cake batter. With the mixer still running, slowly add sugar and beat on high speed until very pale, almost whitened, and voluminous, 3-4 minutes. Add lemon juice, milk, olive oil, vanilla and lemon zest and beat on medium speed until well blended, about 15 seconds. Add the flour mixture and mix on medium speed until well combined and batter is smooth, about 15 seconds. Pour batter into prepared pan and spread it evenly into the corners using an offset spatula. Bake until lightly golden and it springs back when pressed gently with your finger, 12-15 minutes.

Meanwhile, lay a clean cotton tea towel over your work space and sift about ¼ cup of icing sugar over it in an even layer. When cake is baked, carefully turn it out onto the tea towel while warm. Peel off the parchment and immediately roll cake into the tea towel gently, beginning at the narrow end closest to you and rolling away from yourself. Roll as tightly and as evenly as possible. If it cracks slightly, it's OK – just keep rolling gently. Place rolled cake on a wire rack seam-side down and let cool completely so that it holds its shape once you fill it with the lemon curd.

Once cooled, gently unroll the cake. Spread the lemon curd over it leaving about ¾-inch border. Scatter raspberries over the lemon curd and gently roll up the cake again. Some lemon curd might get squeezed out at the seam and from the sides, but that's really no big deal. Wrap cake with parchment paper and refrigerate for 1 hour before serving. Sift a generous amount of icing sugar over the roll immediately before serving and slicing.

Marble Cherry Cheesecake

Makes about 8 servings

For the crust:

1 ½ cups chocolate cookie crumbs (from chocolate pastry scraps)

3 ½ tbsp melted unsalted butter

For the topping:

6 ½ oz/185 g fresh pitted and halved sweet cherries, (about 1 ¼ cups)

2 tbsp granulated sugar

1 tsp freshly squeezed lemon juice

2 tsp corn starch

¼ cup water

For the filling:

2 packages (8.8 oz/250 g each) brick cream cheese, at room temperature

½ cup granulated sugar

2 large eggs, at room temperature

¼ cup full fat (14%) sour cream

½ tsp pure vanilla extract

Preheat your oven to 325°F.

Line the bottom of an 8-inch round non-stick springform pan with a round of parchment paper. Wrap the outside of the pan with a double layer of aluminum foil so that it comes all the way up the sides of the pan for insulation and to protect the crust from the water bath.

In a medium bowl, stir together chocolate crumbs and melted butter until evenly combined. Press the crumbs evenly into the bottom and about ¾-inch up the sides of the pan. Cover loosely with plastic wrap and refrigerate until needed.

To make the topping, combine cherries, sugar and lemon juice in a small saucepan over medium-low heat. Cover and cook until the cherries have released most of their juices and begin to simmer, about 10 minutes.

In a small bowl, whisk together corn starch and water until blended. Remove pan from heat and stir cornstarch slurry into cherry mixture. Return to stove, increase heat slightly and bring to a boil while stirring constantly. Cook until thickened, about 1 minute longer. Remove from heat and allow to cool completely while you make the filling.

To make the filling, beat cream cheese in a large bowl on medium speed until smooth. Add sugar and beat until smooth and creamy, about 30-45 seconds. Do not over-beat because large air bubbles will cause the cheesecake to crack during baking and cooling. Let mixture stand for 5-10 minutes (this allows the sugar to dissolve into the moisture from the cheese). Add one egg and beat on medium speed until well blended, about 10-15 seconds. Scrape down the sides and bottom of the bowl, add the other egg and beat until incorporated, about 15 seconds longer. Add sour cream and vanilla extract and beat just until blended. Again, do not beat the mixture excessively at this point as the eggs will whip up and create air pockets in the batter. Pour into chilled crust, spreading it out evenly and popping any air bubbles that you see. Rap pan down against the counter to release any large air pockets. Spoon cooled cherry topping randomly over the cheesecake batter and swirl it in slightly to create a subtle marbled effect, leaving about ¼-inch border around the edges for easy release once baked.

Place cheesecake in a large, shallow, rimmed baking sheet that is big enough to contain it and place it on the center rack of the oven. Pour about ⅓-inch of boiling water into the baking sheet, close oven door and bake about 40 minutes or until filling is set but the center is slightly wobbly or jiggles when the pan is shaken. Transfer pan to a wire rack to cool. After 10 minutes of cooling, run a knife around the edges of the cake to loosen it and then remove sides of pan. Let cake cool completely before serving.

Dark Chocolate
Truffle Cake

Spiced Sticky Toffee Pudding

Makes 8 servings

Ingredients:

6 oz/170 g pitted dates (about 1 ¼ cups)

1 cup water

1 ½ cups all-purpose flour

1 ½ tsp baking powder

½ tsp baking soda

¼ tsp ground cinnamon

⅛ tsp ground nutmeg

¼ tsp salt

6 tbsp salted butter

¾ cup packed dark brown sugar

2 large eggs, at room temperature

1 recipe Toffee Sauce (page 230)

First, prepare the toffee sauce and keep warm. This can also be prepared days, even weeks, in advance and re-warmed gently in a saucepan when you are ready to use it.

To make the pudding cakes, combine dates and water in a small saucepan over medium-high heat and bring to a boil. Once boiling, reduce heat, cover and simmer until very soft, about 10 minutes. Transfer cooked dates and remaining liquid to a food processor and puree until very smooth. You should have about ¼ cup of this cooking liquid left – if not, compensate with water. Set the puree aside and keep warm.

Preheat your oven to 325°F. Generously grease eight 3-inch round, ½ cup (4 oz) capacity ramekins with butter or cooking spray.

In a medium bowl, whisk together flour, baking powder, baking soda, ground cinnamon, ground nutmeg and salt; set aside.

In a stand mixer fitted with the flat beater/paddle attachment, beat butter until smooth and creamy, about 30 seconds. Add brown sugar and cream together with butter on medium speed until light and fluffy, about 3 minutes. Add eggs, one at a time, beating until well blended (about 30 seconds) after each addition. The mixture may look slightly curdled in some spots but that's ok because it will come together once the dry ingredients are added.

Gradually add dry ingredients while mixing on the lowest speed just until combined. Fold in warm date puree until evenly incorporated and smooth. Set the mixture aside to rest for 5 minutes. The batter will become thick.

Spoon batter into prepared ramekins, filling them two-thirds to three-quarters full. Place ramekins onto a rimmed baking tray and bake until the cakes are evenly browned and cracked at the surface, about 25 minutes. The cakes will spring back when touched when they are done. Transfer ramekins to a wire rack and, while still hot, prick the cakes with a skewer to make lots of small holes. Spoon about 1 or 2 teaspoons of hot toffee sauce over them and let it sink into the cakes.

After about 20 minutes, when the ramekins are cool enough to handle, remove cakes and trim off their peaked tops to make them level. Place them cut-side-down onto your serving plates and douse them with more hot toffee sauce, letting it drip over the sides and onto the plate. Serve immediately.

Black Velvet Cake
with Brown Butter Espresso Frosting

Makes about 10 servings

For the cake batter:

1 oz/28 g unsweetened chocolate, coarsely chopped

1 cup freshly brewed strong hot coffee

1 ⅔ cups all-purpose flour

2 oz/56 g unsweetened Dutch-processed cocoa powder (about ⅔ cup)

1 ½ tsp baking soda

½ tsp baking powder

1 ½ cups granulated sugar, divided

½ tsp salt

¾ tsp espresso coffee grounds

2 large eggs, at room temperature

¼ cup pure sunflower oil

¼ cup unsalted butter, melted and cooled

1 ½ tsp pure vanilla extract

½ cup full fat (14%) sour cream

For the frosting:

⅔ cup unsalted butter, divided and at room temperature

3 large egg whites

⅔ cup packed light brown sugar

¼ tsp espresso coffee grounds

⅛ tsp salt

2 oz/56 g pure milk chocolate, melted and cooled

Preheat your oven to 350°F. Grease two 8-inch round cake pans with butter and dust with cocoa, tapping out excess. Line bottoms with a round of parchment paper and set aside. In a small bowl or volumetric measuring cup, whisk together chocolate and hot coffee until chocolate is melted and the mixture is smooth; set aside to cool completely.

Sift flour, cocoa powder, baking soda and baking powder into a large bowl. Whisk in 1 cup of sugar, salt and coffee grounds until evenly blended and set aside.

In a medium bowl, beat eggs with an electric hand mixer on medium-high speed until frothy, about 30 seconds. Gradually pour in remaining ½ cup sugar while beating and then continue to beat until very pale and thick (ribbon stage), about 3 minutes. The mixture should form a disappearing ribbon on its surface as it falls back into the bowl when the beaters are lifted. With mixer running, very slowly pour in oil and melted butter until well blended and mixture is emulsified. Beat in vanilla and sour cream until well combined. Add flour mixture in three parts, alternating with coffee mixture and beating to incorporate well after each addition. Do not over-mix. Divide batter among prepared pans and bake until a toothpick inserted into the center comes out clean and the cake springs back when pressed gently, about 35 minutes. Transfer cakes to a wire rack and let cool completely in pans. Run a thin knife around the edge of the cake to loosen, invert and remove parchment paper.

To make the buttercream, brown ⅓ cup of butter in a small saucepan over medium-low heat (see page 47). Submerge the bottom of the bowl in a baking dish filled with ice water and stir constantly until completely chilled and firm; set aside.

Whisk together egg whites, brown sugar, coffee grounds and salt in the heatproof bowl of a stand mixer. Place the bowl over a pot with ½-inch of simmering water and whisk constantly until the mixture reaches 162°F (72°C). Remove from heat and attach the bowl to the mixer fitted with the whisk attachment. Beat on high speed until it is completely cooled. This will take 7-8 minutes. The mixture will appear white and fluffy like marshmallow or shaving cream. The bottom of the bowl should feel neutral, not warm. Reduce speed to medium and gradually add remaining ⅓ cup of regular butter, one tablespoon at a time. Scrape down the sides and bottom of the bowl and then add the brown butter one tablespoon at a time. Once all of the butter has been added, increase speed to high and beat until creamy, 1-2 minutes. The mixture will go from looking grainy and soupy to smooth, silky and glossy. Beat in melted chocolate until well blended. If the buttercream is too loose to work with, place the bowl in the fridge for 5 minute intervals and then beat on medium-high speed using the paddle attachment for 15 seconds.

Ginger Pear Cake with Chocolate Glaze

Makes about 8 servings

For the cake batter:

1 ¼ cups all-purpose flour

1 tsp baking powder

¼ tsp baking soda

1 tsp ground ginger

¼ tsp ground cinnamon

¼ tsp salt

⅔ cup granulated sugar

⅓ cup unsalted butter, at room temperature

1 large egg, at room temperature

1 tbsp dark cooking molasses

1 tsp pure vanilla extract

1 tsp freshly grated ginger

½ cup 2% milk, at room temperature

1 large ripe Bosc pear, peeled, cored and diced into ⅓-inch cubes

For the chocolate glaze:

¼ cup 2% milk

1 tbsp unsalted butter

1 tbsp golden corn syrup

pinch of salt

2 ½ oz/70 g semisweet chocolate (54% cocoa), very finely chopped

Preheat your oven to 350°F. Lightly butter the sides of an 8-inch round springform pan or an 8 x 2 ½-inch round cake pan and dust it lightly with flour, tapping out the excess. Line the bottom with a round of parchment paper and set aside.

Sift flour, baking powder, baking soda, ground ginger, ground cinnamon and salt into a large bowl. Whisk in sugar. Add softened butter and beat with an electric hand mixer on medium speed until well incorporated and the mixture resembles soft bread crumbs, about 2-3 minutes.

In a medium bowl, whisk together egg, molasses, vanilla extract, grated ginger and milk. Add to flour mixture all at once and mix on medium-low speed until blended and quite smooth, about 30 seconds. Do not over-beat – if there are still a few tiny lumps, that's OK. Gently fold in chopped pears. The batter will be thick.

Pour batter into prepared pan and spread it out evenly. Bake until evenly golden brown and a toothpick inserted into the center comes out clean, about 35 minutes. Transfer to a wire rack to cool completely.

To make the glaze, combine all ingredients in a small saucepan over medium-low heat and whisk until smooth and glossy. Set aside to cool and thicken, about 20 minutes.

To decorate, remove cake from pan, peel off parchment and place it right-side-up on the wire rack. Lay a piece of parchment paper underneath the rack. Pour the glaze over the cooled cake, spreading it out to the edges to coat all sides, and letting excess drip off onto the parchment paper beneath it. Scrape up the glaze from the parchment, re-warm if necessary and pour it over cake to create a thicker layer of glaze if desired.

Red Grape Olive Oil Cake with White Chocolate Ganache

Makes 8-10 servings

For the cake batter:

1 ¼ cups all-purpose flour

1 ½ tsp baking powder

⅓ cup yellow cornmeal

¼ tsp salt

2 large eggs, at room temperature

1 large egg white, at room temperature

⅔ cup granulated sugar

⅓ cup extra-virgin olive oil

⅓ cup 2% milk

1 tsp finely grated lemon zest

8 oz red seedless grapes (about 1 ½ cups), washed and dried

For the white chocolate glaze:

2 oz/56 g pure white chocolate, very finely chopped

2 tbsp 35% whipping cream

Preheat your oven to 350°F.

Line a 9x5-inch rectangular loaf pan with parchment paper, leaving a 2-inch overhang on opposite ends along the length and butter exposed sides.

Sift flour and baking powder into a medium bowl. Whisk through cornmeal and salt until evenly blended and set aside.

In the bowl of an electric stand mixer fitted with the whisk attachment, beat whole eggs and egg white on medium speed until foamy, about 20 seconds. Gradually add sugar while beating. Increase speed to high and beat until mixture is very pale and almost white in colour, about 5 minutes. The eggs will nearly triple in volume.

In a small bowl, combine olive oil, milk and lemon zest. Whisk it with a fork to blend. Add one-third of the flour mixture to the egg mixture and fold it in gently using a wide rubber spatula or a big balloon whisk. Add half of the olive oil mixture and fold until almost blended. Fold in half of the remaining flour mixture followed by the rest of the olive oil mixture. Finally, gently fold in the last third of the flour mixture.

Place half of the grapes in a bowl and toss with about 1 teaspoon of flour. Gently fold these grapes into the batter and pour it into the prepared pan.

Bake about 12 minutes, then sneak into the oven and scatter remaining grapes on top, poking them in slightly. Continue to bake until the top is golden brown and a toothpick inserted into the center comes out clean, about 30 minutes. Transfer the pan to a wire rack and let cool completely.

To make the glaze, combine chopped white chocolate and cream in a small heatproof bowl set over a pot with ½-inch of barely simmering water and stir until completely melted and smooth. Drizzle over cooled cake.

Chocolate Fudge Almond Torte

Makes 8-10 servings

For the torte batter:

6 oz/170 g bittersweet chocolate (72% cocoa), coarsely chopped

½ cup unsalted butter, at room temperature

5 oz/142 g whole natural almonds (about 1 cup), divided

4 large eggs, separated and at room temperature

¾ cup granulated sugar, divided

¼ tsp salt

¼ cup all-purpose flour

For the fudge glaze:

½ cup 35% whipping cream

¼ cup granulated sugar

1 tbsp light corn syrup

pinch of salt

3 oz/85 g semisweet chocolate (54% cocoa), finely chopped

¼ tsp pure vanilla extract

Butter and flour the sides of a 9-inch springform pan and line the bottom with a round of parchment paper.

Preheat your oven to 350°F.

In a heatproof bowl set over a pot with ½-inch of barely simmering water, stir together chopped chocolate and butter until completely melted and smooth. Remove from heat and set aside to cool for 5-10 minutes.

Place almonds in the bowl of a food processor and process until finely ground, similar to the texture of bread crumbs; set aside.

In a large bowl, whisk egg yolks until smooth. Gradually add all but 2 tablespoons of sugar while whisking constantly until very pale, thick and ribbon-like, about 1 minute. Whisk in salt.

In a separate medium bowl, beat egg whites using an electric hand mixer on medium-high speed until soft peaks form. Gradually add remaining 2 tablespoons of sugar while beating until stiff peaks form; set aside.

Whisk cooled melted chocolate mixture into egg yolk mixture until smooth. Stir in 4 oz (about 1 cup) ground almonds, reserving the rest for garnishing the torte. Using a wide rubber spatula, stir about one-third of the egg whites into the chocolate batter to lighten it. Sift flour over the batter and fold it in until mostly combined but a few streaks remain. Add half of the remaining egg whites and gently yet quickly fold them into the batter until well incorporated. Finally, fold in the rest of the egg whites. It is important to work quickly so that the egg foam does not deflate. Pour batter into prepared pan and bake until it puffs up and forms a firm and crisp crust at the surface, 25-30 minutes. A toothpick inserted into the center of the cake will come out with a few moist crumbs. Transfer cake to a wire rack. Run a knife around the inside edges of the pan and let cool 3 minutes. Then, release and lift off removable sides and let cool completely.

To make the glaze, combine cream, sugar, corn syrup and salt in a small saucepan over low heat and stir until sugar dissolves, about 3 minutes. Add chopped chocolate and stir until the chocolate begins to melt. Increase heat to medium-low and bring mixture to a boil. Cook at a boil for 7 minutes, stirring constantly. The mixture will be thick with a syrup-like consistency. Allow to cool until thickened, about 10 minutes, and then stir in vanilla extract. Pour glaze evenly over torte and gently spread it out to the edges, allowing it to drip over the sides.

Sprinkle reserved ground almonds over top, around the edge of the torte. If not serving immediately, refrigerate and then allow torte to come to room temperature before serving.

Marbled Sour Cream Coffee Cake

Makes 8-10 servings

. . . .

I remember when I first made this cake. It was Christmas break during my freshman year of university and I had just arrived home for the holidays. To my surprise, I came home to a huge Christmas party that my mom failed to mention. All of my closest family was there and my mom prepared an amazing spread including sushi appetizers (her first attempt!). But, she didn't make dessert. So, naturally, as soon as I walked in the door she asked me to go prepare something sweet for after dinner. I came up with this recipe on the spot because I figured a loaf cake would take close to an hour to bake and require little attention, allowing me plenty of time to graze! It turned out fantastic and I still make it regularly for brunch on weekends. The best part is the crunchy chocolate crust – if you happen to eat up the top part fresh from the oven, that's totally normal.

. . . .

Ingredients:

3 oz/85 g dark chocolate (64% cocoa), finely chopped

2 cups all-purpose flour

1 ½ tsp baking powder

¾ tsp baking soda

¼ tsp ground cardamom

¼ tsp freshly grated nutmeg

½ tsp salt

½ cup unsalted butter, at room temperature

½ cup granulated sugar

⅔ cup plus 2 tbsp packed light brown sugar, divided

2 large eggs, at room temperature

1 cup full fat (14%) sour cream, at room temperature

1 ½ tsp pure vanilla extract

Preheat your oven to 350°F. Line a 9x5-inch loaf pan with parchment paper leaving a 2-inch overhang at opposite ends along the lengths and butter exposed sides.

Place chocolate in a heatproof bowl set over a pot with ½-inch of barely simmering water and stir until completely melted and smooth; set aside to cool slightly.

Sift flour, baking powder, baking soda, ground cardamom, nutmeg and salt into a medium bowl and whisk to blend evenly; set aside.

In the bowl of an electric stand mixer fitted with the flat beater/paddle attachment, beat together butter, granulated sugar and ⅔ cup light brown sugar on medium speed until pale and fluffy, 2 to 3 minutes. Beat in eggs, one at a time, mixing thoroughly on medium speed after each addition, about 20 seconds per egg.

Beat in sour cream and vanilla extract until well incorporated. Add half of the flour mixture and mix on low speed until just blended and somewhat smooth, no longer than 20 seconds.

Remove the bowl from the mixer and fold in the remaining flour mixture by hand using a large rubber spatula until well incorporated and smooth. Do not over-mix. The batter will be very thick.

Spoon batter into prepared pan and spread it out evenly. Drizzle melted chocolate randomly over top. Use a butter knife to haphazardly swirl chocolate into the batter, creating a marbled effect. Sprinkle remaining 2 tablespoons of brown sugar evenly over top, patting it down slightly so that it sticks to the surface.

Bake for 30 minutes. Reduce oven temperature to 325°F and bake another 25-30 minutes. The cake will develop a gorgeous brown crust, and a toothpick inserted into the center will come out clean (despite any melted chocolate from the topping). Transfer cake to wire rack and let cool completely in pan. Once cooled, remove from pan using the parchment paper as a handle and use a serrated knife with a gentle sawing motion to slice it.

Peanut Butter Fudge Cheesecake Semifreddo

Makes about 12 servings

....

It's a no-bake dessert in a baking book, so you know it has got to be good for it to make the cut. This is one of those treats that my mom always brought to my grandparents' house for backyard barbeques. Semifreddo means "half cold" in Italian and encompasses a variety of semi-frozen desserts with a mousse-like texture. The air whipped into the eggs and heavy cream prevents it from freezing rock hard. The combination of peanut butter and cream cheese is entirely addictive. Pour it over a nutty oat crust and top it off with homemade hot fudge and you've got one irresistible dessert that I'm not likely to share. Do I even have to go on about chocolate and peanut butter together? Please. They're like the two best friends anyone could ever have and you're about to be a part of that relationship.

....

For the crust:

1 cup old-fashioned large flake rolled oats

¼ cup unsalted peanuts

2 tbsp packed light brown sugar

2 tbsp unsalted butter

2 tbsp all natural smooth peanut butter

For the filling:

2 large eggs

⅓ cup plus 1 tbsp granulated sugar

1 package (8 ¾ oz/250 g) brick cream cheese

¼ cup all natural smooth peanut butter

1 tsp pure vanilla extract

pinch of salt

¾ cup 35% whipping cream

1 recipe Deep Dark Hot Fudge Sauce (page 244)

To make the crust, spread oats in an even layer in a large dry frying pan over medium-low heat and toast until very lightly golden and smells nutty, about 5 minutes. Shake the pan frequently to prevent burning. Transfer oats to the bowl of a food processor and set aside.

Place peanuts in the same frying pan and toast until lightly browned and fragrant, shaking the pan frequently, about 5 minutes. Transfer peanuts to the bowl of the food processor with the oats and pulse several times until the mixture resembles coarse crumbs. Pour the mixture into a small medium bowl and stir in brown sugar. In a small saucepan over medium-low heat, melt together butter and peanut butter until smooth. Pour this over the oat mixture and stir it in until evenly combined. Use your fingertips to blend it together so that the oats are evenly coated with the butter mixture. Pour it into an 8 x 8-inch glass baking dish and press it evenly into the bottom. Cover loosely with plastic wrap and refrigerate while you make the filling.

In a medium heatproof bowl, whisk together eggs and two-thirds of the sugar until blended. Place the bowl over a pot with ½-inch of simmering water and whisk vigorously non-stop until thickened and frothy. The mixture should register at least 162°F (72°C) on an instant-read thermometer to safely cook the eggs. Remove bowl from over the hot water. Use an electric mixer to beat the mixture until cool, thick, and doubled in volume, about 6 minutes. Cover with plastic wrap and refrigerate until chilled.

In a large bowl, beat cream cheese with remaining sugar using an electric hand mixer on high speed until smooth and fluffy, about 1 minute. Beat in peanut butter, vanilla extract and salt until well incorporated. Gradually add the chilled egg mixture in two parts while beating on medium speed until smooth. Increase speed to high and beat until light and fluffy. It should resemble softly whipped cream. Refrigerate this mixture for 20 minutes.

When ready, whip the cream until it forms soft peaks using a whisk or an electric hand mixer on medium speed. Add this mixture all at once to the bowl with the cream cheese mixture and fold it in very gently using a wide rubber spatula until evenly combined. Pour it over the crust in the glass dish and spread it out evenly. Spoon room temperature hot fudge sauce randomly over the surface (you will only need about half of the recipe) and use the blunt end of a knife to swirl it in. Cover the dish with plastic wrap and freeze until firm, about 4 hours or overnight. Transfer to the refrigerator for 30 minutes before serving and cut with a hot dry knife.

Triple Chocolate Apricot Olive Oil Cake

Makes 10-12 servings

....

No eggs! That's right. This cake has no eggs so it keeps for days at room temperature. It also stays incredibly moist and has an almost too perfectly even crumb. The combination of olive oil, chocolate and apricots is so exciting. Olive oil brings peppery undertones and fruitiness, apricots contribute their slight tang and sweetness, while both cocoa and dark chocolate add a hint of bitterness. This cake is so much of a balancing act that it probably belongs in a circus.

....

For the cake batter:

3 oz/85 g coarsely chopped dried apricots (about ½ cup)

1 ¾ cups 2% milk

2 cups plus 1 tsp all-purpose flour, divided

1 ½ oz/42 g unsweetened cocoa powder (about ½ cup)

1 tsp baking soda

½ tsp salt

½ cup extra virgin olive oil

1 cup granulated sugar

½ cup packed dark brown sugar

1 tsp pure vanilla extract

1 tbsp freshly squeezed lemon juice

3.5 oz/100 g dark chocolate (64% cocoa), coarsely chopped

For the chocolate sauce:

⅓ cup water

1 tbsp packed dark brown sugar

1 tbsp golden corn syrup

hefty pinch of salt

4 ½ oz/128 g semisweet chocolate (54% cocoa), very finely chopped

Preheat your oven to 350°F. Generously butter and lightly flour a 10-inch round Bundt pan and set aside. Make sure to get in all the crevices to ensure that your cake releases nicely.

Place chopped apricots in a small bowl, pour 3 tablespoons of boiling water over them and cover with plastic wrap. Let stand about 10 minutes to soften.

In a small saucepan over medium heat, scald the milk so that bubbles just begin to form around the edges and then set it aside to cool slightly.

Sift 2 cups of flour, cocoa powder, baking soda and salt into a large bowl and whisk to blend evenly; set aside.

In a medium bowl, beat the olive oil with both sugars using an electric hand mixer on medium-high speed until fluffy and it looks like wet sand, about 1 minute. Add about half of the hot milk and beat on medium speed until the sugar is dissolved, about 2 minutes. It will look syrupy. Beat in vanilla extract. Add this mixture to the flour mixture and beat on medium-low speed until mostly combined, about 25 seconds. Slowly beat in remaining milk on medium speed until batter is smooth, about 30 seconds. Fold in lemon juice.

Pour batter evenly into your prepared pan. Drain apricots and place them in a dry bowl with chopped chocolate. Sprinkle the remaining teaspoon of flour over it and toss until the chocolate and apricots are evenly coated. Gently scatter this mixture evenly over the surface of the cake batter. Use your fingertips or the tip of a butter knife to gently poke most of the apricots and chocolate chunks into the batter so that the surface does not look too crowded. This will prevent them from sinking to the bottom of the cake as it bakes.

Bake until the surface is cracked and a toothpick inserted into an area of the cake without melted chocolate comes out clean, 40-45 minutes.

Transfer pan to a wire rack and let cool about 30 minutes to 1 hour. Gently run a knife around the inner edges of the cake pan (use the dull side of course, so that you don't scratch your pan) and turn it out onto a plate. To present it, take your serving plate and place it face down over the cake. With a good firm grip on each end of the plate and the cake pan, invert it so that the plate is now flat on the table. Lift off the cake pan and set aside to cool completely.

To make the chocolate sauce, stir together water, brown sugar, corn syrup and salt in a small saucepan and bring it to a boil over medium heat. Remove from heat and add chopped chocolate. Let stand for 3 minutes without stirring and then whisk until smooth and glossy. Let it cool to room temperature or until it thickens, about 25 minutes, stirring frequently. Pour the sauce over the cooled cake, letting it droop over the edges.

Anniversary Cupcakes with Fresh Raspberry Buttercream

Makes about 15 cupcakes

For the cupcake batter:

3 large egg whites, at room temperature

½ cup 2% milk, at room temperature

1 tbsp pure sunflower oil

1 tsp pure vanilla extract

1 cup all-purpose flour

⅓ cup cake & pastry flour

2 tsp baking powder

¼ tsp salt

¾ cup granulated sugar

⅓ cup unsalted butter, at room temperature

For the filling:

2 oz/56 g semisweet chocolate (54% cocoa), finely chopped

⅓ cup 35% whipping cream

For the buttercream:

3 oz/85 g fresh raspberries

½ cup plus 2 tbsp granulated sugar, divided

2 large egg whites

pinch of salt

½ cup plus 1 tbsp unsalted butter, at room temperature

¼ tsp pure vanilla extract

15 fresh raspberries for decorating

These lovely cupcakes stay light and fluffy thanks to a combination of all-purpose and cake & pastry flour. They are also made using the 'one bowl method', which serves to coat flour particles with fat before beating in the liquid ingredients. This creates a protective barrier around wheat proteins to prevent long gluten strands from forming, which can otherwise make the cake tough and dry.

Preheat your oven to 350°F. Line 15 cups from two standard 12-cup muffin pans with paper liners.

In a volumetric measuring cup, whisk together egg whites, milk, sunflower oil and vanilla extract; set aside.

In the bowl of an electric stand mixer fitted with the flat beater/paddle attachment, sift together both flours, baking powder and salt. Attach the bowl to the mixer, add sugar and mix on low to blend ingredients, about 20 seconds. Cut the butter into 5 or 6 pieces and add it to the flour mixture. Beat on low speed for 1 ½ minutes. Increase speed to medium-low and continue to beat until the mixture resembles damp sand or crumbs, another 1-2 minutes. Scrape down the sides of the bowl to make sure all of the butter is worked into the flour mixture and then add half of the milk mixture. Beat on medium-low speed for 30 seconds. Gradually add the remaining milk mixture and beat on medium speed for 30 seconds. The mixture will look satiny. Scrape down the sides and bottom of the bowl and beat for a final 15-20 seconds on medium-high speed. The batter will be white and fluffy.

Divide the batter evenly among the wells of the prepared pan, filling them no more than two-thirds full. Bake about 18 minutes, or until a toothpick inserted in the center comes out clean. Transfer the pan to a wire rack and let cool for 2 minutes, then transfer cupcakes individually to wire rack to cool completely.

To make the filling, place finely chopped chocolate in a small bowl. Scald the cream by heating it in a small saucepan over medium-low heat until bubbles form around the edges. Immediately pour hot cream over chopped chocolate and let stand 1-2 minutes. Gently stir the mixture starting from the center and working your way out to the edges until completely blended, smooth and glossy.

Using a sharp paring knife, cut out a small cone in the center of each cupcake, being careful not to cut too deep (cut just to the center of the cupcake). Snack on the cut-outs. Spoon the warm chocolate ganache into the center of each cupcake, distributing it evenly and filling them so that they are about level with the top. Let cool while you make the buttercream.

To make the buttercream, first place raspberries and 2 tablespoons of sugar in the bowl of a food processor and process until pureed and smooth. If you don't mind the seeds like me, leave them in, but if they bother you, pass the mixture through a fine mesh sieve. You should have about ⅓ cup of raspberry puree. Set this mixture aside for later.

To make the buttercream, whisk together egg whites, ½ cup of sugar and salt in the heatproof bowl of a stand mixer until well blended. Place the bowl over a pot with ½-inch of simmering water and whisk constantly until the mixture reaches 162°F (72°C), about 5 minutes. Remove from heat and attach the bowl to the mixer fitted with the whisk attachment. Beat on high speed until it is completely cooled. This will take about 7 minutes and the mixture will appear white and fluffy like marshmallow or shaving cream.

Do not begin adding butter until the bottom of the bowl feels neutral (not warm). Reduce speed to medium and add the butter slowly, one tablespoon at a time. Once all of the butter has been added, increase speed to medium-high and beat until creamy and smooth, 1-2 minutes, scraping down the bowl as necessary. The mixture will go from looking grainy and soupy to smooth, silky and satiny. Scrape down the sides and bottom of the bowl again. Add vanilla extract and half of the raspberry puree. Beat on high speed until well incorporated, about 1 minute. The mixture will look curdled again at first, but it will come together after some vigorous beating. Add the remaining puree and beat again until very smooth and creamy, about 1 minute more. Taste it – if it still seems a bit bland, add a tiny pinch more salt and beat until combined. Cover with a damp cloth if using shortly.

To decorate cupcakes, fill a piping bag fitted with a medium-sized closed star tip (I use Ateco #843 with a 5/16-inch opening diameter) with buttercream and pipe it in a spiral motion over the tops. First, pipe a small rosette in the center of the cupcake (over the ganache filling) and, without releasing pressure, continue to pipe around it in a spiral motion out to the edges. When you come to the end, ease off the pressure on the piping bag and pull away gently. Place a fresh raspberry at the end of the buttercream swirl to seal and conceal.

Mudslide Cupcakes

Makes about 15 cupcakes

....

This is so much more than just a chocolate cupcake with chocolate frosting. It starts off like a brownie batter by stirring eggs, brown sugar and sour cream into a melted pool of unsweetened chocolate and butter. Then it is lightened by whipped egg whites to create a decadent and moist yet delicately tender cupcake. The rich frosting shows off the beauty of bittersweet chocolate with just enough sugar to make you swoon.

....

For the cupcake batter:

¾ cup all-purpose flour

¾ tsp baking soda

¼ tsp salt, divided

¼ cup unsalted butter, at room temperature

2 oz/56 g unsweetened chocolate, coarsely chopped

½ tsp espresso coffee grounds

2 large eggs, separated and at room temperature

1 tbsp granulated sugar

1 tsp pure vanilla extract

½ cup full fat (14%) sour cream, at room temperature

⅔ cup packed light brown sugar

¼ cup 2% milk, at room temperature

For the Bitter Chocolate Fudge Frosting:

6 oz/170 g bittersweet chocolate (72% cocoa), coarsely chopped

½ cup unsalted butter, at room temperature

2 ½ oz/70 g sifted icing sugar (about ⅔ cup)

1 tsp pure vanilla extract

hefty pinch of salt

4 tbsp 35% whipping cream, at room temperature

Preheat your oven to 325°F. Line 15 cups from two standard 12-cup muffin pans with paper liners; set aside.

Sift flour, baking soda and half of the salt into a small bowl. In a large heatproof bowl set over a pot with ½-inch of barely simmering water, melt together butter, chocolate and coffee grounds until completely melted and smooth, stirring frequently. Set this aside to cool while you whip the egg whites.

In a medium bowl, combine egg whites with remaining salt and beat with a whisk by hand or with an electric hand mixer until they form soft peaks. Gradually sprinkle in granulated sugar while beating on medium speed until stiff (but not dry) peaks form. Set aside.

Whisk egg yolks and vanilla extract into cooled chocolate mixture. Whisk in sour cream until well blended. Whisk in brown sugar until mixture is smooth and no lumps remain.

Gently fold in half of the flour mixture until mostly combined. Gently stir in milk, followed by remaining flour mixture. Now, very gently fold in half of the egg whites to lighten the mixture. Fold in the remaining whites until evenly incorporated.

Divide batter among prepared muffin cups, filling them about halfway to two-thirds full. Bake until a toothpick inserted into the center comes out clean, 20-22 minutes.

To make the frosting, place chocolate in a heatproof bowl set over a pot with ½-inch of barely simmering water and stir occasionally until completely melted and smooth. Remove from the heat and let cool to room temperature, 25-30 minutes.

In the bowl of an electric stand mixer fitted with the flat beater/ paddle attachment, beat butter with icing sugar on medium-high speed until very pale and fluffy, 3-4 minutes. It helps to have the butter just slightly chilled to get maximum aeration. Scrape down the sides of the bowl. Add vanilla extract, salt and 1 tablespoon of cream and beat until well combined, about 20 seconds. Beat in another tablespoon of cream. Remove bowl from the mixer, add cooled melted chocolate and mix on the lowest speed just until blended. Stir in remaining 2 tablespoons of cream by hand until smooth and creamy but not whipped. Mixing gently at this point will maintain the dense, fudge-like texture and dark rich colour of this frosting, whereas beating will incorporate air, lighten the colour and make it stiff. If the frosting is too loose for decorating, place it in the fridge but check on it every 2 minutes. Spoon a dollop of frosting onto each cupcake and use a small offset spatula to spread it out to the edges.

French Vanilla Cupcakes

Makes 15 cupcakes

For the cupcake batter:

¾ cup all-purpose flour

2 tbsp corn starch

¼ tsp baking powder

¼ tsp salt

3 large eggs

⅔ cup granulated sugar

2 tbsp unsalted butter

2 tbsp 2% milk

1 ½ tsp pure vanilla extract

2 tbsp pure sunflower oil

For the buttercream:

3 large egg yolks

½ cup plus 2 tbsp granulated sugar, divided

2 tsp all-purpose flour

¼ cup 35% whipping cream

1 vanilla pod, seeds scraped

3 large egg whites

⅛ tsp salt

⅔ cup unsalted butter, at room temperature and cut into 1 tbsp pieces

Preheat your oven to 350°F. Line 15 muffin cups from two standard 12-cup muffin pans with paper liners and set aside. In a medium bowl, sift together flour, corn starch, baking powder and salt. Whisk to blend and set aside.

In the heatproof bowl of an electric stand mixer, whisk together eggs and sugar. Place the bowl over a pot with ½-inch of simmering water and whisk constantly until sugar dissolves and the mixture reaches 110°F, about 3 minutes. Remove bowl from over water and attach to a stand mixer fitted with a whisk attachment. Beat on high speed until tripled in volume, 5-7 minutes. It should be completely cool, thick, and resemble softly whipped cream. Alternatively, you can beat this mixture using an electric hand mixer in a large heatproof bowl, but it will take you closer to 10 minutes to achieve the desired volume.

While eggs are whipping, melt butter over low heat in a small saucepan with milk and vanilla extract. Once melted, stir in oil and set aside but keep slightly warm. Sift flour mixture over whipped eggs and very, very carefully fold it in using the whisk attachment until the flour is no longer visible, making sure to fold to the bottom of the bowl. Do not over-mix or the batter will deflate. You want to minimize the loss of volume so be sure to have a light hand. Scoop about one cup of batter into the pan

with the warm melted butter mixture and stir together until well blended. Add this mixture to the remaining batter and continue to fold gently using a wide rubber spatula until evenly incorporated.

Spoon or scoop batter into prepared muffin cups filling them two-thirds to three-quarters full. Bake until golden brown and the top of the cake springs back when pressed with your finger, 13-15 minutes. Let cupcakes cool for 2 minutes in the pan before transferring to a wire rack to cool completely.

To make the buttercream, whisk together egg yolks, 2 table-spoons of sugar and flour in a small bowl until smooth. In a small saucepan, combine cream with scraped vanilla bean (reserve seeds for later) and bring to a simmer over medium-low heat to infuse the cream with the vanilla flavour. Remove vanilla bean and gradually whisk hot cream into egg yolk mixture until smooth. Return mixture to pan and cook gently over low heat, whisking constantly, until thick and paste-like, about 5-7 minutes. Pay much attention to it as the egg yolks can curdle very easily. Resist the temptation to increase the heat. When it is ready, you should be able to see the bottom of the pan as you whisk. Remove from heat and whisk vigor-ously to make it smooth – the heat of the pan will continue to cook it. Push mixture through a fine mesh sieve and into a clean bowl. It will look like lemon curd at this stage. Cover with plastic wrap and let cool completely at room temperature.

In the heatproof bowl of a stand mixer, whisk together egg whites, remaining ½ cup of sugar and salt. Place the bowl over a pot with ½-inch of simmering water and whisk constantly until the mixture reaches 162°F (72°C). Remove from heat and attach the bowl to the mixer fitted with the whisk attachment. Beat on high speed until completely cooled and the bottom of the bowl feels neutral, 7-8 minutes. The mixture will appear white and fluffy like marshmallow. Reduce speed to medium and add the butter one tablespoon at a time. Increase speed to high and beat until creamy and smooth, 1-2 minutes. The mixture will go from look-ing grainy and soupy to smooth, silky and glossy. Scrape down the sides and bottom of the bowl, add scraped vanilla bean seeds and beat on high until well incorporated. Switch to the flat beater attachment and gradually add cooled egg yolk mixture in two additions while beating on high speed until fluffy and smooth.

To decorate, fill a piping bag fitted with a large round tip (Ateco #806 with ½-inch opening diameter) with buttercream and pipe it in a spiral motion over the tops, starting at the edges and working your way in towards the center.

Real Red Velvet Cupcakes with Silken Butterscotch Frosting

Makes about 12 cupcakes

For the cupcake batter:

3 tbsp full fat (14%) sour cream

⅓ cup 2% milk

2 ½ tbsp natural unsweetened cocoa powder ❓

3 tbsp boiling water

1 ¼ cups all-purpose flour

¾ tsp baking soda

¼ tsp salt

⅓ cup unsalted butter, at room temperature

¾ cup granulated sugar

1 tsp pure vanilla extract

1 large egg, at room temperature

1 tsp distilled white vinegar

Silken Butterscotch Frosting:

3 tbsp all-purpose flour

½ cup packed light brown sugar

⅔ cup 2% milk

⅓ cup unsalted butter, at room temperature

4 oz/113 g brick cream cheese, at room temperature

½ tsp pure vanilla extract

pinch of salt

Preheat your oven to 325°F. Line a standard 12-cup muffin pan with paper liners and set aside.

In a small bowl, whisk together sour cream and milk until well blended and set aside. In a volumetric measuring cup, whisk together cocoa powder and boiling water until smooth and no lumps remain. Gradually pour in the milk mixture while whisking constantly until evenly combined; set aside.

In a medium bowl sift together flour, baking soda and salt. Whisk to blend and set aside.

In another medium bowl, beat butter using an electric hand mixer on medium-high speed until creamy, about 20 seconds. With mixer on low speed, gradually add sugar and then beat on medium-high speed until pale and fluffy, about 3 minutes. Scrape down the sides and bottom of the bowl and beat in vanilla extract. Add egg and beat on medium-high speed until well incorporated, smooth and a bit fluffy, about 30 seconds. With mixer on low speed, add one-third of the flour mixture and beat until it is mostly blended. Pour half of the cocoa mixture into the batter and beat on medium speed until fluffy and no longer appears curdled, about 10 seconds. Scrape down the sides and bottom of the bowl. Beat in half of the remaining flour mixture on low speed followed by the remaining cocoa mixture and white vinegar, mixing no longer than 15 seconds between additions. Finally, add the last of the flour mixture and fold it in gently using a rubber spatula until evenly combined. Do not over-mix.

Spoon or scoop batter into prepared muffin cups filling them about two-thirds full and bake until a toothpick inserted into the center comes out clean, 18-20 minutes. Transfer cupcakes to a wire rack to cool completely.

To make the frosting, whisk together flour and brown sugar in a 1 or 2-quart saucepan until even blended and no lumps remain. Gradually whisk in milk and then place pan over medium heat. Bring the mixture to a boil, whisking constantly. Once the mixture comes to a boil, continue to cook another 3 minutes while whisking constantly. It will turn into a thick, smooth, opaque paste. It should be as thick as butterscotch sauce. Remove this mixture from heat and pass it through a fine mesh sieve and into a clean bowl. Let it cool at room temperature until completely cool, about 30 minutes. You can refrigerate the mixture to speed up the process, but make sure to check up on it and stir it frequently. It should be cool, not cold. The ingredients need to be at the same temperature for them to emulsify properly.

In a large bowl, beat butter with cream cheese until very smooth and creamy using an electric hand mixer on medium-high speed. Add half of the cooled milk mixture and beat on medium-high speed for about 45 seconds. Add the remaining milk mixture and beat until light, fluffy and smooth, about 1 minute. Finally, beat in vanilla extract and salt. To decorate cupcakes, fill a piping bag fitted with a large open star tip (I use Ateco #825 with a 7/16-inch opening diameter) with frosting and pipe it in a spiral motion over the tops, starting at the edges and working your way in towards the center. Decorate with gold sugar pearls to make them look extra fancy.

....

⭐ How it works:

The obsession with Red Velvet cake has always baffled me. At its core, it's just a vanilla cake made with a touch of cocoa powder and overdosed on red food colouring. I've seen recipes that call for a whole bottle of Red#40. Some are so bright that you need sunglasses to eat the dang thing. Other traditional ingredients include buttermilk and vinegar. Word has it that, like Devil's Food cake, Red Velvet cake got its name from the reaction between acidic natural cocoa powder and alkaline baking soda, which changes the colour pigments in cocoa from brown to brick-red. The problem is that traditional recipes don't contain enough cocoa to produce this brick-red colour (1 tablespoon per cup of flour), so a hefty dose of red dye is added to compensate. That doesn't fly with me, so I made a few changes.

❓ This recipe for Real Red Velvet Cupcakes relies solely on science for its colour and contains no artificial dye. Now, don't expect a vivid crimson red but a rusty brownish red hue. I've also used sour cream instead of buttermilk for added richness while still providing the required acidity. The other great thing about this recipe is that you can actually use a light Dutch-processed cocoa powder, such as Fry's, since natural cocoa is rather difficult to find in your local supermarket. The addition of white vinegar and sour cream in this recipe will provide enough acidity to react completely with the baking soda so that you are not left with a bitter, soapy taste. These little cakes are paired with a rich Silken Butterscotch Frosting to put a twist on your traditional cream cheese frosting.

Chocolate Chip Cookie Cupcakes

Makes 15 cupcakes

For the cupcake batter:

1 ¼ cups all-purpose flour

½ tsp baking powder

½ tsp baking soda

¼ tsp salt

6 tbsp unsalted butter, at room temperature

½ cup packed light brown sugar

¼ cup packed dark brown sugar

2 large eggs, at room temperature

1 tsp pure vanilla extract

½ cup 2% milk, at room temperature

2 ½ oz/70 g semisweet chocolate (54% cocoa), finely chopped

For the Boiled Brown Sugar Frosting:

2 tbsp plus 1 tsp all-purpose flour

½ cup plus 1 tbsp packed dark brown sugar, divided

½ cup 2% milk

½ cup unsalted butter, at room temperature

1 tsp pure vanilla extract

hefty pinch of salt

1 oz/28 g semisweet chocolate (54% cocoa), very finely grated

Preheat your oven to 350°F. Line 15 cups from two standard muffin pans with paper liners and set aside.

Sift flour, baking powder, baking soda and salt into a medium bowl and whisk to blend evenly; set aside.

In a large bowl, beat butter using an electric hand mixer on medium speed until creamy, about 20 seconds. Add both brown sugars and beat on medium-high speed for 3 minutes so it is pale and fluffy. Scrape down the bottom and sides of bowl halfway through beating, and again after fully creamed. Add one egg and beat until well incorporated and smooth, about 25 seconds. Scrape down the sides of the bowl. Add vanilla extract and remaining egg and beat until the batter is light and fluffy, like softly whipped cream, about 45 seconds on medium-high speed.

Add one-third of the flour mixture and beat on low speed until just barely moistened, about 10 seconds. Add half of the milk and beat on low until mostly blended. Add half of the remaining flour mixture and beat for 10 seconds. Add remaining milk and beat on medium speed until the batter is smooth but no more than 10 seconds. Add chopped chocolate and remaining flour and gently fold it into the batter by hand using a wide rubber spatula until well incorporated. Do not over-mix. Divide batter evenly among muffin cups, filling them about halfway. Bake until a toothpick inserted into the center comes out clean, about 15 minutes. Transfer pan to a wire rack to cool about 2 minutes before transferring individually to wire rack to cool completely.

To make the frosting, whisk together flour and 1 tablespoon of brown sugar in a small 1-quart saucepan to break down any lumps and then slowly whisk in milk until smooth. Place the pan over medium heat and cook, stirring constantly, until it comes to a gentle boil, about 5 minutes. Immediately reduce heat to medium-low and continue to cook and whisk vigorously until the mixture thickens considerably, about 2 minutes longer. You want it to be almost paste-like, to the point where you can see the bottom of the pan as you whisk and webs are forming along the sides of the pan. Remove from heat and pass mixture through a fine mesh sieve and into a clean bowl. Let it cool to room temperature.

In the bowl of a stand mixer fitted with the flat beater/paddle attachment, beat butter with ½ cup of brown sugar on medium-high speed for 5 minutes, stopping occasionally to scrape down the sides of the bowl. The mixture will be pale and creamy. Scrape down the sides of the bowl and beat in vanilla extract and salt. You will notice that the sugar granules will become finer. Gradually add the completely cooled milk mixture and beat on medium-high speed until light, fluffy and smooth, 2-3 minutes. Remove bowl from mixer and fold in finely grated chocolate. Use a small offset spatula to frost cupcakes and decorate with dark chocolate buttons.

Coconut Chiffon Cupcakes with Lime Glaze

Makes about 15 cupcakes

For the cupcake batter:

¾ cup plus 2 tbsp all-purpose flour

1 ¼ tsp baking powder

¼ tsp plus ⅛ tsp salt, divided

3 large eggs, separated and at room temperature

⅔ cup granulated sugar

¼ tsp cream of tartar

3 tbsp pure sunflower oil

⅓ cup coconut milk (use a high-quality brand that contains minimum 55% coconut milk)

¼ tsp pure vanilla extract

For the glaze:

5 oz/142 g sifted icing sugar (about 1 ¼ cups)

1 ½ - 2 tbsp freshly squeezed lime juice

½ cup sweetened flaked coconut

Preheat your oven to 325°F. Line 15 cups from two standard 12-cup muffin pans with paper liners; set aside.

Sift flour, baking powder and ¼ teaspoon of salt into a medium bowl and whisk to blend evenly; set aside.

Place egg yolks in a medium bowl and whisk until blended. Gradually add ½ cup of the sugar in a slow stream while whisking vigorously or beating on medium speed using an electric hand mixer. Once all the sugar is added, continue to whisk vigorously or beat on high speed until very pale yellow, thick and ribbon-like, about 2 minutes. At this stage, the egg yolks are thoroughly aerated and the mixture will form a slowly disappearing ribbon on the surface as it falls back into the bowl after lifting the beaters. Set this mixture aside.

Combine egg whites with cream of tartar and remaining ⅛ teaspoon of salt in the bowl of a stand mixer fitted with the whisk attachment and beat on medium speed until foamy, about 20 seconds. Increase speed to medium-high and beat until they form soft peaks, 1-2 minutes. When you lift the beater, the tips of the peaks should droop over and be quite wobbly. Decrease speed to medium and gradually beat in remaining sugar, ½ tablespoon at a time, just until stiff (not dry) and glossy peaks form; set aside.

Whisk vegetable oil into egg yolk mixture until well incorporated. Add coconut milk and vanilla extract and whisk until well combined. Sift flour mixture over the wet ingredients in two parts and use the whisk to gently stir it in just until the batter is smooth. It will be thick and sticky at this point. Do not over-mix or the cupcakes will become tough.

Turn the stand mixer on high speed for a few seconds to perk up the whites. Briskly fold one-third of beaten whites into egg yolk mixture to lighten it, then gently fold in the rest in two batches until just combined. The batter will be goopy and foamy. Use a 1 ½-oz quick-release ice cream scoop to divide batter among prepared muffin cups, filling them halfway to two-thirds full and bake until lightly golden and a toothpick inserted into the center comes out clean, 17-20 minutes. Under-baking can cause them to sink, but over-baking will make them dry, so watch closely. Let cupcakes cool in pan for about 2 minutes before transferring individually to a wire rack to cool completely.

To make the glaze, whisk together icing sugar and 1 ½ tablespoons of lime juice in a small bowl until smooth. It should be opaque and thick, but still thin enough to spoon over the cupcakes. Add another ½ tablespoon of lime juice if necessary to achieve the desired consistency. Spoon icing over cupcakes and spread it out to the edges. Sprinkle with flaked coconut while still wet.

....

✪ Ribbon Stage & Flour Choices:

To proudly beat egg yolks and sugar to the ribbon stage, make sure you use a bowl that is not too large. The bottom of the beaters or your whisk should be sufficiently submerged in order to incorporate enough air into the yolks. Many chiffon cake recipes use cake flour for an extra light and tender texture, but I use all-purpose flour in this recipe so that the cupcakes don't crumble apart, and to give them more strength so that they don't shrink excessively during cooling.

Cinnamon Roll Cupcakes

Makes 12 cupcakes

For the cinnamon swirl:

3 tbsp unsalted butter

3 tbsp packed dark brown sugar

1 tsp ground cinnamon

1 tsp water

1 tbsp 2% milk

For the cupcake batter:

1 ¼ cups all-purpose flour

1 tsp baking powder

¼ tsp baking soda

¼ tsp salt

⅛ tsp freshly grated nutmeg

⅓ cup unsalted butter, at room temperature

⅓ cup packed light brown sugar

⅓ cup granulated sugar

1 tsp pure vanilla extract

1 large egg, at room temperature

⅓ cup full fat (14%) sour cream, at room temperature

¼ cup 2% milk, at room temperature

For the Cinnamon Cream Cheese frosting:

6 oz/170 g brick cream cheese

2 tbsp unsalted butter

1 tsp cinnamon swirl mixture (reserved from making cupcakes)

½ tsp pure vanilla extract

6 oz/170 g sifted icing sugar (about 1 ½ cups)

1-2 tsp 2% milk

To make the swirl, melt butter in a small saucepan over medium heat. Add brown sugar, cinnamon and water and bring to a boil while whisking constantly. Reduce heat slightly and boil gently for 1 minute, whisking constantly. It should resemble dark caramel sauce. Set aside to cool slightly (the milk is to be added later).

Preheat your oven to 350°F. Line a standard 12-cup muffin pan with paper liners and set aside.

Sift flour, baking powder, baking soda, salt and nutmeg into a medium bowl and whisk to blend evenly; set aside.

In a large bowl, beat butter with both sugars on medium-high speed until pale and fluffy, about 3 minutes, scraping down the bowl halfway through mixing. Beat in vanilla extract and egg until well incorporated, about 30 seconds. Add sour cream and beat until batter is light, fluffy and smooth, about 1 minute. If the mixture appears curdled, it's probably because the sour cream is cold and not at room temperature (sigh). Remember, room temperature ingredients make for a more homogeneous batter. Gently fold half of the flour mixture into the wet batter by hand using a wide rubber spatula until mostly combined and a few streaks of flour remain. Stir in milk. Gently fold in remaining dry ingredients until the batter is smooth. It will be rather thick.

Place 1 tablespoon of batter into each prepared muffin cup, spreading it out slightly to fill the edges. If the cinnamon swirl mixture has hardened and appears grainy, place it over medium-low heat and stir in 1 tablespoon of milk until smooth and pourable. Spoon about ¾ teaspoon of it over the batter in each cup and use a toothpick to swirl it in. Spoon another tablespoon of batter into each cup and repeat the filling/swirling process, reserving about 1 teaspoon of the swirl mixture for the frosting. Make sure the cups are no more than three-quarters full. Bake until a toothpick inserted in the center comes out clean, about 17 minutes. Transfer pan to a wire rack and let cupcakes cool for 2 minutes before transferring them individually to wire rack to cool completely.

To make the frosting, beat cream cheese and butter in a medium bowl until smooth. Beat in reserved cinnamon swirl mixture and vanilla. Gradually beat in icing sugar on medium-high speed until fluffy, 1-2 minutes. Drizzle in milk, ½ teaspoon at a time, until it reaches a thick spreading consistency. You may not need all of it or any at all depending on how humid it is that day. Cover the bowl loosely with plastic wrap and refrigerate frosting for 20-30 minutes to let it firm up. Spoon a dollop of frosting onto each cupcake and use a small offset spatula to spread it out to the edges.

Golden Vanilla
Purist Cupcakes
with Vanilla Roux-Meringue
Buttercream

Makes about 15 cupcakes

For the cupcake batter:

1 cup all-purpose flour

½ cup cake & pastry flour

½ tsp baking powder

½ tsp baking soda

¼ tsp salt

1 cup superfine sugar

¼ cup unsalted butter, at room temperature

1 large egg, at room temperature

1 large egg yolk

¼ cup full fat (14%) sour cream, at room temperature

2 tbsp sunflower oil

1 ½ tsp pure vanilla extract

⅓ cup 2% milk, at room temperature

For the Vanilla Roux-Meringue Buttercream:

2 tbsp all-purpose flour

⅔ cup plus 1 tbsp granulated sugar, divided

⅔ cup 2% milk

3 large egg whites

⅛ tsp salt

⅔ cup unsalted butter, at room temperature and cut into 1 tbsp pieces

1 tsp pure vanilla extract

To decorate:

white sprinkles or nonpareils

Just wait until you try these cupcakes! This is my absolute favourite frosting recipe. It combines the techniques of a traditional Swiss Meringue Buttercream and an old-fashioned cooked frosting. I start by making a marshmallow-like meringue from a mixture of warmed egg whites and sugar before beating in butter until it is smooth and silky. Then, I beat in a thickened cooked mixture of flour and milk to lighten it – that's where the "roux" part of the name comes from. A roux is traditionally a cooked mixture of fat and flour that acts as a thickening agent for sauces, soups and gravies. This gives the buttercream a cloud-like airy texture and luscious creamy flavour, making it taste like pure ice cream on top of fluffy yellow cake!

Preheat your oven to 350°F. Line 15 muffin cups from two standard muffin pans with paper liners and set aside.

In the bowl of an electric stand mixer fitted with the flat beater/paddle attachment, sift together both flours, baking powder, baking soda and salt. Attach the bowl to the mixer, add sugar and mix on low speed until evenly blended, about 30 seconds.

Add softened butter and beat on low speed for 1 minute. The mixture will become less dusty as the butter becomes coated with flour and broken down into small pieces. Increase speed to medium-low and continue to beat until the mixture resembles damp sand or fine bread crumbs, about 2 minutes.

In a medium bowl, whisk together egg, yolk, sour cream, sunflower oil and vanilla extract until smooth. Add it to the flour mixture and beat on medium-low speed until moistened, sticky and the batter just begins to form webs along the sides of the bowl and the beater, about 20 seconds. With mixer running on low, gradually add milk and then beat on medium speed for 20 seconds. Stop the mixer to scrape down the sides and bottom of the bowl, and then beat on medium speed for another 15 seconds. Do not over-mix. The batter will be smooth, satiny and creamy-looking. Gently fold the batter a few times with a rubber spatula to incorporate any ingredients stuck at the bottom of the bowl.

Spoon or scoop batter into lined muffin cups, filling them no more than halfway full (these cupcakes will rise quite a bit). Bake until evenly golden on top, the cake springs back when pressed gently with your finger and a toothpick or wooden skewer inserted into the center comes out clean, about 18 minutes. Transfer cakes to a wire rack to cool completely.

To make the buttercream, whisk together flour and 1 tablespoon of sugar in a small 1 or 2-quart saucepan until evenly blended. Gradually whisk in milk until smooth. Place over medium heat and cook, whisking constantly, until it begins to thicken and nearly comes to a boil. Reduce heat to medium-low and continue to cook, while whisking constantly, until very thick and paste-like. When it is ready, the mixture will resemble white glue and you should be able to see the bottom of the pan as you whisk. This will take about 10 minutes all together.

Pass the mixture through a fine mesh sieve and into a small bowl. This serves to remove any lumps and it helps the mixture cool down faster. Place plastic wrap directly over the surface and set aside to cool completely at room temperature.

In the heatproof bowl of a stand mixer, whisk together egg whites, remaining ⅔ cup of sugar and salt. Place the bowl over a pot with ½-inch of simmering water and whisk constantly until the mixture reaches 162°F (72°C), about 5 minutes. Remove from heat and immediately attach the bowl to the mixer fitted with the whisk attachment. Beat on high speed until it is completely cooled. This will take 7-8 minutes and the mixture will appear white and fluffy like marshmallow or shaving cream.

147

Do not begin adding butter until the bottom of the bowl feels neutral (not warm). Reduce speed to medium and add the butter slowly, one tablespoon at a time. Increase speed to medium-high and beat until creamy and smooth, 1-2 minutes. The mixture will go from looking grainy and soupy to smooth, silky and glossy. Scrape down the sides and bottom of the bowl.

At this point the cooled flour/milk mixture will be stiff. So, with a wooden spoon or a spatula, beat it vigorously until it is smooth and creamy. Add half of the cooled flour mixture to the buttercream and beat on medium-high until smooth, about 30 seconds. Add the remaining flour mixture and vanilla extract and beat until whipped and creamy, about 1 minute more. Cover with a damp cloth if using shortly.

To decorate cupcakes, fill a piping bag fitted with a medium-sized closed star tip (I use Ateco #844 with a 3/8-inch opening diameter) with buttercream and pipe rather generously in a spiral motion over the tops starting at the outer edges and working your way toward the center. When you come to the center, release pressure and pull the tip away gently but swiftly. Decorate with white non-pareils or sprinkles for fun!

Banana Cupcakes
with PB Cocoa Frosting

Makes 12 cupcakes

For the cupcake batter:

1 ¼ cups all-purpose flour

1 ½ tsp baking powder

¼ tsp salt

⅓ cup unsalted butter, at room temperature

⅔ cup granulated sugar

1 large egg, at room temperature

½ tsp pure vanilla extract

1 medium very ripe banana (about 100 g flesh), previously frozen,❓ thawed and at room temperature

¼ cup full fat (14%) sour cream, at room temperature

¼ cup 2% milk, divided and at room temperature

For the PB Cocoa Frosting:

6 oz sifted icing sugar (about 1 ½ cups)

1 oz/28 g unsweetened Dutch-processed cocoa powder, (about 5 tbsp)

½ cup unsalted butter, at room temperature

2 tbsp all natural smooth peanut butter

2 tbsp 35% whipping cream, at room temperature

½ tsp pure vanilla extract

⅛ tsp salt

Preheat your oven to 350°F. Line a standard 12-cup muffin pan with paper liners.

Sift flour, baking powder and salt into a medium bowl and whisk to blend evenly; set aside.

In a large bowl, beat butter until smooth and creamy using an electric hand mixer on medium speed. Add sugar and beat on medium-high speed until pale and fluffy, about 2 minutes. Add egg and vanilla extract and beat until well incorporated, fluffy and cloud-like, about 30 seconds, scraping down sides and bottom of the bowl as needed. In a food processor, puree banana with 1 tablespoon of milk until very smooth and liquefied. Add banana mixture to butter mixture and beat until well combined.

With mixer on medium-low speed, add one-third of the flour mixture to the butter mixture and mix until just combined. Add sour cream and beat until smooth, about 15 seconds. Beat in half of the remaining dry ingredients, followed by the milk, beating no longer than 10 seconds between additions. Finally, fold in the last of the flour mixture until well combined. The batter will be thick. Spoon or scoop batter into muffin cups, filling each one about two-thirds full. Bake until a toothpick inserted into the center comes out clean, 18-20 minutes. Transfer pan to a wire rack and let cool 2 minutes before transferring individual cupcakes to a wire rack to cool completely.

To make the frosting, sift icing sugar and cocoa powder into a medium bowl and whisk to blend evenly. In a separate medium bowl, beat butter and peanut butter until smooth and creamy using an electric hand mixer on medium speed. Slowly add icing sugar mixture in three parts, beating until well incorporated after each addition. Very slowly pour in cream while beating on medium to medium-high speed until smooth, fluffy and well blended. Gradual additions of cream will ensure that the frosting does not split from fat separation (make sure the cream is at room temperature). Beat in vanilla extract.

Fill a pastry bag fitted with a 1-cm open star tip with frosting and pipe roses on top of each cooled cupcake. To do this, pipe a small rosette in the center of the cupcake, and without releasing pressure on the pastry bag (i.e. in a continuous motion), create a spiral working around the rosette and out toward the edges of the cupcake.

❓ Previously frozen bananas make a lovely smooth batter because freezing breaks down the dark fibers, which creates a uniform, pale yellow and downright fluffy crumb in the baked cake.

Crème Brûlée Cupcakes

Makes about 12 cupcakes

For the cupcake batter:

1 ¼ cups all-purpose flour

1 ¼ tsp baking powder

¼ tsp salt

6 tbsp unsalted butter, at room temperature

1 vanilla bean pod, seeds scraped

⅔ cup granulated sugar

1 large egg, at room temperature

½ cup 2% milk, at room temperature

1 tbsp pure sunflower oil

For the filling & topping:

⅔ cup 35% whipping cream

⅔ cup 2% milk

1 vanilla bean pod, seeds scraped

4 large egg yolks

⅓ cup granulated sugar

pinch of salt

1 tbsp plus 1 tsp corn starch

1 tbsp plus 1 tsp all-purpose flour

½ cup coarse sugar, such as turbinado

This recipe is inspired by my friends Sylvie and Mike. We came up with the idea over one of our many dinner dates – leave it to me to discuss food while eating food. Mike envisioned a lot of custard and wanted it to explode from the center as well as adorn the top to really make this cupcake about the "crème". Then he thought, "maybe that's too much?" I can reassure him that there is never too much of a good thing when it comes to rich and silky vanilla bean custard combined with utterly soft and tender cake. Alas, the Crème Brûlée Cupcake was born and I dedicate this recipe to the sinful act of indulgence!

Preheat your oven to 350°F.

Line a standard 12-cup muffin pan with paper or foil liners and set aside.

Sift flour, baking powder and salt into a medium bowl and whisk to blend evenly; set aside.

In a separate medium bowl, beat butter with the scraped vanilla bean seeds (reserve the spent bean for the custard filling) using an electric hand mixer on medium-high speed until creamy and whipped, about 30 seconds. Add sugar and beat until light and fluffy, about 3 minutes on high. Add egg and beat until well incorporated and fluffy, about 30 seconds on medium-high speed.

In a small bowl or volumetric measuring cup, whisk together milk and oil with a fork. Add one-third of the flour mixture to the butter mixture and beat on medium-low speed until mostly incorporated. Add half of the milk mixture and beat until well blended, 10-15 seconds. Beat in half of the remaining flour mixture followed by the last of the milk mixture on medium speed just until the batter is smooth, but do not over beat. Finally, fold in the rest of the flour mixture by hand until evenly combined. Divide the batter among prepared muffin cups, filling them about two-thirds full and bake until a toothpick inserted into the center comes out clean, 16-18 minutes. Transfer them to a wire rack to cool completely.

Meanwhile, make the custard filling. In a small 1-quart saucepan, combine cream, milk, vanilla bean seeds and split pods over medium-low heat. Scald the mixture by heating it just before it comes to a boil, keeping a close eye on it so that it doesn't boil over. Bubbles will form around the edges and it will show signs of foaming up when ready. In the meantime, whisk together egg yolks, sugar and salt until pale in a heat-proof medium bowl. Sift in corn starch and flour and whisk until smooth and there are no lumps; set aside. Remove cream mixture from heat, discard vanilla bean pod and slowly pour it into the egg mixture in a thin stream while whisking constantly to prevent cooking the egg yolks. This gradual addition of hot liquid to eggs is called tempering, and it is a way of slowly and gently increasing the temperature of the egg yolks before they are placed over direct heat on the stove. Pour the whole mixture back into the saucepan and cook over medium to medium-low heat while whisking constantly until it thickens considerably and begins to boil, about 5-7 minutes. Once boiling, cook 30 seconds longer.

Immediately pass the mixture through a fine mesh sieve to remove any curdled egg pieces. Pour it into a clean bowl and place a piece of plastic wrap directly in contact with the surface to prevent a skin from forming. Refrigerate until cool, about 20 minutes. Once cool, whisk vigorously to smoothen the texture. If it is too thick (you want it to be the consistency of pudding), whisk in ½ to 1 teaspoon of milk. Avoid stirring in any vanilla extract, as it will discolour the whole batch and change it from a lovely pale yolky yellow to murky greyish-brown.

Using a sharp paring knife, cut out a small cone in the center of each cooled cupcake, being careful not to cut too deep (cut just to the center of the cupcake). Snack on the cut-outs.

Spoon the custard into the center to fill the well of each cupcake and then spoon another dollop of custard over the tops, dividing it evenly among them. Use a small offset spatula to spread the custard to the edges. Place cupcakes on a baking sheet and refrigerate until custard is firm and the surface has dried out a bit, about 15 minutes. Sprinkle or gently dip in sanding sugar, and then flame with a torch until caramelized. Don't be alarmed if you torch the paper liners a bit because I do it all the time and it's kinda fun – the singed edges add character. Let the sugar harden and serve immediately. If the cupcakes sit for too long before they are served, the hard sugar layer will become soft as it dissolves into the custard, but it will still have an incredibly complex burnt sugar flavour. So, if you won't miss the crunchy top, then you can prepare these in advance and they will still taste incredible.

Black Tie Cupcakes
with White Chocolate Swiss Meringue Buttercream

Makes about 12 cupcakes

....

As the name suggests, these cupcakes bake up really dark brown, almost black! They are simple to make and have intense chocolate flavour from both bittersweet chocolate and unsweetened cocoa powder. Using sunflower oil creates very moist cupcakes and also allows the cocoa flavours to shine through cleanly. Just make sure your oil is fresh because if it is even slightly rancid, it can taint the whole batch.

....

For the cupcake batter:

1 cup all-purpose flour

¼ cup unsweetened Dutch-processed cocoa powder

¾ tsp baking soda

¾ cup granulated sugar

¼ tsp salt

2 ½ oz/70 g bittersweet chocolate (72% cocoa), finely chopped

¾ cup boiling water

1 large egg, at room temperature

¼ cup pure sunflower oil

¾ tsp pure vanilla extract

For the White Chocolate Buttercream:

3 large egg whites

⅔ cup granulated sugar

⅛ tsp salt

⅔ cup unsalted butter, at room temperature

1 tsp pure vanilla extract

3 ½ oz/100 g pure white chocolate, melted and cooled

Preheat your oven to 325°F. Line a standard 12-cup muffin pan with paper liners and set aside.

Sift flour, cocoa powder and baking soda into a large bowl. Whisk through sugar and salt until evenly blended; set aside.

In a small bowl, whisk together chocolate and half of the boiling water until completely melted and smooth; set aside to cool for 10 minutes. In another small bowl, whisk together egg, sunflower oil and vanilla extract until smooth. Whisk in cooled chocolate mixture. Add this mixture to the bowl with the dry ingredients and beat on low speed using an electric hand mixer just until moistened, about 15 seconds. Gradually pour in remaining warm water while mixing on low speed. Once all of the water has been added, beat on medium-low speed for 45 seconds, stopping halfway to scrape down the sides and bottom of the bowl. The batter will be smooth and rather wet. Do not over-beat or the cupcakes will become tough and gummy.

Scrape the batter into a 2-cup (500 ml) volumetric measuring cup and pour it into prepared muffin cups, filling them about halfway. Do not over-fill or you will end up with a bunch of cone heads rather than softly curved domes. Bake until a toothpick inserted into the center comes out clean, 18-20 minutes. Transfer cupcakes to a wire rack to cool completely, about 1 hour.

To make the buttercream, whisk together egg whites, sugar and salt in the heatproof bowl of a stand mixer. Place the bowl over a pot with ½-inch of simmering water and whisk constantly until the mixture reaches 162°F (72°C). Remove from heat and attach the bowl to the mixer fitted with the whisk attachment. Beat on high speed until it is completely cooled. This will take about 7-8 minutes. The mixture will appear white and fluffy like marshmallow or shaving cream. The bottom of the bowl should feel neutral, not warm.

Reduce speed to medium and gradually add the butter, one tablespoon at a time. Once all of the butter has been added, increase speed to high and beat until creamy and smooth, 1-2 minutes. The mixture will go from looking grainy and soupy to smooth, silky and glossy. Scrape down the sides and bottom of the bowl, add vanilla extract and beat another 15 seconds. Add melted and cooled white chocolate and beat on medium-high until well incorporated, fluffy and smooth. Use immediately to generously frost your cupcakes using a small offset spatula, or cover with a damp cloth if using shortly. Decorate cupcakes with some grated dark chocolate.

PIES
and
TARTS

fig. 3

SIMPLE AS PIE

tender flaky crust
sweet juicy filling

The Secret Life of Pastry

Making pastry is one of my most favourite things to do. The beauty of it is that it doesn't require many ingredients, you don't need a lot of equipment and there are few steps. It can be made entirely by hand. There are, however, a few tricks to keep in mind so that you end up with tender and flaky crusts.

I never use or recommend using food processors for making pastry. I know that this can be a touchy subject because it's just so easy, right? I know you might hate me for saying this but it just produces a very less than desirable crust. Plus, the best part of making pies and tarts is making the pastry! You can really get in there with your hands and get the feel of the dough. Also, the smell of butter worked into flour is so incredibly dreamy. If you are used to making pastry in the food processor then I hope this will change you. You will soon see that the interactive old-fashioned hand-made version will win the battle of flakiness hands-down. I find it very easy to overwork the dough in a food processor, and most of the time the butter is nearly invisible by the time the dough has "come together". I have no doubt that you will agree after you try it out and hopefully you won't think I'm some sort of crazy scientist lady trying to make your life harder. Truly, I'm just trying to make your life tastier.

In this book, I mainly work with two types of pastry: pie dough and tart dough. Pie crust is more flaky than tart crust, which is more of a balance between crumbly tenderness and flakiness. When making any type of pastry, it is important to remember the following tips:

1. Have all ingredients as cold as possible, especially the fat

2. Handle the dough mixture lightly and work quickly

3. Keep the fat in solid pieces

4. Use just enough water to bind the mixture

5. Bake in a very hot oven

Most of these "rules" apply more strictly to pie pastry, which relies heavily on flakiness for its appeal. Tart pastries are sometimes more similar to cookie dough and benefit from the addition of eggs to give it a stronger texture in order to contain cooked fillings and achieve clean slices.

KEY INGREDIENTS:

1

FAT (LARD, SHORTENING AND BUTTER)

Fat tenderizes pastry because it is insoluble in water, so it coats flour particles and helps to prevent the proteins in the flour from coming together and forming an elastic material called gluten, which can make pastry tough. Fat is described as having a "shortening" effect, as it essentially shortens these gluten-forming protein strands by preventing them from linking together and elongating.

Lard:

Of the main fats used to make pastry, lard has the highest melting temperature due to its crystalline structure. That means it will withstand the temperature of your fingers (assuming you are making the dough by hand) and resist melting more so than butter. This provides more insurance that your fat will remain solid in the dough, and solid fat is required for flakiness. Lard is 100% rendered pig fat and is softer than butter when cold, making it a bit trickier to work with when making pie dough. Nonetheless, this softness makes it easy to finely integrate with flour and create a tender crust. Keeping larger flakes of lard in pie dough will make a flaky crust because it keeps the layers of flour separate due to its higher melting temperature. These layers of flour will set before the lard melts, creating individual laminated sheets of dough. Fat also acts as a water barrier. So, as the crust bakes, the little water that is in the dough turns to steam and further separates the layers of flour and fat. When working with lard, make sure it is fresh and store it in an airtight container as it can develop off-flavours fairly quickly.

Shortening:

Vegetable shortening is made from vegetable oils, and like lard, it is 100% fat. It is made through a high pressure process called hydrogenation which converts unsaturated fatty acids in liquid oils to saturated fatty acids. This creates a solid fat that is softer than butter when cold. During this process, certain compounds called trans fats can form, and I'm sure you've heard of these by now. So, when buying shortening, look for "trans-fat free" on the label, as these types of fats are linked to a variety of health risks. Shortening works in the same way as lard in creating a flaky crust. Its high melting point will allow the crust to hold its structure long enough for the flour layers to set before the fat melts.

Butter:

Butter has a lot to offer pastry due to its incredibly rich flavour. However, it is not the best fat for flakiness. Butter is made up of a variety of fatty acids which makes it soft at room temperature and melt over a wide temperature range. Unlike the other fats, butter contains only about 82% fat. The rest consists of mostly water, some proteins and trace amounts of milk sugars (lactose). These sugars and proteins interact in browning reactions when the crust is baked, adding both flavour and colour. Although butter has a lower melting temperature than lard and shortening, it has the benefit of being chilled to a rock hard consistency so large pieces of solid butter worked into the flour will create long striated pieces of fat when rolled out in the final dough. As they melt, the dough around it sets and creates flakes. It is important to work quickly and be aware of the temperature of your butter when making pastry – if you feel that your dough mixture becomes oily, place it in the freezer for a few minutes until the fat firms up. Remember that making pie dough is a balancing act between function and flavour, so although flaky all-butter pie doughs can be achieved with the right technique, sometimes it is best to use a fraction of lard or shortening. On the other hand, don't replace all of the butter with shortening because shortening is flavourless and butter is sensational.

2

ACID

Lemon juice or white vinegar will lower the pH (increase the acidity) of the dough. Acidity may interfere with bond formation between gluten proteins in the flour, resulting in a softer, more tender texture. An acidic dough also sets more quickly.

3

ALCOHOL

I know, strange right? But it's technically true. Using a strong hard liquor, such as triple distilled vodka, will help to make a crispier and flakier crust. That is because around 40-50% of this vodka is alcohol which will evaporate during baking, leaving you with far less water in the final dough. So, you're less likely to wind up with a soggy crust.

Make it Cold and Bake it Hot!

THERE ARE FEW KEY INGREDIENTS IN A TENDER, FLAKY PIE CRUST. THE MAJOR SECRETS ARE IN THE TECHNIQUE.

1 KEEP IT COLD!

The bowl, the flour, the fat, the water, your hands – keep them cold! Flaky pastry requires pliable solid fats so the trick is to avoid melting. Melted fat becomes oily, leaks water (in the case of butter) and tends to stick to the dough. Naturally, the warmth of our fingers can heat up the fat and create an oily texture if over-worked. To prevent this, begin incorporating the fat using a cold, metal pastry blender or bench scraper to literally cut the fat into the dry ingredients. Once most of the fat is broken down, you can use your fingers to incorporate more of the flour so that the mixture is not too dry. Use ice cold water to bring the dough together.

2 VISIBLE PIECES OF FAT

Tender and flaky can coexist in the same crust. Finely dispersing some of the fat evenly into the dough (so that it resembles coarse crumbs) will coat and separate small particles of flour from each other to achieve a tender texture. Larger visible pieces of fat will melt with the heat of the oven and create pockets in the crust that separate surrounding layers of flour from each other to achieve flakiness. The water in butter, specifically, will turn into steam and expand these pockets even further.

For tarts, a more tender rather than flaky crust is desired, so it is important to incorporate most of the fat rather finely until it resembles bread crumbs with some larger pieces the size of oat flakes. Due to the finer dispersion of fat in tart pastry, the final dough appears more smooth compared to pie dough.

To achieve a flakier crust for pie pastry, the fat should be left in larger pieces ranging from green peas to chickpeas. There should also be a higher ratio of large fat pieces in the crumbly mixture compared to tart dough. If working with your fingers, it is best to move quickly by rubbing, pinching and squeezing pieces of the fat and flour in between your fingertips and thumb to create flattened pieces of fat. Then let it drop back into the bowl and repeat until all of the ingredients are evenly distributed. Round pieces will flatten out between layers of dough upon rolling.

HOW DO I KNOW WHEN IT IS READY?

When the fat and flour are properly combined, there should be visible pieces of fat but the mixture should not be floury or dusty. Overworked dough will be heavy and leave you with a soggy crust. So, if you feel that the fat is getting too warm at any time, place the dough mixture in a bowl, cover with plastic wrap and refrigerate or freeze until thoroughly chilled (about 10 minutes).

On the other hand, fat that is inadequately distributed can pose more of an issue than fat that is over-worked. Oversized pieces of fat will make the dough difficult to roll out as they will stick to the rolling pin. During baking, the fat will melt and leave large holes or tears in the crust. Hence, you should be able to see visible flecks (not large chunks) of fat in the final dough.

3 JUST ENOUGH ICE COLD LIQUID

The goal is to use just enough liquid to make a dough that barely holds together when pinched or squeezed in your hand – it should be able to hold the impressions of your fingers when you let go. In the case of tart pastry, liquid can come from water, milk or eggs. Too much moisture will create a sticky dough and promote gluten formation, giving it a tough and elastic texture. It will also make a less than crispy and flaky crust. Take care not to over-work the dough. Add liquid by gradually sprinkling or drizzling it into the flour/fat mixture a couple of teaspoons at a time while gently tossing it with a fork. Be sure to reach down into the bottom of the bowl to hydrate the very dry sections.

4 TENDER LOVING HANDS

After just the right amount of cold liquid has been added to the flour/fat mixture, the mass needs to be brought together so that if forms a cohesive dough (the exception to this is if you choose to use the fraisage technique). Gently gather the dough and press it together using cupped hands. You may fold it over itself a couple of times if necessary. Avoid kneading and never expect it to be completely smooth.

5 CHILL THE DOUGH

Resting the dough in the refrigerator will firm up the fat, relax the gluten, and allow the moisture from eggs, milk or water to become absorbed and more evenly distributed. This makes the dough easier to work with and prevents it from contracting when rolled and shrinking when baked. Rolling chilled dough will press solid fat into thin disks that will separate flattened layers of dough for flakiness. The end result is a laminating effect with layers of flour aggregates that are mostly untouched by the fat alternating with layers of fat particles embedded with flour. Some gluten develops in the layers of flour and the fat layers melt upon baking to leave spaces between sheets of dough. For round pies and tarts, always shape the finished dough into a flat disk (not a ball) before wrapping and chilling. This not only creates a larger surface area so that it chills evenly and quickly, but it makes it easier to roll into a circle.

6 HOT! HOT! HOT!

Initially it is important to bake pastries at high temperatures (375-425°F) to both set the dough layers before the fat melts completely and to set the crust before the filling makes it soggy. This rapid heating also causes water in the dough to evaporate so that the resulting steam separates dough layers.

7 FRAISAGE

Fraisage is a method of blending dough by smearing it across a work surface with the heel of the hand before gathering it up into a ball to form a cohesive mass. This is optional and not completely necessary as the dough can be formed by pressing it together firmly with some gentle folding. Many French pastry chefs use the fraisage technique to achieve a very delicate flaky texture in all-butter pie crusts and egg-based tart pastry without the addition of shortening or lard. Traditionally, it is performed by using the heel of your hand (not the palm which is too warm) to smear the dough little by little across a floured board until the whole mass has been smeared. Blending the dough together in this way creates long alternating streaks of butter and dough. As the crust bakes, moisture turns to steam and expands to form pockets between the striations. Using fraisage also makes a good crust for free-form tarts where leaking might be a concern. Because you are smearing the butter, you are less likely to get a clump of fat that will melt during baking and form a hole in your crust as it bakes.

Fraisage may not be desired for tart crusts that are made to hold a moist or cooked filling, such as fruit fillings, custards or curds, because it lacks strength due to its very delicate and flaky texture. As a result, it may just break apart and crumble when sliced.

How to "Fraisage":

Pile dry ingredients on a clean work surface. Toss butter in flour mixture to coat and use a pastry blender or a bench scraper to cut the butter into the flour mixture until it is the size of large peas. Use your cold fingertips to quickly work the butter further into the flour until it resembles oat flakes with some pea-sized pieces remaining. Gradually sprinkle in ice cold water until the mixture just barely clings together. Gather the dough into a shaggy mass. Beginning at the end farthest from you, use the heel of your hand to smear the dough bit by bit (two or three tablespoon portions at a time) against the work surface, pushing it away from you in a 4 or 5-inch streak. Repeat until all dough has been smeared, but only go over each portion once. Use the bench scraper to gather all of the smeared dough into a mass and form it into a ball. The dough should now be cohesive and almost smooth. Form dough into a disk, wrap in plastic, and refrigerate until cold and firm but malleable. This usually takes about 2 hours.

STEAM ROLLER METHOD:

For most pie crusts in this book, I use a technique that combines the effects of both American-style pastry and fraisage. American-style pastry is formed by simply cutting butter into the dry ingredients until it resembles large pea and hazelnut-sized pieces. After the water is sprinkled in, the dough is brought together by gently folding and forming by hand.

In my Steam Roller method, I use the rolling pin to flatten chunks of cold fat into thin sheets (like a steam roller, get it?). I repeat this rolling motion 3 or 4 times, gathering the flour/fat mixture and scraping down the rolling pin as necessary, until most of the flour is embedded in the fat. Then I use minimum water to glue the shaggy dough together and form it into a mass by hand. You need a lot of space, a clean work surface and a big smile. This is fun, I promise.

The Facts

butter vs lard

Butter has incredible flavour and contains small amounts of sugar and protein, which promote browning during baking. It is absolutely superior for making cookies, brownies and cakes. For pastries, a combination of butter and lard or shortening works best when flakiness is desired. Lard has a higher melting temperature than butter, which prevents it from becoming oily when making the dough by hand. It also gives time for the flour portions in the dough to set before the fat melts to create striations, which translates to flakiness in the final crust.

cold fat vs soft fat

Very cold, solid fat is almost always used to make pastry for pies and tarts. When cold, these solid fats are malleable so they can get worked into dry ingredients, such as flour and sugar, in a way that allows it to hold its shape. The end result is a crumbly mixture with bits of solid butter throughout, which serve to create flakes in the final pastry. Softened fat is most often used to make cookies and cakes. At room temperature, fat can be beaten and whipped to retain more air. This is especially evident in the "creaming" technique where soft fat is beaten with sugar until very pale and fluffy. This marks the first step in many cake and cookie recipes and creates structure, lightness and a fine-textured crumb. Remember, room temperature means 23°C (73°F), at which butter is soft and malleable but not oily. If it is too warm, butter can leak water and become greasy which hinders its ability to become fully aerated during creaming.

glass *vs* metal

Glass and metal bakeware cannot always be used interchangeably in a recipe without adjusting the baking time. Metal is an excellent conductor of heat so it heats up and cools down very quickly. Glass is a poor heat conductor but a great insulator. So, it absorbs and holds heat very well, but will take longer to heat up and cool down. This makes glass great for pies because it heats evenly and keeps them warm for hours, but not great for cakes and brownies that need to cool quickly so that they don't over-bake and dry out. To compensate for longer heating times, you might have to extend baking times by 5-10 minutes when using glass in place of metal, but I always recommend using the vessel specified in the recipe for best results.

baking powder *vs* soda

Both baking powder and baking soda are leavening agents that are added to batters and doughs to cause them to rise during baking. However, the proportions in which they are used in a recipe can have a significant effect on the taste, colour and texture of the final product. Baking powder contains baking soda, but the two materials are used under different circumstances. Baking soda is pure sodium bicarbonate and reacts chemically with acidic ingredients (such as yogurt, honey, brown sugar, sour cream, cocoa powder and buttermilk) to produce bubbles of carbon dioxide gas that expand during heating and cause baked goods to rise. The reaction begins immediately upon mixing the acidic wet and dry ingredients, so you need to bake recipes which call for baking soda immediately, or else they can sink in the middle. Baking powder contains sodium bicarbonate, but it also contains the acidifying agent in dry form (such as cream of tartar) and a drying agent like corn starch that keeps it fresh. So, baking powder does not require an acidic ingredient in the recipe to react – it only needs to be hydrated. It is available as single-acting or double-acting. Single-acting baking powder is activated by moisture; so, like baking soda, recipes that use this product must be baked immediately after mixing. Double-acting baking powder reacts in two phases: some gas is released at room temperature when the powder is hydrated during mixing, but majority of gas is released during heating as the product bakes in the oven. I use double-acting baking powder for all the recipes in this book. Make sure to store it in an airtight container in a cool, dry place because even if a drop of water gets in, it can deactivate the batch.

Summer Berries & Vanilla Bean Cream Tart

Makes about 10 servings

For the pastry:

1 cup plus 3 tbsp all-purpose flour

2 tbsp granulated sugar

¼ tsp salt

6 tbsp very cold butter, cut into ½-inch cubes

1 large cold egg

½ tsp pure vanilla extract

For the filling:

7 oz/200 g brick cream cheese, at room temperature

1 vanilla pod, seeds scraped ❷

2 ½ tbsp amber honey

1 large egg yolk

2 tbsp full fat (14%) sour cream, at room temperature

For the topping:

8 oz/227 g fresh blueberries (about 1 ⅔ cups)

7 oz/200 g freshly hulled and sliced strawberries (1 ½ cups)

¼ cup granulated vanilla sugar (see page 227)

1 ½ tbsp corn starch

To make the pastry, whisk together flour, sugar and salt in a large bowl. Add cold butter and toss to coat. Using a pastry blender or your fingertips, cut or rub butter into flour mixture until it resembles coarse crumbs. The butter should be well dispersed so that there is no dusty flour left in the bowl, but there should still be some larger oat flake-sized pieces remaining. In a small bowl, beat egg with vanilla using a fork until rather fluid and drizzle into flour mixture while gently tossing with the fork until dry ingredients are moistened and it holds together in clumps. Turn dough out onto a clean work surface and bring it together

in a ball with your hands, turning it frequently and pressing in loose bits until it is cohesive. Fold the dough over itself a couple of times to bring it together if necessary. Flatten into a disk, wrap well with plastic wrap and refrigerate until firm, about 2 hours.

On a lightly floured work surface, roll the dough out into a 12-inch circle with just over ⅛-inch thickness. Carefully fit it into a 9-inch round fluted tart pan with removable bottom. Press the dough into the corners and up the sides of the pan. Trim off excess dough, leaving about ¾-inch overhang. Fold overhang dough back over the sides to create a stronger edge crust, pressing it firmly against the sides of the pan to seal it. Refrigerate until firm, about 20 minutes.

Preheat your oven to 375°F.

To make the filling, beat cream cheese until smooth in a medium bowl using an electric hand mixer on medium speed. Add vanilla pod seeds and honey and beat on medium speed until smooth and creamy. Add egg yolk and beat just until well blended, about 15 seconds. Stir in sour cream until incorporated. Do not beat with the mixer at this point as you want to avoid excessive air incorporation which can cause your filling to over-expand in the oven.

To make the topping, place berries in a large bowl. In a small bowl, whisk together sugar and corn starch until no lumps remain. Gently fold this mixture into the berries until they are evenly coated and the corn starch is hydrated. Spread cream cheese mixture evenly into the bottom of the chilled, unbaked tart shell. Spoon berry mixture with its juices evenly over cream cheese layer. Place tart on a baking sheet to capture any juices that may leak out during baking and bake on bottom-third rack of your oven for 20 minutes. Reduce oven temperature to 350°F, transfer tart to middle rack and bake until juices are bubbling around the edges, 20-25 minutes longer. Transfer tart to a wire rack to cool completely before slicing.

....

❷ Wiggle, bend and roll the vanilla bean between your thumbs and forefingers of both hands to make it pliable. Lay it flat on a cutting board and use a paring knife to slice it in half lengthwise. Lay each half flat with the cut side facing up, hold down one end against the board with your index finger and use the knife to scrape away from you along the cut surface. Repeat scraping a couple of times to extract as many seeds as possible without tearing the pod.

White Peach Raspberry Pie

Makes about 8 servings

For the pie dough:

⅔ cup very cold unsalted butter, cut into ¾-inch pieces

3 tbsp ice cold water

1 tbsp freshly squeezed lemon juice

1 ¾ cups all-purpose flour

2 tbsp granulated sugar

½ tsp salt

For the filling:

2 ½ lbs (40 oz/1.15 kg) mixed yellow and white-fleshed peaches (6-8 large peaches)

¼ cup plus 1 tbsp granulated sugar, divided

¼ cup packed light brown sugar

2 tbsp corn starch

2 tbsp all-purpose flour

½ tsp ground cinnamon

¼ tsp ground ginger

pinch <u>each</u> ground coriander and ground clove

4 oz/113 g fresh raspberries (1 cup)

For the topping:

1 large yolk

2 tsp 2% milk

1 tsp granulated sugar

To make the pie dough, first place the butter in the freezer for 15 minutes. Mix together ice cold water and lemon juice and place it in the freezer.

In a large bowl, whisk together flour, sugar and salt. Add 3 tablespoons of the cold butter and rub it into the flour mixture rapidly using your fingertips until it resembles coarse crumbs. The butter should be well dispersed so that the mixture feels mealy and the flour is less dusty. This will create a tender crust as the fat coats the gluten-forming proteins in the flour to prevent the dough from becoming tough.

Add the remaining cold butter and toss it in flour mixture to coat. Using a pastry blender or a bench scraper, cut the fat into flour to break it down into hazelnut and marble-sized pieces. Turn this crumbly mixture out onto a clean work surface and use a rolling pin to roll over it in several rocking motions to flatten pieces of fat into thin disks. Be sure to go over all portions of the dough. Scrape down the rolling pin and gather the mixture into a pile using the bench scraper. Repeat this process 3 or 4 more times until most of the flour is incorporated into the fat and the dough looks shaggy. You'll notice that there is very little dusty flour. Run your bench scraper over the entire mixture in a chopping-like motion to break down any excessively large pieces of fat. Scoop this crumbly dough back into the bowl and place the bowl in the freezer for 10 minutes to allow the fat to firm up.

Gradually sprinkle water/lemon juice mixture over the chilled shaggy dough, one tablespoon at a time, while gently tossing with a fork until it is moistened and it barely clings together in clumps. The dough will hold together when squeezed or pressed when it is ready, but it should not form a ball.

Turn dough out onto a work surface and bring it together with your hands slightly cupped, turning it frequently and pressing firmly to hold in loose bits until it is cohesive and forms a mass but is not completely smooth. Fold the dough over itself one or two times to bring it together if necessary. Separate slightly more than one-third of the dough (for the top crust) and press each portion firmly to form a roughly-shaped ball. Flatten each one into a disk, wrap well with plastic wrap and refrigerate at least 2 hours or overnight.

To peel peaches, bring a large pot of water to a boil and fill a large bowl with ice cold water. Use a paring knife to score a small 'x' at the base of each peach and lower them into boiling water with a large slotted spoon or skimmer. Blanch them by boiling until the skins are loose, about 30 seconds. Transfer peaches to ice water and submerge them to stop their cooking, about 1 minute. The skins should now slip off very easily. Starting from the scored 'x', peel each peach, cut them in half, remove the stones and slice them into just under ¼-inch crescents. Place the sliced peaches in a large bowl and set aside.

Whisk together ¼ cup granulated sugar, brown sugar, corn starch, flour and spices until no lumps remain and set aside. You will fold this together with the peaches immediately before filling the pie.

Preheat your oven to 425°F and place a baking sheet on the bottom rack. Let dough sit at room temperature for about 10 minutes before working with it. On a lightly floured work surface, roll the larger half of dough into a 13-inch circle, rotating the dough and adding more flour as necessary to prevent sticking. Carefully drape the dough over an 8x2-inch round pie dish and gently press it into the corners and up the sides. Refrigerate until firm, about 15 minutes. This allows the rolled layers of gluten and fat to relax so that the pastry doesn't shrink during baking, creating a more flaky crust.

Once the bottom layer is chilled, begin to roll the other portion of dough out into a 10 to 11-inch circle. Add sugar mixture to the bowl with the peaches and fold them together to combine. Spoon the mixture into chilled pie crust, tucking it in gently to fill all the spaces (this will prevent the top crust from sinking as the pie cools). Gently toss raspberries with remaining tablespoon of sugar and scatter them over, around and under the peaches. In a small bowl, beat egg yolk with milk until blended and lightly brush it around edges of bottom pastry layer before carefully draping the top layer over the filled pie. Press edges of top layer against bottom layer edges to seal. Trim off excess dough leaving ½-inch overhang and then tuck it in by rolling it underneath itself (top and bottom crusts together) so that it sits against the edge of the pie dish. This ensures a tight seal on your pie. Using a large dessert spoon, hold it upside down (convex side facing up) and make crescent-shaped indentations all around the edge. Place the pie in the freezer for 10 minutes.

Lightly brush the top and edges of chilled pie with egg wash and sprinkle it all over with sugar. Place pie on baking sheet and bake on bottom rack of oven for 20 minutes. Reduce oven temperature to 350°F and bake until juices have been bubbling for at least 5 minutes, about 40 minutes longer.

White Chocolate Lemon Tarts

Makes six 4-inch tarts

For the pastry:

1 cup plus 2 tbsp all-purpose flour

3 tbsp granulated sugar

¼ tsp salt

6 tbsp very cold unsalted butter, cut into ½-inch cubes

1 large egg yolk

1 ½ - 2 tbsp ice cold water

For the filling:

5 oz/142 g pure white chocolate, very finely chopped

⅓ cup 35% whipping cream

pinch of salt

For the topping:

1 recipe Zesty Lemon Curd (page 225)

To make the pastry, whisk together flour, sugar and salt in a large bowl. Add butter and toss to coat in flour mixture. Using your fingertips, rub butter into flour mixture until it resembles coarse crumbs. The butter should be well dispersed with some larger oat flake-sized pieces remaining and there should be very little dusty flour in the bowl. Whisk egg yolk with 1 ½ tablespoons of water in a small bowl until well blended and drizzle into flour mixture while gently tossing with a fork. Continue to stir until dry ingredients are moistened and it holds together in clumps. If the dough still feels quite dry, sprinkle in another ½ tablespoon of water.

Turn dough out onto a clean work surface and bring it together in a ball with your hands slightly cupped, turning it frequently and pressing in loose bits until it is cohesive. Flatten dough to shape it into a disk, wrap well with plastic wrap and refrigerate until firm, at least 2 hours.

Allow dough to rest at room temperature for about 10 minutes before rolling to take the chill off of it and make it easier to work with.

On a lightly floured work surface, roll the dough out to just over ⅛-inch thickness. Cut out as many 5-inch circles as you can and fit each circle into a 4-inch round fluted tart pan with removable bottom. You can either use a 5-inch round cookie cutter or trace the circumference of a 4-inch tart pan with a knife keeping about ½-inch border all the way around. Gather the trimmings and re-roll it so that you have six circles in total. Rest the rolling pin over each tart pan so that it is held up by the sides and roll it across the top so that the weight of the pin cuts the pastry flush with the rim. Pull away excess dough. Place tarts on a baking sheet and refrigerate until pastry is very firm, at least 30 minutes (this prevents the dough from shrinking or puffing up in the center during baking).

Preheat your oven to 350°F. Prick pastry all over with a fork and bake until golden brown, 18-20 minutes. Remove from oven and transfer to a wire rack to cool completely.

To make the ganache filling, place chopped chocolate in a small heatproof bowl. Combine cream and salt in a small saucepan and heat it over medium-low heat until bubbles begin to form around the edges (just before it reaches a boil). Remove from heat and immediately pour over chocolate. Let stand about 1 minute and then slowly stir using a rubber spatula until completely melted and smooth. If chocolate is not completely melted, place bowl over a pot with ½-inch of barely simmering water and heat gently until melted. Divide ganache evenly among baked tart shells and refrigerate until completely set, 30 minutes to 1 hour.

Once set, spread 2-3 tablespoons of lemon curd over the chocolate layer and garnish with white chocolate curls.

....

✪ NOTE: To make chocolate curls, place a 6-8 oz bar of white chocolate in the microwave on 50% power for 10 to 20 seconds to soften (but not melt) it slightly. Then use a Y-shaped potato peeler to peel strips of chocolate along the edge of the bar as you would peel a potato. The chocolate will curl back onto itself to form beautiful spirals curls. Carefully transfer them over the tarts using a tooth-pick or a wooden skewer.

Black Forest Tart

Makes about 10 servings

For the pastry:

1 cup all-purpose flour

¼ cup unsweetened Dutch-processed cocoa powder

3 tbsp granulated sugar

¼ tsp salt

¼ tsp freshly cracked black pepper

7 tbsp very cold unsalted butter, cut into ½-inch cubes

1 large cold egg

½ tsp pure vanilla extract

For the cherry topping:

8 oz/227 g pitted fresh cherries (about 1 ½ cups)

3 tbsp granulated sugar

2 ¼ tsp corn starch

⅓ cup water

2 tsp freshly squeezed lemon juice

For the chocolate filling:

⅓ cup all-purpose flour

¼ tsp baking powder

¼ tsp salt

¼ cup unsalted butter, at room temperature

7 tbsp granulated sugar

1 large egg

2 oz/56 g bittersweet chocolate (72% cocoa), melted and slightly cooled

⅓ cup 35% whipping cream for topping

To make the pastry, whisk together flour, cocoa powder, sugar and salt in a large bowl. Add cold butter and toss to coat. Using a pastry blender or your fingertips, cut or rub butter into flour mixture until it resembles coarse crumbs. The butter should be well dispersed so that the mixture looks uniformly brown and there is no dusty flour left in the bowl, but there should still be some larger oat flake and pea-sized pieces remaining. In a small bowl, beat egg with vanilla and drizzle into flour mixture while gently tossing with a fork. Continue to mix until dry ingredients are moistened and it holds together in clumps but does not yet form a ball. Turn the crumbly dough out onto a clean work surface and gather it together in a ball with your hands, turning it frequently and pressing in loose bits until it forms a mass.

Now use the fraisage technique to form a cohesive dough. Use the heel of your hand to push portions of dough away from you, smearing it along the work surface to distribute fat into the flour. Repeat this process up to 5 times total, but only go over each portion of dough once or the pastry will become tough. You should be able to see faint streaks of butter marbled throughout the dough, which will give it a slightly flaky texture. Gather dough into a ball using a bench scraper, flatten into a disk, wrap tightly with plastic wrap and refrigerate until firm, about 2 hours.

Roll the dough out into a 12-inch circle between two large pieces of parchment paper. This eliminates the need for extra flour during rolling, which helps to prevent cracks and maintains the rich dark colour of the dough. Remove the top piece of parchment and turn rolled dough over onto a 9-inch round fluted tart pan with removable bottom so that it is centered and the other piece of parchment is facing up. Carefully peel off the paper and gently press dough into the corners and up the sides of the pan. Push or tuck some of the overhanging dough back down the sides of the pan to create a thicker edge crust. Balance the rolling pin over the pan and roll it over the top so that it cuts the excess pastry flush with the rim. Pull away excess dough. Cover loosely with plastic wrap and refrigerate until firm, about 30 minutes.

Preheat your oven to 375°F.

Prick bottom and sides of pastry all over with a fork and bake on center rack until dry but still soft, about 10 minutes. Transfer to a wire rack to cool.

To make the cherry topping combine cherries and sugar in a small saucepan over medium-low heat. Cover the pan and cook while stirring frequently until cherries release most of their juices and begin to simmer but not boil, about 10 minutes. In a separate bowl, whisk together corn starch, water and lemon juice. Remove the pan from heat and stir in corn starch mixture. Return to medium heat and bring to a boil while stirring constantly. Once boiling, cook until mixture is thick and juices are clear, about 1 minute longer. Remove from heat and let cool completely.

Preheat your oven to 325°F.

To make the chocolate filling whisk together flour, baking powder and salt in a small bowl and set aside. In a medium bowl, beat butter with sugar on medium speed using an electric hand mixer until light and fluffy, about 2 minutes. Add egg and beat until well blended and fluffy, about 1 minute. Beat in flour mixture on low speed until smooth, about 30 seconds. Add melted chocolate and beat on medium speed until evenly incorporated. Spread batter into prebaked tart shell and make a depression or well in the center about 5-inches in diameter, leaving a 1 ½-inch border. Spoon the cooled cherry filling evenly into the well, reserving about ⅓ cup for later.

Bake until the chocolate filling is puffed, shiny and crackly on top, about 20-25 minutes. Let cool completely before removing the sides of the pan.

Spoon reserved cooled cherry topping over the cooked cherry filling in the tart. Whip up the whipping cream in a small bowl using a whisk until it forms soft to stiff peaks (do not over-beat or it will become dry and grainy). Fill a pastry bag fitted with a large star tip with whipped cream and pipe it around the border of the cherries. For a finishing touch, finely grate some dark chocolate over top using a fine hand-held grater.

Coconut Cream Cheese Mango Tart

Makes 8-10 servings

For the pastry:

¼ cup sweetened flaked coconut

1 cup all-purpose flour

2 tbsp granulated sugar

¼ tsp salt

6 tbsp very cold unsalted butter, cut into ½-inch cubes

1 large egg yolk

2 tbsp ice cold water

For the filling:

7 oz/200 g brick cream cheese, at room temperature

3 tbsp granulated sugar

pinch of salt

1 large egg yolk

¼ cup coconut cream (use a high quality brand that contains minimum 30% coconut fat)

For the topping:

1 perfectly ripe mango, peeled

1 tbsp golden honey

1 tbsp freshly squeezed lime juice

To make the pastry, first toast the coconut. Spread it in a single layer in a dry frying pan over medium heat and cook until golden brown, shaking the pan frequently for even browning. Keep a close eye on it so that it doesn't burn. This will take 5-7 minutes. Transfer toasted coconut to a bowl and let cool completely.

Whisk together flour, cooled coconut, sugar and salt in a large bowl. Using a pastry blender or your fingertips, cut or rub butter into flour mixture until it resembles coarse crumbs. The butter should be well dispersed with some larger oat flake-sized pieces remaining. Whisk egg yolk with water in a small bowl until well blended and drizzle into flour mixture while gently tossing with a fork. Continue to mix until dry ingredients are moistened and it holds together in clumps but does not yet form a ball. Turn the crumbly dough out onto a clean work surface and gather it together in a ball, turning it frequently and pressing in loose bits until it is cohesive. Shape dough into a disk, wrap tightly with plastic wrap and refrigerate until firm, at least 2 hours.

On a lightly floured work surface, roll the dough out into a rectangle with just over ⅛-inch thickness and fit it into a 14x5-inch rectangular fluted tart pan with removable bottom, pressing it into the corners. Push overhang dough down the sides of the pan to reinforce the edge crust. Rest the rolling pin over top of the pan so that it is held up by the sides and roll it across so that the weight of the pin cuts the pastry flush with the rim. Pull away excess dough. Press the dough firmly against the sides of the pan to make sure it fits snuggly into the corners. Place tart on a baking sheet and refrigerate until very firm, at least 30 minutes (this will prevent it from shrinking or puffing up in the center during baking).

Preheat your oven to 375°F. Prick pastry all over with a fork and bake until golden brown, 15-18 minutes. Transfer to a wire rack to cool completely. Reduce oven temperature to 325°F.

To make the filling, beat cream cheese in a medium bowl until smooth and creamy using an electric hand mixer on medium speed. Gradually beat in sugar and salt until glossy. Beat in egg yolk just until well blended. With mixer on low speed, slowly add coconut cream and beat until well combined. Do not over-beat as this will incorporate too much air and make the filling puff up excessively as it bakes, leading to overflowing cream cheesiness. Spread filling evenly over cooled crust and bake until filling is just set but not browned, 10-12 minutes. Transfer tart to a wire rack to cool completely.

Carefully cut the sides of the peeled mango off the pit so that you have two lobes. Place them on a cutting board, cut-side-down, so that they lay flat and slice into ⅛-inch thick pieces. Arrange slices so that they overlap each other over the filling. In a small bowl, whisk together honey and lime juice and brush it evenly over the mangoes. Serve chilled or at room temperature.

Salted Chocolate Caramel Tartlets

Makes 24 tartlets

For the pastry:

1 cup plus 1 tbsp all-purpose flour

3 tbsp unsweetened cocoa powder

3 tbsp granulated sugar

¼ tsp salt

6 tbsp very cold unsalted butter, cut into ½-inch cubes

1 large egg yolk

2 tbsp ice cold water

For the filling:

1 cup granulated sugar

2 tbsp light corn syrup

2 tbsp water

1 tbsp unsalted butter

¼ cup 35% whipping cream

1 tbsp full fat (14%) sour cream

½ tsp pure vanilla extract

¼ tsp salt

For the topping:

4 oz/113 g dark chocolate (64% cocoa), very finely chopped

⅓ cup 35% whipping cream

1 tbsp full fat (14%) sour cream, at room temperature

½ tsp flaked sea salt

To make the pastry, whisk together flour, cocoa powder, sugar and salt in a large bowl. Add butter and toss to coat in flour mixture. Using your fingertips, rub butter into flour until it resembles coarse crumbs. The butter should be well dispersed with some larger oat flake and pea-sized pieces remaining. Whisk egg yolk with water in a small bowl and drizzle into flour mixture while gently tossing with a fork until dry ingredients are moistened and it holds together in clumps when squeezed in your hand. If dough still seems rather dry, drizzle in another teaspoon of water. Turn dough out onto a clean work surface and bring it together to form a mass. Apply the fraisage technique by smearing portions of dough along your work surface (see page 159). Gather it in a ball, shape into a disk, wrap in plastic wrap and refrigerate at least 2 hours.

Lightly dust a work surface with flour or cocoa powder and roll the dough out to ⅛-inch thickness, rotating it frequently and using more flour/cocoa as needed to prevent sticking. Cut out as many circles as you can using a 2.75-inch round. Gather the scraps, re-roll and make enough cut-outs so that you have 24 circles in total and fit them into the wells of a 24-cup miniature muffin pan. Gently press the dough into the bottom and up the sides to form little cups. Refrigerate at least 30 minutes (this helps to prevent shrinking during baking).

Preheat your oven to 350°F. Remove pan from fridge, liberally prick bottoms of tart shells with a fork and bake until lightly browned, 10-13 minutes. Transfer pan to a wire rack to cool about 3 minutes, then remove tarts from pan and let them cool completely on rack.

To make the caramel filling, pour sugar in a single layer in a 1 or 2-quart saucepan. Add corn syrup and drizzle water around the inside edges of the pan. Bring to a boil over medium heat without stirring, washing down sides of pan with a wet pastry brush to dissolve any crystals that form. Boil until caramel is a dark amber color, 10-15 minutes, swirling pan to colour evenly. Really have the confidence to let the caramel get dark for a truly complex, burnt sugar taste. The bubbling will subside, the bubbles will become smaller and a golden foam will begin to form when the caramel is ready. Remove from heat and very carefully stir in butter, whipping cream and sour cream, in that order. The mixture will bubble up violently and a cloud of steam will erupt so wear an oven mitt for protection. Return pot to heat and boil another 30 seconds, stirring constantly. Remove from heat, stir in vanilla and salt and then pour caramel into a heatproof volumetric measuring cup with a spout. Pour caramel into cooled tart shells, filling them about two-thirds full. Let cool until set, about 20 minutes.

To make the ganache topping, place chopped chocolate in a heatproof bowl. In a small saucepan, heat the cream over medium-low heat until bubbles begin to form around the edges (just before it comes to a boil) and then pour it immediately over chocolate. Let stand for 1-2 minutes before gently stirring with a rubber spatula until smooth and glossy. Gently stir in sour cream until blended. Make sure that the sour cream is at room temperature, otherwise it will cause the mixture to split.

Spoon ganache into tartlets, dividing it evenly and spreading it out to the edges to cover the caramel layer. Let stand until set, but just before it begins to lose its sheen and set up completely, sprinkle some flaked sea salt over each tart.

Triple Berry Crostata

Makes about 8 servings

For Italian pastry (pasta frolla):

1 ¼ cups all-purpose flour

⅓ cup sifted icing sugar

¼ tsp salt

7 tbsp very cold unsalted butter, cut into ½-inch cubes

1 ½ tsp finely grated lemon zest

2 large egg yolks

1 tbsp cold 35% whipping cream or milk

For the filling:

10 oz/284 g hulled, halved or quartered strawberries, depending on size

¼ cup granulated sugar

1 tbsp freshly squeezed lemon juice

For the topping:

5 oz/142 g fresh blueberries (1 cup)

5 oz/142 g fresh raspberries (about 1 heaped cup)

3 tbsp granulated sugar

1 tbsp corn starch

1 large egg, well beaten

To make the pastry, whisk together flour, icing sugar and salt in a large bowl. Add butter and lemon zest and toss it in flour mixture to coat. Using your fingertips, rub butter into flour mixture until it is well dispersed and resembles coarse crumbs with some pieces of butter the size of oat flakes. There should be no dusty flour left in the bowl.

In a small bowl, beat egg yolks with cream or milk using a fork until rather fluid and drizzle into flour mixture while gently stirring with the fork until the dry ingredients are moistened and it holds together in clumps. Turn the crumbly dough mixture out onto a clean work surface and bring it together in a ball with your hands slightly cupped, turning it frequently and pressing in loose bits. Unlike regular tart pastry, pasta frolla has a more cohesive texture, so you can knead it gently at this point by folding the dough over itself 3 or 4 times to bring it together. It should be smooth and pliable with a rich yellow colour. Gather the dough together with your hands to form a ball. Separate about one-third of it (for the lattice top), flatten each portion into a disk, wrap well with plastic wrap and refrigerate for at least 2 hours.

Let pastry sit at room temperature for about 20 minutes before rolling to make it easier to work with.

On a lightly floured work surface, roll two-thirds of the dough out into an 11-inch circle with just over ⅛-inch thickness. Carefully fit it into an 8-inch round fluted tart pan with removable bottom. Press the dough into the corners and up the sides of the pan and then trim off the excess, leaving about ¾-inch overhang. Fold overhang dough back over the sides and press firmly to reinforce the edge crust, making sure to keep it level with the rim of the pan. Refrigerate until very firm, about 20 minutes.

To make the filling, place strawberries in a 2-quart saucepan over medium-low heat. Cover and cook gently until they begin to release their juices and look soupy, 5-7 minutes. This will extract pectin from the fruit into the juices released during heating. Uncover the pot and stir in sugar. Increase heat to medium and bring mixture to a gentle boil. Reduce heat to medium-low and simmer until thickened, about 15 minutes. Use a potato masher to break down the large pieces of fruit, leaving it rather chunky still. Stir in lemon juice and continue to cook until thickened even more, about 5 minutes. The mixture should be the consistency of runny jam. Remove from heat and let cool completely.

Preheat your oven to 375°F.

To make the topping, place blueberries and raspberries in a large bowl. In a separate small bowl, stir together sugar and corn starch until evenly blended and no lumps remain. Add this mixture to the bowl with the berries and fold together gently until all of the berries are evenly coated. Let stand for 3 minutes to let the juices leach out slightly.

Meanwhile, on a lightly floured work surface, roll out the other third of dough into a 10-inch circle with ⅛-inch thickness. Cut it into ½-inch wide strips, making sure you have 10 or 12 strips in total.

Retrieve the tart from the refrigerator and prick it a few times with a fork. Spread cooled strawberry filling evenly into the bottom of the unbaked tart shell. Spoon the berry mixture evenly over strawberry layer. Brush the edges of pastry with beaten egg. Lay five or six strips of dough evenly-spaced across the top of the pie and let the ends hang off the sides. Repeat this with another five or six strips, placing them at a 45 degree angle from the first layer of strips so that the open spaces are in the shape of diamonds. Press ends against the edge crust to seal and trim off excess dough.

Place the tart on a baking sheet to capture any juices that may leak out during baking and lightly brush the strips of dough with beaten egg. Bake on bottom-third rack of the oven for 20 minutes. Transfer tart to the middle rack and bake until juices are bubbling around the edges, about 15 minutes longer. Transfer tart to a wire rack to cool completely before slicing.

Marbled Blueberry & Creamy Lemon Tart

Makes 8-10 servings

For the pastry:

1 cup plus 2 tbsp all-purpose flour

3 tbsp granulated sugar

½ tsp ground cardamom

¼ tsp salt

6 tbsp very cold unsalted butter, cut into ½-inch cubes

1 tsp finely grated lemon zest

1 large egg yolk

2 tbsp cold 2% milk

For the blueberry filling:

5 ½ oz/156 g fresh blueberries (about 1 cup)

2-3 tbsp granulated sugar

1 tsp corn starch

For the lemon filling:

⅓ cup granulated sugar

1 tsp corn starch

pinch of salt

2 large eggs

¼ cup freshly squeezed lemon juice

⅓ cup full fat (14%) sour cream

For the topping:

8 oz/227 g fresh blueberries (about 1 ½ cups)

To make the pastry, whisk together flour, sugar, cardamom and salt in a large bowl. Add cold butter and lemon zest and toss to coat. Using a pastry blender or your fingertips, work quickly to cut or rub butter into flour mixture until it resembles coarse crumbs. The butter should be well dispersed so that there is no dusty flour left in the bowl, but there should still be some larger oat flake-sized pieces remaining. Whisk egg yolk with milk in a small bowl until thoroughly blended and drizzle into flour mixture while gently tossing with a fork so that it is evenly distributed. Continue to mix until dry ingredients are moistened and it holds together in clumps when squeezed in your hand but does not yet form a ball.

Turn the crumbly dough out onto a clean work surface and gather it together in a ball with your hands, turning it frequently and pressing in loose bits until it forms a mass. Use the heel of your hand to push 3 tablespoon portions of dough away from you, smearing it along the work surface to distribute fat into the flour. Repeat this process until all of the dough is smeared, 5-6 times total, but only go over each portion once. You should be able to see faint streaks of butter marbled throughout the dough, which will give it a slightly flaky texture. Gather dough into a ball, flatten it into a rectangle, wrap tightly with plastic wrap and refrigerate at least 2 hours.

Let dough sit out at room temperature for about 10 minutes before rolling to make it a bit easier to work with. On a lightly floured work surface, roll the dough out into an 18x9-inch rectangle with about ⅛-inch thickness and fit it into a 14x5-inch rectangular fluted tart pan with removable bottom. Press dough into the corners and up the sides of the pan. Trim away excess dough leaving ½-inch overhang. Fold overhang dough over the sides and press together firmly to seal and create a stronger edge crust. Cover dough loosely with plastic wrap and refrigerate until very firm, about 30 minutes.

Preheat your oven to 375°F.

Prick the bottom and sides of pastry all over with a fork and bake on the center rack of your oven until the edges are golden brown, about 15 minutes. The pastry will pull away from the sides of the pan slightly. Reduce oven temperature to 325°F and transfer tart to a wire rack to cool completely.

To make the blueberry filling, place blueberries, 2-3 tablespoons of sugar (depending on how sweet your blueberries are) and corn starch in the bowl of a food processor and puree until smooth. If some pieces of blueberry skins remain, that's OK. Pour this mixture into cooled prebaked crust and spread it out in an even layer. Place tart on a large baking sheet and set aside.

To make the lemon filling, whisk together sugar, corn starch and salt in a medium bowl to remove any lumps. Add eggs and whisk until smooth. Whisk in lemon juice and sour cream until smooth. Very carefully pour this mixture in a slow stream over the blueberry mixture in an even layer – its weight will displace some of the blueberry filling so it will rise to the top and create a beautiful marbled effect. Return to oven and bake an additional 20-25 minutes, or until the filling is set around the edges but still very slightly wobbly in the center. Let cool completely at room temperature. Once cooled, pile blueberries on top and serve chilled or at room temperature.

Chocolate Truffle Brownie Tartlets

Makes 24 tartlets

For the pastry:

1 cup plus 3 tbsp all-purpose flour

1 ½ oz/42 g sifted icing sugar (about ⅓ cup)

¼ tsp salt

6 tbsp very cold unsalted butter, cut into ½-inch cubes

2 large egg yolks

1 ½ tbsp cold 2% milk

1 tsp pure vanilla extract

For the filling:

4 oz/113 g bittersweet chocolate (72% cocoa), coarsely chopped

3 tbsp unsalted butter

½ cup superfine sugar

¼ tsp salt

1 large egg yolk

1 large egg, lightly beaten and at room temperature

½ tsp pure vanilla extract

1 tbsp full fat (14%) sour cream

2 tbsp corn starch

For the topping:

3 oz/85 g bittersweet chocolate (72% cocoa), finely chopped

⅓ cup 35% whipping cream

½ tsp light corn syrup

pinch of salt

To make the pastry, whisk together flour, sugar and salt in a large bowl. Add butter and use your fingertips to rub it into flour until it resembles coarse crumbs. The butter should be well dispersed with some larger oat flake-sized pieces remaining. Whisk egg yolks, milk and vanilla in a small bowl and drizzle into flour mixture while gently tossing with a fork. Continue to mix until dry ingredients are moistened and it holds together in clumps but does not yet form a ball. Turn the crumbly dough out onto a clean work surface and gather it together in a ball with your hands, turning it frequently and pressing in loose bits until it is cohesive. Use the heel of your hand to push portions of dough away from you, smearing it along the work surface to distribute fat into the flour. Repeat this process up to 5 times total, but only go over each portion once or the pastry will become tough. Gather dough into a ball, shape into a disk, wrap tightly with plastic wrap and refrigerate at least 2 hours.

On a lightly floured work surface, roll dough out to ⅛-inch thickness, using more flour as needed to prevent sticking. Use a 2.75-inch round to cut out circles. Gently fit dough circles into the cups of a 24-cup miniature muffin pan, gently pressing it into the bottom and up the sides. Refrigerate until firm, about 15 minutes.

To make the filling, stir together chocolate and butter in a medium heatproof bowl set over a pot with ½-inch of barely simmering water until completely melted and smooth. Add sugar and salt and stir constantly for 30 seconds while still over the heat. Remove bowl from over the pot and let cool about 3 minutes. Whisk in egg yolk until well blended. Add whole beaten egg and vanilla and whisk until well incorporated and smooth. Stir in sour cream. Add corn starch and stir until well combined. Spoon about 2 teaspoons of brownie filling into each unbaked tart shell. Refrigerate until filling is slightly firm, about 15 minutes. Meanwhile, preheat your oven to 350°F. Bake until crust is golden brown and filling is puffed and glossy, 12-15 minutes. Let cool for 5 minutes in the pan before transferring to a wire rack to cool completely.

To make the topping, place chocolate in a small heatproof bowl. Combine cream, corn syrup and salt in a small saucepan and place over medium-low heat until it just begins to boil. Immediately pour over chopped chocolate. Let stand for 2 minutes and then slowly stir using a rubber spatula until completely melted, smooth and glossy. Let cool at room temperature until thick, about 30 minutes. Fill a piping bag fitted with a 1-cm closed star tip with ganache and pipe rosettes over each tartlet.

Two-way Brown Sugar Cherry Pie

Makes about 8 servings

For the pie dough:

⅓ cup very cold butter, cut into ¾-inch pieces

⅓ cup very cold pure lard, cut into ¾-inch pieces

3 tbsp ice cold water

2 tbsp triple distilled vodka

1 ¾ cups all-purpose flour

2 tbsp granulated sugar

½ tsp salt

For the cooked filling:

10 oz/284 g pitted and halved sweet cherries (about 2 cups)

3 tbsp packed light brown sugar

1 tbsp corn starch

3 tbsp water

For the fresh filling:

1 lb (16 oz/454 g) pitted and halved sweet cherries (about 3 cups)

⅓ cup packed light brown sugar

¼ tsp ground cinnamon

1 tbsp corn starch

2 oz/56 g whole almonds (about ⅓ cup) or ½ cup ground almonds

For the topping:

1 well beaten large egg

1 tsp granulated sugar

To make the pie dough, first place the butter and lard in the freezer for 15 minutes. Mix together the ice cold water and vodka and place in the freezer.

In a large bowl, whisk together flour, sugar and salt. Add 3 tablespoons of cold fat (a mix of butter and lard) and rub it into the flour mixture using your fingertips until it resembles coarse crumbs. The fat should be well dispersed so that the mixture feels mealy and the flour is less dusty. This will create a tender crust as the fat coats the gluten-forming proteins in the flour to prevent the dough from becoming tough and elastic.

Add the remaining cold butter and lard and toss it in flour mixture to coat. Using a pastry blender or a bench scraper, cut the fat into the flour to break it down into hazelnut and marble-sized pieces. Turn this crumbly mixture out onto a clean work surface and use a rolling pin to roll over the whole mixture in several rocking motions to flatten pieces of fat into thin disks. Be sure to go over all portions of the dough. Scrape down the rolling pin and gather the mixture into a pile using the bench scraper. Repeat this process 3 or 4 more times until most of the flour is incorporated into the fat and the dough looks shaggy. You'll notice that there is very little dusty flour. Run your bench scraper over the entire mixture in a chopping-like motion to break down any excessively large pieces of fat. Scoop this crumbly dough back into the bowl and place the bowl in the freezer for 10 minutes to allow the fat to firm up.

Gradually sprinkle the cold water/vodka mixture over shaggy dough while gently tossing with a fork until the it is moistened and it holds together in clumps. You may not need all of the liquid. The dough will hold together when squeezed or pressed when it is ready, but it should not form a ball. Turn dough out onto a clean surface and bring it together with your hands, pressing in loose bits until it is evenly moist and cohesive but not completely smooth. Separate about one-third of the dough (for the lattice top), flatten each portion into a disk, wrap well with plastic wrap and refrigerate at least 2 hours or overnight.

To make the cooked cherry filling, combine cherries and sugar in a small saucepan over medium-low heat. Cover and cook, stirring frequently, until cherries become soft and release most of their juices, about 10 minutes. In a separate bowl, whisk together corn starch and water. Remove pan from heat and stir in corn starch mixture. Place pan back over the heat and bring to a boil, stirring constantly. Once boiling, cook until thick and juices are clear, about 1 minute. Remove from heat and set aside to cool.

Preheat your oven to 425°F and place a baking sheet on the bottom rack.

On a lightly floured work surface, roll larger portion of dough out into a 12 to 13-inch circle with ⅛-inch thickness, rotating the dough and adding more flour as necessary to prevent sticking. Loosely roll it around the rolling pin, slide an 8x2-inch round glass pie dish under the rolling pin and unroll the dough over the dish. Fit the dough gently into the edges and up the sides, allowing the excess to hang over the edges. Refrigerate until firm, about 15 minutes. This lets the rolled layers of gluten and fat to relax, creating a more flaky crust. Roll the other portion of dough out to a 10-inch wide round with ⅛-inch thickness and slice it into ¾-inch strips. You should have 12 strips.

To make the fresh cherry filling, stir together brown sugar, cinnamon and cornstarch with a fork in a small bowl. Add to cherries in a large bowl and fold together gently until evenly blended. Work quickly at this point because you don't want the pastry to sit at room temperature for too long.

Sprinkle ground almonds in an even layer over bottom of pie crust and pat them down gently. Spoon fresh cherry filling evenly over ground almonds. Spoon cooked filling evenly over fresh cherries. Arrange strips over top in a lattice pattern. Press edges of lattice strips against bottom crust edges to seal. Trim off excess dough around the edges leaving a ½-inch overhang and then tuck it in by rolling it underneath itself so that it sits against the edge of the pie dish. Crimp decoratively if desired, or press the edge crust down firmly against the edge of the pie dish and use a fork to crimp. Place the pie in the freezer for 10 minutes.

Brush top and edges of chilled pie lightly with beaten egg and sprinkle evenly with sugar. Place pie on baking sheet and bake on bottom rack of oven for 25 minutes. Reduce oven temperature to 350°F and bake until juices have been bubbling for at least 5 minutes, about 40 minutes longer.

....

✪ Why two ways?

It might seem like extra work, but I like to use both cooked and fresh fillings for a couple of worth-while reasons. I like the contrasting texture of some slightly firm fruit and some soft, saucy fruit. Most importantly, cooking part of the filling allows you to fit more cherries into the pie without having a totally mushy interior as you could have with 100% cooked cherries.

Ultimate Candy Bar Tart

Makes about 10 servings

For the pastry:

6 tbsp unsalted butter, at room temperature

1 ½ oz/42 g sifted icing sugar (about ⅓ cup)

2 large egg yolks

¼ tsp salt

1 tsp pure vanilla extract

1 cup all-purpose flour

For caramel layer:

⅔ cup 35% whipping cream

¾ cup granulated sugar

¼ cup light corn syrup

2 tbsp water

2 tbsp full fat (14%) sour cream

1 tbsp unsalted butter

¼ tsp fine sea salt

½ tsp pure vanilla extract

For chocolate layer:

½ cup sweetened condensed milk

½ tsp pure vanilla extract

3 ½ oz/100 g unsweetened chocolate, very finely chopped

For the topping:

2 tbsp 35% whipping cream

1 tbsp golden honey

1 ½ oz dark chocolate (64% cocoa), finely chopped

2 tsp warm water

¼ cup roasted and salted pistachios, coarsely chopped

flaked sea salt (such as Maldon) for sprinkling

To make the pastry, combine butter, icing sugar, egg yolks, salt and vanilla extract in a medium bowl and mash it all together with a wooden spoon until well blended and smooth. Add flour and fold it in gently using a rubber spatula until well incorporated and dough is smooth. Turn dough out onto a piece of plastic wrap, shape it into a disk, wrap tightly and refrigerate at least 2 hours.

Let pastry sit at room temperature for 10 minutes before rolling. On a lightly floured work surface or between two pieces of parchment paper, roll dough out into a circle with just over ⅛-inch thickness and fit it into an 8-inch round fluted tart pan with removable bottom. Fold overhang dough over the sides and press firmly to create a thicker edge crust. Pull away excess dough that gets pushed up over the edge to keep it level with the rim of the pan, or roll your rolling pin over the pan to cut the excess dough flush with the rim. Refrigerate until dough is very firm, at least 30 minutes.

Preheat your oven to 350°F. Line chilled pastry shell with aluminum foil, fill with baking beads or dried beans and bake for 15 minutes. Remove foil with baking beads and continue to bake until edges are golden brown, 5-10 minutes longer. Transfer to a wire rack to cool completely.

To make caramel layer, heat cream in a small saucepan over medium-low heat until it barely simmers, but don't let it boil. In the meantime, combine sugar, corn syrup and water in a heavy-bottomed 2-quart saucepan with tall sides over medium heat without stirring until sugar is dissolved and mixture begins to boil. Continue to cook, swirling the pan occasionally, until it changes to a light golden colour. Reduce heat to control the colouring and continue cooking until the foam subsides and it turns amber. Remove pan from heat and very carefully stir in the warm cream – be careful as the mixture will bubble up violently, so pour slowly and stir constantly. Whisk in butter and sour cream until smooth. Return pan to medium heat and cook, stirring constantly, until it registers 236-238°F on an instant-read thermometer (5-8 minutes). Remove from heat, stir in vanilla extract and salt and pour into cooled pastry crust without scraping bottom of pan. Let stand at room temperature undisturbed until completely cooled and set, about 4 hours.

To make chocolate cream layer, place condensed milk and vanilla extract in a medium heatproof bowl set over a pot with ½-inch of simmering water. Add chopped chocolate and heat the mixture very gently while stirring frequently until completely melted and smooth. It will be thick. Use an offset spatula to spread it out evenly over the caramel layer.

To make chocolate glaze, bring cream and honey to a boil in a small saucepan over medium-low heat. Once boiling, remove from heat and add chocolate. Swirl the pan to bring all chocolate in contact with cream and let stand for a minute to let the heat melt the chocolate. Stir until smooth and glossy. Stir in warm water until combined and shiny. Pour over cooled chocolate cream layer, and then tilt and rotate the tart so the glaze can coat the surface evenly. Do not use a spoon or spatula to spread it out so that you get a streak-free shine. Let stand at room temperature to set slightly, about 10 minutes, before topping with pistachios and sea salt. Slice with a hot, dry knife and serve at room temperature.

Cinnamon Peach Galette

Makes 8-10 servings

For the pie dough:

6 tbsp very cold unsalted butter, cut into ¾-inch cubes

2 tbsp very cold pure lard, cut into ¾-inch cubes

1 ½ cups all-purpose flour

1 ½ tbsp granulated sugar

¼ tsp salt

4 tbsp ice cold water

For the filling:

1 lb (16 oz/454 g) ripe and fragrant peaches (about 3 large peaches), sliced to just under ¼-inch thickness

1 tbsp corn starch

1 tbsp freshly squeezed orange juice

1 tsp ground cinnamon

2 tbsp granulated sugar

For the topping:

1 large egg

1 tbsp 2% milk

1 tsp granulated sugar

2 tsp unsalted butter, cut into small pieces

1 sprig of fresh basil

To make the pastry, first place the butter and lard in the freezer for 15 minutes. In a large bowl, whisk together flour, sugar and salt. Add cold lard and rub it into the flour mixture completely using your fingertips so that it is well dispersed. The mixture should look crumbly and the flour will be less dusty. This will create a tender crust as the fat coats the gluten-forming proteins in the flour to prevent the dough from becoming tough.

Add the cold butter and toss in flour mixture to coat. Using a pastry blender or a bench scraper, cut the fat into flour

to break it down into hazelnut or marble-sized pieces. Use your fingertips to further rub fat into flour until it resembles a coarse, crumbly mixture. There should be pieces of butter that are the size of oat flakes and bigger pieces the size of large peas. Place the bowl in the freezer for 5-10 minutes to allow the fat to firm up. Slowly drizzle cold water over dough mixture, one tablespoon at a time, while gently tossing with a fork until the flour is moistened and it holds together in clumps. Add another ½ to 1 tablespoon of ice cold water if necessary. The dough will hold together when squeezed or pressed when it is ready, but it should not form a ball. Turn dough out onto a clean work surface and bring it together with your hands, pressing in loose bits. You should be able to see solid bits of fat in the dough. Flatten it into a disk, wrap in plastic wrap and refrigerate at least 2 hours or overnight.

Preheat your oven to 400°F. Line a large 17x11-inch baking sheet with parchment paper. Place the sliced peaches in a large bowl and set aside. Whisk together corn starch and orange juice and set aside as well.

On a lightly floured work surface, roll the dough out into a 16x10-inch rectangle. Carefully transfer dough to prepared baking sheet and sprinkle cinnamon evenly in a 12x4-inch space in the center of the rectangle.

Re-whisk the corn starch/lime mixture to make a slurry, drizzle it over peaches and sprinkle sugar over top. Gently fold it together until the peaches are evenly coated. Arrange peaches snuggly in two rows over the cinnamon-dusted area, allowing them to overlap (reserve the liquid in the bowl from the peaches). Fold the edges of the dough over the peaches allowing the fruit to peak through in the middle. Place the baking sheet with the tart in the freezer for 5 minutes.

Beat together egg and milk and lightly brush it evenly over the chilled pastry. Lightly brush the fruit with some of the reserved orange/cornstarch mixture from the bowl that the peaches were tossed in. Sprinkle the entire tart evenly with sugar and scatter little dots of butter over the peaches. Place on bottom rack of your oven and bake for 10 minutes. Reduce oven temperature to 350°F and bake until crust is golden brown and juices have been bubbling for at least 5 minutes, 20-25 minutes longer. Loosely cover the edges with aluminum foil midway through baking to protect them from over-browning if necessary. Transfer galette to a wire rack to cool completely before slicing. Serve with fresh basil. I know this sounds weird...but the pungent licorice flavour is lovely when paired with the sweet peaches.

White Chocolate Raspberry Tart

Makes about 8 servings

For the pastry:

1 cup all-purpose flour

4 tbsp unsweetened cocoa powder

3 tbsp granulated sugar

¼ tsp salt

7 tbsp very cold unsalted butter, cut into ½-inch cubes

1 large cold egg, well beaten

1 tbsp cold 2% milk

For the filling:

7 oz/200 g pure white chocolate, finely chopped

½ cup 35% whipping cream

2 strips fresh lemon zest

pinch of salt

For the topping:

8 oz/227 g fresh raspberries, rinsed and dried (about 2 cups)

dark chocolate curls for garnish

To make the pastry, whisk together flour, cocoa powder, sugar and salt in a large bowl. Add butter and toss to coat in flour mixture. Using your fingertips, rub butter into flour mixture until it resembles coarse crumbs. The butter should be well dispersed with some larger oat flake-sized pieces remaining. Whisk together egg and milk until rather fluid and drizzle it into flour mixture while gently tossing with a fork. Continue to stir until dry ingredients are moistened and it holds together in clumps. Turn dough out onto a clean work surface and bring it together in a ball with your hands, turning it frequently and pressing in loose bits until it is cohesive. Fold the dough over itself a couple of times to bring it together if necessary. Shape it into a disk, wrap well with plastic wrap and refrigerate until firm, at least 2 hours.

Let pastry sit at room temperature for 10 minutes before working with it. On a lightly floured work surface, roll the dough out into a 12-inch circle with just over ⅛-inch thickness. Fit it into an 8-inch round fluted tart pan with removable bottom. Press the dough into the corners and up the sides of the pan. Tuck or push some overhang dough back down the sides to reinforce the edge crust. Roll the rolling pin over top of the pan to cut the excess dough flush with the rim. Refrigerate until firm, about 20 minutes (this prevents the dough from shrinking or puffing up excessively during baking).

Preheat your oven to 350°F. Prick the bottom and sides of pastry liberally with a fork and bake until dry but still soft, 18-20 minutes. Remove from oven and transfer to a wire rack to cool completely.

To make the filling, place chocolate in a medium heatproof bowl. Combine cream, lemon zest and salt in a small saucepan over medium-low heat and bring to a boil. Remove from heat, cover and let stand for about 10 minutes to infuse the citrus flavours. Re-heat the mixture just until bubbles form around the edges, remove lemon strips and immediately pour over chopped chocolate. Slowly stir the mixture using a rubber spatula until completely melted and smooth. If chocolate is not completely melted, place bowl over a pot with ½-inch of barely simmering water and heat gently until melted. Pour this ganache into the baked tart shell and refrigerate until completely set, about 1 hour. Pile raspberries on top and garnish with chocolate curls if desired.

✪ Chocolate Curls

Place a large thick (10 oz) block of dark chocolate in the microwave and warm it at 50% power for 10-second intervals until soft and sort-of pliable but not melted. If it melts too fast, leave it at room temperature to set back up slightly. When ready, use a Y-shaped potato peeler to peel strips of chocolate as you would peel a potato. The chocolate will curl back onto itself to form beautiful spirals curls. Carefully transfer them over the tart using a toothpick or a wooden skewer.

Caramel Apple Tart

Makes about 10 servings

For the pastry:

1 ½ cups all-purpose flour

¼ cup granulated sugar

¼ tsp salt

½ cup very cold unsalted butter, cut into ½-inch cubes

2 large egg yolks

3 tbsp ice cold water

For the filling:

1 lb (16 oz/454 g) firm apples (about 3), peeled, cored and sliced to about ¼-inch thickness

2 tbsp granulated sugar

1 tsp ground ginger

½ tsp ground cinnamon

⅛ tsp ground nutmeg

1 tbsp unsalted butter

For the caramel:

¼ cup 35% whipping cream

1 tsp dark cooking molasses

⅛ tsp salt

½ cup granulated sugar

1 tsp golden corn syrup

½ tsp distilled white vinegar

1 tbsp water

To make the pastry, whisk together flour, sugar and salt in a large bowl. Add cold butter and toss to coat. Using your fingertips, rub butter into flour mixture until it resembles coarse crumbs. The butter should be well dispersed so that there is no dusty flour left in the bowl, but there should still be some larger oat flake-sized pieces remaining. Whisk egg yolks with water in a small bowl and drizzle into flour mixture while gently tossing with a fork until dry ingredients are moistened and it holds together in clumps but does not yet form a ball (you may not need to use all of the liquid). Turn the crumbly dough out onto a clean work surface and gather it together in a ball with your hands slightly cupped, turning it frequently and pressing in loose bits until it is cohesive. Separate about one-third of the dough (for the lattice top), shape each portion into a disk and wrap tightly with plastic wrap. Refrigerate for at least 2 hours.

Let pastry sit at room temperature about 10 minutes before rolling to make it easier to work with. On a lightly floured work surface, roll two-thirds of pastry into a 12-inch circle with just over ⅛-inch thickness. Fit it into a 9-inch round fluted tart pan with removable bottom. Press the dough into the corners and up the sides of the pan. Tuck or push some overhang dough back down the sides of the pan to reinforce the edge crust. Rest the rolling pin over the pan so that it is held up by the sides and roll it across the top so that the weight of the pin cuts the pastry flush with the rim. Pull away excess dough and refrigerate until firm, about 20 minutes.

To make the filling, fold together apples, sugar, ground ginger, ground cinnamon and ground nutmeg in a large bowl. In a frying pan, heat butter over medium heat until the foam subsides and it begins to smell toasty. Add apples and cook until tender, 3-5 minutes, tossing frequently. Transfer apples back to the bowl and let cool in the refrigerator while you prepare the rest of the tart.

To make the caramel, first combine cream, molasses and salt in the smallest saucepan you can find. Place it over medium-low heat and stir until molasses is dissolved; set aside.

Pour sugar in an even layer in a 1-quart saucepan. Add corn syrup and vinegar. Drizzle water around the edges of the sugar and bring the mixture to a boil over medium heat without stirring. Cook until caramel is a dark amber colour, swirling the pan periodically to colour evenly, 10-15 minutes. The sugar may look grainy before it turns into a clear syrup.

Wash down the sides of pan with a pastry brush dipped in water to dissolve any crystals that may form around the sides of the pan. When caramel is almost ready, the large bubbles will subside and a golden foam will appear at the surface. Remove caramel from heat and very carefully stir in the cream mixture until smooth. Be cautious as the caramel will bubble up violently once you add the cream. Pour caramel into a heatproof volumetric measuring cup and let cool about 15 minutes.

Preheat your oven to 375°F.

On a lightly floured work surface, gather scraps from bottom crust and remaining one-third of pastry dough and roll it into a 9 ½ to 10-inch circle. Use a sharp knife to slice the circle into ½ to ¾-inch strips.

To assemble the tart, arrange cooled apples in an even layer over chilled pastry shell. Drizzle slightly cooled caramel evenly over apples. Brush edges of pastry with water and weave strips of pastry over the tart to create a lattice pattern, pressing strip ends onto bottom crust edges to seal.

Place the tart on a baking tray to capture any juices that may leak out and bake for 20 minutes on bottom-third rack of the oven. Reduce oven temperature to 350°F, transfer tart to middle rack and continue baking until caramel is bubbling, about 10 minutes longer. Transfer tart to a wire rack to cool at least 1 hour before serving.

Sour Cream Custard Tart with Vanilla-Poached Cherries

Makes about 8 servings

For the pastry crust:

6 tbsp unsalted butter, at room temperature

1 ½ oz/42 g sifted icing sugar (about ⅓ cup)

2 large egg yolks

¼ tsp salt

1 tsp milk

1 cup all-purpose flour

For the filling:

1 ¼ cups full fat (14%) sour cream

⅓ cup granulated sugar

⅛ tsp salt

1 vanilla pod, seeds scraped

1 large egg, lightly beaten

For the topping:

8 oz/227 g whole pitted cherries (about 1 ½ cups)

2 tbsp vanilla sugar, divided (see page 227)

2 cardamom pods, gently crushed with the back of a knife

¾ tsp corn starch

To make the pastry, combine butter, icing sugar, egg yolks, salt and milk in a medium bowl and mash it all together with a wooden spoon until well blended and smooth. Add flour and fold it in gently using a rubber spatula until well incorporated. Turn dough out onto a clean work surface and gather it together in a smooth ball with your hands. Shape into a disk, wrap tightly with plastic wrap and refrigerate at least 2 hours.

On a lightly floured work surface, roll dough out into a circle with just over ⅛-inch thickness and fit it into an 8-inch round fluted tart pan with removable bottom. Fold overhang dough over the sides and press firmly to create a thicker edge crust. Pull away excess dough that gets pushed up over the edge to keep it level with the rim of the pan or roll your rolling pin over the pan to cut the excess dough right off. Cover with plastic wrap and refrigerate until very firm, about 30 minutes.

Preheat oven to 350°F. Line chilled pastry shell with aluminum foil, fill with baking beads or dried beans and bake 15 minutes. Remove foil with baking beads and bake until edges are golden, about 5 minutes longer. Transfer tart to a wire rack to cool completely. Reduce oven temperature to 325°F.

To make the filling, whisk together sour cream, sugar, salt and vanilla pod seeds in a medium bowl until blended (reserve vanilla pod for the topping). Whisk in beaten egg until smooth. Do not over-beat because this will create large air bubbles in the filling. Pour mixture into cooled, baked crust and spread it out evenly, popping any air bubbles that rise to the surface. Place the tart on a baking sheet and bake until filling is slightly puffed, 25-30 minutes. The filling should be set around the edges and slightly wobbly in the center. Transfer tart to a wire rack to cool completely. Refrigerate at least 1 hour before adding the cherry topping.

To make the topping, gently toss together cherries, 1 tablespoon of vanilla sugar, cardamom pods and scraped vanilla pod in a small 2-quart saucepan. Let stand until cherries begin to release some juices, about 5 minutes. Place pan over medium-low heat, cover and cook while stirring frequently until cherries become slightly soft and release most of their juices, 5-6 minutes. Use a slotted spoon to transfer cherries to a fine-mesh sieve placed over a bowl to catch any juices. Pour whatever juice is left in the pan into a volumetric measuring cup and discard cardamom pods. Pour in juices that drained from the reserved cherries (they will release more juices as they cool slightly). Add water until it reaches the ⅓ cup marking. Stir in remaining tablespoon of vanilla sugar until dissolved. In a separate small bowl, whisk together cornstarch with about 1 tablespoon of this cherry juice liquid until well combined and then stir it back into the rest of the liquid. Pour this syrup into the pan and bring it to a boil while whisking constantly over medium-low heat. Once boiling, cook for one more minute. Pour it into your volumetric measuring cup and let cool for 2 minutes. It will thicken as it cools. Spoon cooled poached cherries over the cooled tart and pour syrup over and around the cherries.

Tuxedo Tartlets

Makes about 24 tartlets

For the pastry:

1 cup plus 2 tbsp all-purpose flour

3 tbsp granulated sugar

¼ tsp salt

6 tbsp very cold unsalted butter, cut into ½-inch cubes

1 large egg yolk

1 ½ - 2 tbsp ice cold water

For the filling:

⅔ cup 2% milk

⅓ cup 10% half & half cream

1 vanilla bean pod, seeds scraped

3 large egg yolks

¼ cup granulated sugar

pinch of salt

1 tbsp <u>each</u> corn starch and all-purpose flour

For the topping:

5 oz/142 g semisweet chocolate (54% cocoa), finely chopped

⅓ cup 10% half & half cream

1 tbsp unsalted butter

pinch of salt

⅓ cup unsweetened shredded, toasted coconut

To make the pastry, whisk together flour, sugar and salt in a large bowl. Quickly rub butter into flour mixture using your fingertips until it resembles coarse crumbs with some larger oat flake-sized pieces but no dusty flour is left in the bowl. Whisk egg yolk with 1 ½ tablespoons of water in a small bowl and drizzle into flour mixture while gently tossing with a fork until dry ingredients are moistened and it holds together in clumps when squeezed in your hand. Sprinkle in another ½ tablespoon of water if necessary. Turn crumbly dough out onto a clean work surface and gather it together to form a mass. Use the heel of your hand to push 3 tablespoon portions of dough away from you, smearing it along the work surface to distribute fat into the flour. Repeat this process until all of the dough is smeared, 5-6 times total, but only go over each portion once. Gather dough into a ball, flatten it into a disk, wrap tightly with plastic wrap and refrigerate at least 2 hours.

On a lightly floured work surface, roll dough out to ⅛-inch thickness, rotating it frequently and using more flour as needed to prevent sticking. Cut out as many circles as you can using a 2 ½-inch round. Gather scraps, re-roll pastry and cut out enough circles so that you have 24 total. Fit them into the cups of a 24-cup miniature muffin pan, gently pressing the dough into the bottom and up the sides. Refrigerate at least 15 minutes. Preheat your oven to 350°F. Prick bottoms of chilled pastry a few times with a fork and bake until golden brown, about 10 minutes. Transfer pan to a wire rack to cool for 3 minutes. Remove tarts from pan and let cool completely on rack.

To make the filling, heat milk, cream, vanilla bean seeds and split pods in a small 1-quart saucepan over medium-low heat until it just barely comes to a simmer. Meanwhile, whisk together yolks and sugar in a sturdy heatproof medium bowl. Sift in corn starch and flour and whisk until smooth and there are no lumps; set aside. Extract vanilla pods from scalded milk mixture and slowly pour it into the egg mixture in a thin stream while whisking constantly to prevent cooking the yolks. Pour the whole mixture back into the saucepan and cook over medium to medium-low heat, whisking constantly, until it thickens to the consistency of pudding and begins to boil, about 5 minutes. Once boiling, cook 30 seconds longer. Immediately pass the mixture through a fine mesh sieve and into a clean bowl. Place a piece of plastic wrap directly in contact with the surface of the custard to prevent a skin from forming. Refrigerate until firm, about 1 hour.

To make the topping, place chocolate in a small heatproof bowl. Heat cream, butter and salt in a small saucepan over medium-low heat until it just barely simmers, stirring frequently. Immediately pour over chocolate. Let stand 2 minutes. Gently stir with a spatula until smooth and glossy. Beat the chilled custard with a wooden spoon to loosen it and spoon about 1 teaspoon into each tart. Generously spoon warm ganache over top, letting it fill the crevices and seal in the custard. Sprinkle toasted coconut over each tart and let stand until ganache is set. Store in the fridge.

Classic Blueberry Pie

Makes about 8 servings

For the pie dough:

⅓ cup very cold unsalted butter, cut into ¾-inch cubes

⅓ cup very cold pure lard, cut into ¾-inch cubes

3 tbsp ice cold water

1 tbsp distilled white vinegar

1 ¾ cups all-purpose flour

2 tbsp granulated sugar

¼ tsp salt

For the filling:

1 ½ lbs (24 oz/700 g) fresh blueberries (about 5 cups)

½ cup granulated sugar

2 tbsp corn starch

1 tbsp all-purpose flour

⅛ tsp ground cardamom

pinch of freshly grated nutmeg (about 3 grates on a fine handheld grater)

For the topping:

1 large egg, well beaten

1 tbsp coarse sanding sugar

To make the pie dough, first place the butter and lard in the freezer for 15 minutes. Mix together the ice cold water and vinegar and place it in the freezer.

In a large bowl, whisk together flour, sugar and salt. Add about 3 tablespoons of fat (a mix of butter and shortening) and rub it into the flour mixture using your fingertips until it resembles coarse crumbs. The fat should be well dispersed so that the mixture feels mealy and the flour is less dusty. This will create a tender crust as the fat coats the flour particles and acts as a barrier to prevent the development of gluten proteins that can make the dough tough.

Add the remaining cold butter and shortening and toss it in flour mixture to coat. Using a pastry blender or a bench scraper, cut the fat into the flour to break it down into hazelnut and marble-sized pieces. Turn this crumbly mixture out onto a clean work surface and use a rolling pin to roll over the whole mixture in several rocking motions to flatten pieces of cold fat into thin disks. Be sure to go over all portions of the dough. Scrape down the rolling pin and gather the mixture into a pile using the bench scraper. Repeat this process 3 or 4 more times until most of the flour is incorporated into the fat and the dough looks shaggy. You'll notice that there is very little dusty flour. Run your bench scraper once over the entire mixture in a chopping-like motion to break down any excessively large pieces of fat. Scoop this crumbly dough back into the bowl and place it in the freezer for 10 minutes to allow the fat to firm up.

Gradually sprinkle cold water/vinegar mixture over the chilled shaggy dough, one tablespoon at a time, while gently tossing with a fork until the dough is moistened and it barely clings together in clumps. The dough will hold together when squeezed or pressed when it is ready, but it should not form a ball. Turn dough out onto a clean surface and bring it together with your hands, pressing in loose bits until it is evenly moist and cohesive but not completely smooth. Divide the dough almost in half (one half slightly larger than the other), flatten each portion into a disk, wrap well with plastic wrap and refrigerate at least 2 hours or overnight.

Preheat your oven to 425°F and place a baking sheet on the bottom rack.

To make the filling, place the blueberries in a large bowl and set aside. Whisk together sugar, corn starch, flour, ground cardamom and ground nutmeg until no lumps remain and set aside. You will fold this together with the blueberries immediately before filling the pie.

On a lightly floured work surface, roll the larger half of the dough into a 12 to 13-inch circle, rotating it and adding more flour as necessary to prevent sticking. Carefully drape the dough over an 8x2-inch round glass pie dish. Gently press it into the corners and up the sides of the dish. Refrigerate until firm, about 15 minutes, while making the filling and rolling out the top crust. Chilling allows the rolled layers of gluten and fat to relax and firm up, preventing shrinkage during baking and resulting in a flakier crust.

Once the bottom pastry layer is chilled, roll the other portion of dough out into a 10 to 11-inch circle. Add sugar mixture to the bowl with the berries and fold them together to combine. Pour into chilled pie crust. Brush edges with beaten egg and carefully drape top layer over the filled pie. Press edges of top layer against bottom layer edges to seal. Trim away excess dough leaving a ½-inch overhang and then tuck it in by rolling it underneath itself (top and bottom crusts together) so that it sits against the edge of the pie dish. This ensures a tight seal on your pie. Crimp decoratively using three fingers. Using your thumb and index finger from one hand, push from the outside edge of the crust toward the inside of the pie while pushing at the same time with the index finger of the other hand in the opposite direction between the other two fingers. Place the pie in the freezer for 10 minutes.

Brush top and edges of chilled pie lightly with beaten egg and sprinkle with sanding sugar. Make six 1 ½-inch incisions in an asterisk pattern on the top crust to let steam escape during baking.

Place pie on baking sheet on bottom rack of oven and bake for 25 minutes. Reduce oven temperature to 350°F and bake until juices have been bubbling for at least 5 minutes, 35-40 minutes longer. Loosely cover the edges with aluminum foil midway through baking to protect them from over-browning if necessary. Transfer pie to a wire rack to cool completely before slicing.

Spiked Silk Chocolate Tart

Makes about 8 servings

For the crust:

¾ cup plus 1 tbsp all-purpose flour

1 oz/28 g unsweetened cocoa powder (about ⅓ cup), plus extra for rolling out the dough

¼ tsp salt

6 tbsp unsalted butter, at room temperature

¼ cup granulated sugar

½ tsp pure vanilla extract

1 large chilled egg

For the filling:

4 oz/113 g semisweet chocolate (54% cocoa), coarsely chopped

2 oz/56 g bittersweet chocolate (72% cocoa), coarsely chopped

⅓ cup 35% whipping cream

⅓ cup 2% milk

2 tsp coffee liqueur

pinch of salt

2 large egg yolks

To make the crust, whisk together flour, cocoa powder and salt in a medium bowl until well blended and no lumps of cocoa powder remain; set aside.

In another medium bowl, cream together butter, sugar and vanilla extract using a rubber spatula until light and fluffy. Add egg and whisk rather vigorously until well combined and somewhat smooth. The mixture may look slightly curdled with small bits of butter because the egg is cold, but that's OK. Add flour mixture all at once and fold it in gently until a soft dough forms. Place dough on a piece of plastic wrap, form into a disk, wrap well and refrigerate until firm, about 1 hour.

Preheat your oven to 350°F.

On a work surface dusted lightly with cocoa powder (or between two pieces of parchment paper), roll dough out to just over ⅛-inch thickness and gently fit it into an 8-inch round fluted tart pan with removable bottom. Press dough into the corners and up the sides. Tuck or push some overhang dough back down the sides of the pan to reinforce the edge crust. Roll the rolling pin over top of the pan to cut the excess dough flush with the rim. Refrigerate until firm, about 30 minutes (this prevents the dough from shrinking or puffing up excessively during baking). Prick chilled pastry all over with a fork and bake until it pulls away from the sides, 17-20 minutes. The crust will feel soft but dry. Transfer to a wire rack and let cool slightly while making the filling.

Reduce oven temperature to 325°F.

To make the filling, place chopped chocolate in a large heat-proof bowl set over a pot with ½-inch of barely simmering water and stir until completely melted, smooth and glossy; set aside. Combine cream and milk in a small saucepan and scald it by heating it over medium-low heat just until bubbles begin to form around the edges and steam appears at the surface. Gradually pour this hot liquid into melted chocolate while stirring constantly until smooth. Let cool slightly, about 3 minutes. Stir in coffee liqueur and salt. Stir in egg yolks, one at a time, until mixture is smooth. Do not over-mix in order to prevent excessive air incorporation. Pour into pre-baked crust, rap it down on the counter to remove air bubbles and place it onto a 13x9-inch baking sheet. Bake until filling is set around the edges but still very slightly wobbly in the center, 10-13 minutes. Transfer tart pan to a wire rack and let cool completely. Serve at room temperature or refrigerate for 1 hour and slice with a hot, dry knife for clean lines.

Strawberry Curd Truffle Tarts

Makes six 4-inch tarts

For the pastry:

¾ cup plus 2 tbsp all-purpose flour

4 tbsp unsweetened cocoa powder

¼ cup sifted icing sugar

¼ tsp salt

6 tbsp very cold unsalted butter, cut into ½-inch cubes

1 large cold egg

For the strawberry filling:

8 oz/227 g hulled and quartered strawberries

2 large egg yolks

⅓ cup granulated sugar

pinch of salt

1 tbsp corn starch

3 tbsp freshly squeezed lemon juice

For the ganache topping:

4 oz/113 g semisweet chocolate (54% cocoa), very finely chopped

⅓ cup 35% whipping cream

1 tsp light corn syrup

flaked sea salt for topping

To make the pastry, whisk together flour, cocoa powder, sugar and salt in a large bowl. Add butter and toss to coat in flour mixture. Using a pastry blender or your fingertips, cut or rub butter into flour mixture until it resembles coarse crumbs. The butter should be well dispersed with some larger oat flake-sized pieces remaining. In a small bowl, beat the egg with a fork until it is runny and drizzle into flour mixture while gently tossing with the fork. Continue to stir until dry ingredients are moistened and it holds together in clumps. Turn dough out onto a clean work surface and bring it together in a ball with your hands, turning it frequently and pressing in loose bits until it is cohesive. Shape dough into a disk, wrap well with plastic wrap and refrigerate until firm, at least 2 hours.

To make the strawberry filling, place strawberries in medium saucepan. Without adding any liquid, cover and cook over medium to medium-low heat until soupy, 7-10 minutes (watch carefully so it does not stick or burn); set aside.

Meanwhile, whisk together egg yolks, sugar and salt in a medium bowl until well blended. Whisk in corn starch until smooth. Whisk in lemon juice, and then gradually pour in hot strawberries and their liquid while whisking constantly until evenly combined.

Pour this mixture back into the saucepan and cook over medium-low heat for 5 minutes, stirring constantly with a rubber spatula. Increase heat to medium and continue cooking until it reaches a boil. Once boiling, cook for 1 minute longer while stirring constantly. The mixture will be thick. Pour curd into a clean bowl and place a piece of plastic wrap directly over the surface of the curd to prevent a film from forming. Refrigerate until thoroughly chilled, about 1 hour.

Let pastry sit at room temperature about 10 minutes before working with it. On a lightly floured work surface, roll the dough out to just over ⅛-inch thickness. Cut out as many 5-inch circles as you can. You can either use a 5-inch round cookie cutter or trace the circumference of a 4-inch tart pan with a knife keeping about ½-inch border all the way around. Gather the dough and re-roll it so that you have six circles in total.

Fit each round into a 4-inch fluted tart pan with removable bottom. Rest the rolling pin over each tart pan so that it is held up by the sides and roll it across the top so that the weight of the pin cuts the pastry flush with the rim. Pull away excess dough and then press firmly against the edge crust all around the tart to make sure the dough is fit snuggly into the corners and against the sides of the pan. Place tarts on a baking sheet and refrigerate until dough is very firm, at least 30 minutes (this will prevent it from shrinking or puffing up in the center during baking).

Preheat your oven to 375°F. Prick the bottom of pastry shells all over with a fork and bake until dry but still soft, about 15 minutes. Transfer to a wire rack to cool completely.

To make the ganache topping, place chocolate in a medium heatproof bowl. Combine cream and corn syrup in a small saucepan and heat it over medium-low heat until bubbles begin to form at the surface (just before it reaches a boil). Remove from heat and immediately pour over chopped chocolate. Let stand for 2-3 minutes and then slowly stir the mixture using a rubber spatula until completely melted, smooth and glossy.

Using a pastry brush or the back of a spoon, brush or spread about 1 teaspoon of ganache in a thin layer over the base of each cooled tart crust. This will serve as a moisture barrier to prevent the crusts from getting soggy once the strawberry curd is added. Place the tarts in the freezer for 5 minutes to allow the ganache to set up until firm.

Divide the curd among the tart shells and spread it out in an even layer. Spoon ganache over the strawberry curd layer, gently spreading it out to the edges to cover the curd completely. Sprinkle with flaked sea salt and serve immediately or refrigerate until set, about 30 minutes. Serve with fresh strawberries!

Custard Tart with Mulled Wine-Glazed Grapes

Makes about 10 servings

For the pastry:

1 cup plus 2 tbsp all-purpose flour

3 tbsp granulated sugar

¼ tsp salt

6 tbsp very cold unsalted butter, cut into ½-inch cubes

1 large egg yolk

2 tbsp ice cold water

For the filling:

½ cup 35% whipping cream

½ cup 2% milk

1 large egg plus 2 large egg yolks

¼ cup granulated sugar

pinch of salt

¼ tsp pure vanilla extract

For the glazed grapes:

⅔ cup good quality dry red wine

4 tbsp granulated sugar

3-inch piece cinnamon stick

2 2-inch strips of orange zest

2 cups seedless red grapes

¼ cup sliced almonds for topping

To make the pastry, whisk together flour, sugar and salt in a large bowl. Add butter and use your fingertips to rub it into flour mixture until it resembles coarse crumbs. The butter should be mostly dispersed with some larger oat flake-sized pieces remaining. Whisk egg yolk with water in a small bowl and drizzle into flour mixture while gently tossing with a fork until the dry ingredients are moistened and it holds together in clumps when squeezed in your hand. Turn dough out onto a clean work surface and bring it together in a ball with your hands slightly cupped, turning it frequently and pressing in loose bits until it is cohesive. Shape into a disk, wrap well with plastic wrap and refrigerate until firm, at least 2 hours.

On a lightly floured work surface roll pastry into an 11-inch circle. Fit it into a 9-inch round fluted tart pan with removable bottom, pressing it firmly into the corners and up the sides. Pull away excess dough that comes up over the sides. Cover with plastic wrap and refrigerate until firm, about 15 minutes.

Preheat your oven to 375°F. Prick chilled pastry liberally with a fork and bake until golden brown, 15-20 minutes. Transfer to a wire rack to cool completely. Reduce oven to 350°F.

To make the filling, combine cream and milk in a small saucepan over medium-low heat. Bring mixture just to a boil and remove from heat. In a medium bowl, whisk together egg, yolks, sugar and salt until pale and thick, about 1 minute. Slowly pour about ¼ cup of hot cream mixture into egg mixture while whisking constantly until smooth. Gradually whisk in remaining cream until blended. Pour mixture back into saucepan and cook over medium-low heat, stirring constantly with a wooden spoon or spatula until thick enough to coat a spoon, 10-15 minutes. Make sure to stir around the edges of the pan where it tends to over-cook. Pour mixture through a sieve and into a clean bowl. Stir in vanilla extract and set aside to cool.

To make glazed grapes, combine wine, sugar, cinnamon and orange zest in a 2-quart saucepan over medium heat. Cover pan, bring to a gentle boil, remove lid and continue to cook until thickened and reduced by about half, around 10 minutes. You should be left with ¼ to ⅓ cup of liquid. Reduce heat to medium-low, add grapes, cover and cook gently until slightly tender, no longer than 4 minutes. Immediately remove grapes with a slotted spoon and transfer to a plate. Reserve wine syrup and set aside to cool (it will thicken as it cools). The grapes should be glazed and sticky – that's how you know your syrup will be the right consistency. Evenly spread custard into parbaked tart shell and scatter grapes on top, pressing them in slightly. Bake until custard is set around the edges but slightly loose in the center, 10-12 minutes. Transfer to a wire rack and sprinkle sliced almonds over top. Let cool at room temperature until set, 1-2 hours, and then spoon reserved wine syrup over it.

German Chocolate Tarts

Makes 12 tarts

For the pastry:

1 cup all-purpose flour

4 tbsp unsweetened Dutch-processed cocoa powder

3 tbsp granulated sugar

¼ tsp salt

6 tbsp very cold unsalted butter, cut into ½-inch cubes

1 large egg

For the filling:

3 oz/85 g bittersweet chocolate (72% cocoa), coarsely chopped

2 tbsp unsalted butter

½ cup granulated sugar

⅛ tsp salt

2 large eggs, at room temperature

2 tbsp full fat (14%) sour cream

½ tsp pure vanilla extract

⅓ cup all-purpose flour

For the topping:

2 ½ oz/70 g sweetened shredded coconut (about ⅔ cup)

¾ cup evaporated milk

½ cup granulated sugar

2 large egg yolks

pinch of salt

1 tbsp unsalted butter

2 oz/56 g coarsely chopped pecans (about ½ cup)

3 oz/85 g semisweet chocolate (54% cocoa), coarsely chopped for drizzling

To make the pastry, whisk together flour, cocoa, sugar and salt in a large bowl. Add butter and use your fingertips to rub it into flour mixture until it resembles coarse crumbs. The butter should be well dispersed with some larger oat flake-sized pieces remaining. Beat egg with a fork in a small bowl until very fluid and drizzle into flour mixture while gently tossing with the fork until dry ingredients are moistened and it holds together in clumps. Turn dough out onto a work surface and bring it together in a ball with your hands, turning it frequently and pressing in loose bits until it is cohesive. Fold the dough over itself a few times so that it is evenly hydrated. Shape dough into a disk, wrap in plastic wrap and refrigerate at least 2 hours.

On a lightly floured work surface, roll dough out to ⅛-inch thickness. Use a 3 ½ to 4-inch round to cut out 12 circles (re-roll scraps if necessary) and fit each round into the base of each cup in a standard 12-cup muffin pan. Press pastry into the bottom and up the sides of the cups. Cover loosely with plastic wrap and refrigerate until firm, about 15 minutes. Preheat your oven to 350°F.

To make the filling, stir together chocolate and butter in a heatproof bowl set over a pot with ½-inch of barely simmering water until completely melted and smooth. Remove bowl from heat and stir in sugar and salt. Stir in eggs, one at a time, until well incorporated. Stir in sour cream and vanilla extract. Fold in flour until batter is smooth and set aside briefly.

Prick bottoms of chilled, unbaked tart shells a few times with a fork. Spoon batter into tart shells, filling them about halfway and bake on bottom-third rack of oven until batter puffs up and pastry is crisp, about 15 minutes. Let cool in pan at least 10 minutes before transferring to a wire rack to cool completely. Use a small offset spatula to help release them from the pan. Reduce oven to 325°F.

To make the topping, spread coconut in a single layer on a baking sheet and bake until lightly golden, about 5 minutes, stirring once. Transfer coconut to a bowl and let cool completely. Meanwhile, in a small saucepan, whisk together evaporated milk, sugar, egg yolks and salt over medium-low heat. Continue to cook, stirring constantly, until it thickens considerably and reaches the consistency of sweetened condensed milk or pouring custard, 10-15 minutes. Stir in butter until smooth. Remove from heat and stir in toasted coconut and chopped pecans. Let mixture cool for 5-10 minutes before spooning about 1 tablespoon of it over each tart.

Place chocolate in a heatproof bowl set over a pot with ½-inch of barely simmering water and stir until completely melted and smooth. Using a fork, drizzle warm chocolate over tarts as you wish.

Pear Apple & Oat Pie

Makes about 8 servings

For the pie dough:

1 recipe for pie dough from *White Peach Raspberry Pie* (page 164)

½ tsp ground cinnamon

For the filling:

1 ½ lbs (24 oz/700 g) tart apples (about 4-5), such as a mix of Granny Smith and Northern Spy

1 lb (16 oz/454 g) ripe but firm pears (about 2-3), such as Bosc

1 tbsp freshly squeezed lemon juice

⅓ cup packed light brown sugar

2 tbsp granulated sugar

2 tsp freshly grated ginger

¾ tsp ground cinnamon

¼ tsp ground nutmeg

¼ tsp ground cardamom

¼ cup old-fashioned large flake rolled oats

For the topping:

1 large egg, well beaten

2 tsp granulated sugar

¼ tsp ground cinnamon

To make the pie dough, follow the recipe for pie dough on page 164 for the 'White Peach Raspberry Pie', but add ground cinnamon to the bowl with the flour, sugar and salt before incorporating the butter.

Divide the dough almost in half (one half slightly larger than the other), flatten each portion into a disk, wrap well with plastic wrap and refrigerate at least 2 hours or overnight.

Preheat your oven to 425°F and place a baking sheet on the bottom rack.

Peel, core and chop the apples and pears into ¾-inch chunks. Place them in a large bowl and toss with lemon juice so they are well coated. Add both sugars, grated ginger, ground cinnamon, ground nutmeg and ground cardamom and toss until evenly combined. Fold in rolled oats and set aside while you roll out the dough.

On a lightly floured work surface, roll the larger half of dough into a 12 to 13-inch circle, rotating it and adding more flour as necessary to prevent sticking. Carefully drape the dough over an 8x2-inch round glass pie dish, and gently press it into the bottom edges and up the sides of the dish. Refrigerate until firm, about 10 minutes, while making the filling and rolling out the top crust. This allows the rolled layers of gluten and fat to relax and firm up, creating a more flaky crust.

Once the bottom layer is chilled, begin to roll the other portion of dough out into a 10 to 11-inch circle. Lightly brush the rim of the bottom layer with beaten egg and pour the apple mixture into it, gently pressing and tucking the fruit in so it fits snuggly – this will help to reduce the gap between the fruit and top crust of the pie once baked since the fruit will shrink as it cooks. Carefully drape top pastry layer over the filled pie. Press edges of top layer against bottom layer edges to seal. Trim away excess dough leaving about ½-inch overhang and then fold and roll it over itself (top and bottom crusts together) so that it sits against the edge of the pie dish. This ensures a tight seal on your pie. Crimp decoratively if desired using three fingers – your thumb and index finger on one hand and the index finger of the other hand. Place the pie in the freezer for 10 minutes.

In a small bowl, stir together sugar and cinnamon for topping. Brush top and edges of chilled pie lightly with beaten egg and sprinkle with cinnamon sugar. Make three 1-inch incisions in the center of the top crust to let steam escape during baking.

Place pie on baking sheet on bottom rack of oven and bake for 20 minutes. Reduce oven temperature to 350°F and bake until juices have been bubbling for at least 5 minutes, about 50 minutes longer. Loosely cover the edges with aluminum foil midway through baking to protect them from over-browning if necessary. Transfer pie to a wire rack to cool completely before slicing.

Milk Jam Chocolate Tarts with Toasted Hazelnuts

Makes 12 tarts

For the pastry:

1 cup plus 2 tbsp all-purpose flour

3 tbsp packed dark brown sugar

¼ tsp salt

6 tbsp very cold unsalted butter, cut into ½-inch cubes

1 large egg yolk

2 tbsp cold 2% milk

For the filling:

2 ⅔ cups 2% milk

⅓ cup 35% whipping cream

¾ cup granulated sugar

¼ tsp baking soda

½ tsp pure vanilla extract

heaped ⅛ tsp salt

1 oz/28 g bittersweet chocolate (72% cocoa), very finely chopped

For the topping:

1 oz/28 g whole hazelnuts (about ¼ cup), coarsely chopped

2 tbsp 35% whipping cream

1 ½ oz/42 g bittersweet chocolate (72% cocoa), very finely chopped

1 tbsp 2% milk

I bet you're sold on this recipe already based on the title. Milk jam just sounds so decadent doesn't it? And it is exactly that. The French refer to this as "confiture de lait" and it is very similar to South American dulce de leche. It has a rich caramel flavour with nutty undertones. Baking soda helps to promote Maillard browning for both colour and flavour development. Don't skimp on the salt when seasoning this divine spread at the end because it really enhances it like nothing else.

To make the pastry, whisk together flour, brown sugar and salt in a large bowl. Add butter and toss to coat in flour mixture. Using your fingertips, quickly rub butter into flour until it resembles coarse crumbs. The butter should be well dispersed with some larger oat flake and pea-sized pieces remaining, and there should be no dusty flour left in the bowl. Place the bowl in the freezer for 5 minutes to let the fat firm up again.

Beat together egg yolk and milk in a small bowl and drizzle into cold flour/butter mixture while gently tossing with a fork. Continue to stir until dry ingredients are evenly moistened and it holds together in clumps. The dough will hold together when squeezed in your hand when ready. Turn the crumbly dough out onto a clean work surface and gather it together in a pile. Apply the fraisage technique: use the heel of your hand to push portions of dough away from you, smearing it along the work surface to distribute fat into the flour. Repeat this process up to 5 times total, but only go over each portion once or the pastry will become tough. You should be able to see faint streaks of butter marbled through the dough, which will give it a slightly flaky texture. Gather the dough and press it firmly to form a roughly-shaped ball – it should be pliable but not sticky. Shape it into a disk, wrap well with plastic wrap and refrigerate until firm, at least 2 hours.

To make the milk jam, whisk together milk, cream, sugar and baking soda in a heavy bottomed 5-quart saucepan and bring it to a gentle boil over medium heat. Watch it carefully as it will bubble up and boil over quickly and uncontrollably if it gets too hot. When the mixture just begins to boil, quickly turn the heat down to medium-low and simmer gently until very thick and dark caramel coloured, stirring occasionally, about 1 ¼ hours depending on the diameter of your pot. The consistency should be somewhere between caramel and jam. As it begins to get thick, stir often to prevent it from scorching on the bottom of the pot. Remove from heat and pour into a heatproof bowl. Stir in vanilla extract and salt. Let cool completely at room temperature before storing in the fridge. This should make 1 cup of milk jam.

On a lightly floured work surface, roll out the dough to about ⅛-inch thickness. Use a 3 ½ to 4-inch round to cut out as many circles as you can. Gather the scraps into a ball, re-roll and cut out enough rounds so that you have 12 in total. Fit each circle into the cups of a standard 12-cup muffin pan, pressing the dough into the corners and up the sides. Refrigerate until very firm, about 30 minutes.

Preheat your oven to 350°F.

Prick chilled pastry all over with a fork and bake until golden brown, 13-15 minutes. Remove from oven, transfer pan to a wire rack and immediately divide the 1 oz of finely chopped chocolate among the tarts, sprinkling it evenly into the bottom of each one. Let the chocolate melt and then gently spread it around using the back of a spoon. Remove tarts from pan and transfer to a wire rack. Let cool until chocolate is set.

To toast hazelnuts, spread them on a baking sheet and roast at 375°F for 7 minutes, shaking pan half-way through. Or, toast in a dry frying pan over medium heat, shaking the pan frequently, about 6 minutes. Rub them around in a dry dish towel to remove skins and then chop them up coarsely.

To make the chocolate topping, place whipping cream in the smallest saucepan you can find and heat it gently over medium-low heat until you see steam coming up from the surface. Add chocolate and remove from heat. Let it stand for 1 minute and then stir gently until completely melted and smooth. The mixture may look a bit grainy. Add milk and stir until smooth and glossy.

To assemble tarts, spread about 1 ½ tablespoons of milk jam into the bottom of each tart. Drizzle with warm chocolate sauce, reserving some for later. Sprinkle some hazelnuts over top and then drizzle a touch more chocolate sauce over the nuts.

Raspberry Macaroon Tarts

Makes six 4-inch tarts

For the crust:

¾ cup plus 2 tbsp all-purpose flour

2 oz/56 g ground almonds (about ½ cup)

3 tbsp granulated sugar

¼ tsp ground cardamom

⅛ tsp salt

6 tbsp unsalted butter, melted and slightly cooled

For the filling:

⅓ cup sweetened condensed milk

¼ tsp pure vanilla extract

4 oz/113 g sweetened shredded coconut (about 1 cup)

2 large egg whites

⅛ tsp salt

½ tsp distilled white vinegar

2 tsp granulated sugar

1 cup fresh raspberries, rinsed and dried

1 ½ oz/42 g semisweet chocolate (54% cocoa), finely chopped

Preheat your oven to 350°F. Have ready six 4-inch round fluted tart pans with removable bottoms.

To make the crust, whisk together flour, ground almonds, sugar, ground cardamom and salt in a large bowl. Stir in melted butter using a wooden spoon until dough is moistened and crumbly without any dusty flour remaining. Use your fingertips to work the butter into the mixture and press it together so that it is cohesive. The dough will be crumbly but moist. Divide portions of dough evenly among six tart pans and press it firmly and evenly into the bottom and up the sides. Place the tarts on a baking sheet, cover them loosely with plastic wrap and refrigerate until firm, about 20 minutes.

Prick the tarts all over with a fork and bake until golden brown around the edges, 12-13 minutes. Transfer tarts to a wire rack to cool completely.

To make the filling, stir together condensed milk, vanilla extract and coconut in a medium bowl. In a separate bowl, beat egg whites with salt using an electric hand mixer on medium speed until foamy, about 20 seconds. Add vinegar and beat until soft peaks form. Then, slowly add sugar while beating until it holds stiff peaks.

Quickly fold one-third of the egg whites into the coconut mixture to lighten it. Gently fold in the remaining egg whites in 2 batches. The mixture will be quite loose, foamy and creamy-looking. Spoon this mixture evenly into the cooled tart shells, filling them almost to the rim. Scatter 5 or 6 raspberries over the filling, poking them in gently. Bake until the coconut filling is golden brown around the edges but still a bit sticky in the middle, 12-15 minutes. Transfer tarts to a wire rack to cool completely.

To make the chocolate drizzle, place chopped chocolate in a heatproof bowl set over a pot with ½-inch of barely simmering water and stir until melted and smooth. Use a spoon or a fork to drizzle chocolate over the tarts. For a more precise drizzle, fill a small plastic sandwich bag with melted chocolate, pushing it into one of the bottom corners. Snip the tip off of that corner with scissors and squeeze the bag from the top while swaying your hand in a zig-zag pattern over the tarts.

Toffee Chocolate Crumb Tart with Red Wine Caramel

Makes 8-10 servings

For the crust:

1 cup all-purpose flour

½ cup packed light brown sugar

¼ tsp salt

⅓ cup very cold butter, cut into ½-inch pieces

2 tbsp 10% half & half cream

For the caramel & topping:

1 cup granulated sugar

1 tbsp light corn syrup

⅛ tsp salt

2 tbsp water

¼ cup 35% whipping cream

1 tbsp unsalted butter

2 tbsp dry red wine (such as Cabernet Sauvignon or Shiraz)

3 oz/85 g bittersweet chocolate (72% cocoa), coarsely chopped

Preheat your oven to 325°F.

Have ready a 14x5-inch rectangular fluted tart pan with removable bottom.

To make the toffee crust, combine flour, brown sugar and salt in a food processor and pulse to blend. Add cold butter and pulse until it resembles coarse crumbs. Add cream, one tablespoon at a time, and pulse just until it holds together in loose clumps. Pour crumbs into the bottom of the rectangular tart pan and gently press it evenly into the corners and three-quarters of the way up the sides, reserving about ⅓ cup of crumbs for the topping. Refrigerate until firm, about 15 minutes. Keep crumbs refrigerated in the meantime.

Prick the dough several times with a fork and bake until lightly golden, 15-17 minutes. Transfer pan to a wire rack to cool completely.

To make the caramel filling, pour sugar in an even layer in a 1 or 2-quart heavy-bottomed metal saucepan with high sides. Add corn syrup and salt. Drizzle water around the outer edges of the sugar and bring the mixture to a boil over medium heat without stirring. Cook until caramel is a rich amber colour, swirling the pan periodically to colour evenly, 10-15 minutes. Wash down the sides of pan with a pastry brush dipped in water to dissolve any crystals that may form. When the caramel is almost ready, the large bubbles will subside and a golden foam will begin to appear at the surface. Remove caramel from heat and very carefully stir in cream and butter until smooth. Be cautious as the caramel will bubble up violently once you add the cream (wear an oven mit to protect your hand from the hot steam). Stir in red wine and return caramel to the heat to boil for another 2 minutes while stirring constantly. The mixture should reach 234°F on a candy thermometer. Pour caramel into a heatproof volumetric measuring cup and let cool for 5 minutes. Pour caramel over baked crust and set aside to cool for 15-20 minutes.

While it cools, preheat your oven again to 375°F. Evenly scatter chopped chocolate over cooled caramel and then sprinkle reserved dough crumbs over top. If the crumb is too fine, squeeze some bits together to form larger, pea-sized pieces if necessary to achieve a chunkier look. Bake 5-7 minutes to gently melt the chocolate and set the crumbs. Transfer tart to a wire rack to cool completely.

Serve tart at room temperature or make homemade candy bars. To do this, refrigerate the cooled tart for 30 minutes before slicing it into 1-inch wide bars and wrap each bar in waxed paper to prevent the caramel from spreading.

CONFECTIONERY

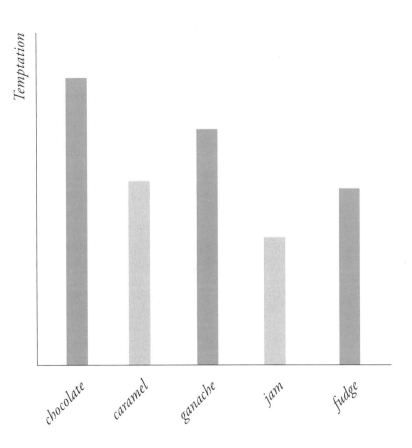

fig. 4

The Secret Life of Confectionery

The first thing that comes to mind when I think of candy is chocolate and this chapter wouldn't be complete without a thorough rundown on the science behind this food of the Gods.

How Chocolate is Made:

Let me begin by saying that chocolate is made from seeds (cocoa beans) found within cocoa pods, which are gorgeous large, oblong fruits that grow on cocoa trees. Hello! Cocoa is a fruit! How about that for a fun fact and a great excuse to eat more of it?

Cocoa pods are first harvested from trees of the species Theobroma cacao. They are split lengthwise and the seeds are removed from within their white pulp, which has a lovely mild sweet flavour. These seeds are immediately fermented under the sun for several days, during which the chocolate flavour begins to develop. At this stage, the fermented seeds are called cocoa beans.

Cocoa beans are then dried, cleaned and roasted. Once cooled, roasted cocoa beans are cracked to remove their outer shell and expose the interior kernels, called cocoa nibs. These cocoa nibs are the basis of chocolate-making, and once ground up, they form a paste referred to as chocolate liquor.

Further processing of chocolate liquor separates cocoa butter from cocoa solids, which are then combined in different proportions with sugar to produce semisweet, dark or bittersweet chocolate. The cocoa solids can also be alkalized, crushed and ground into fine powder to create cocoa powder. Alkalization involves treating cocoa solids with an alkali salt such as sodium or potassium carbonate to neutralize its acidity, resulting in a softer flavour and darker colour. Personally, I prefer the taste of natural, non-alkalized cocoa for its complexity and bitterness; however, it is quite difficult to find it in supermarkets these days.

Tempering Chocolate:

Melting chocolate is an essential aspect of making candy. It is used to drizzle, dip, curl and swirl. Tempering is a controlled heating and cooling technique applied to melted chocolate that is necessary for it to reset quickly into a glossy state with a crisp snap. Couverture chocolate is a high quality type that has better flow and melting properties due to its increased cocoa butter content, making it ideal for coating. If chocolate is simply melted any old way and then used for dipping or decorating, it can develop a dull, matte surface with white film or streaks.

The basic principle of tempering chocolate relies on the stabilization of cocoa butter crystals. Fat takes on crystal structures when set into a solid, and cocoa butter in particular is a mixture of triglycerides with different crystallization temperatures. As a whole, chocolate has a wide temperature range over which fat crystallization occurs, and this is called polymorphism. Cocoa butter has six different crystal forms (called polymorphs) and tempering is designed to stimulate it to crystallize in Form V. Form V (five), also known as "beta 2", is the fat crystal structure that produces the glossy sheen and crisp snap of high quality, melt-in-your-mouth chocolate. Chocolate manufacturers practice special mixing techniques (conching) that last for days to ensure the development of Form V crystals and produce smooth, creamy chocolate. If you've ever seen a white film coating your chocolate, this is likely caused by changes in cocoa butter composition. This white film is called bloom and it is perfectly safe to eat but can have an unpleasant mouthfeel. Most of the time it is due to:

1. Incorrect or incomplete tempering

2. Age: over time, cocoa butter crystals convert to Form VI, which scatter light and appear white at the surface

3. High humidity or condensation: sugar in chocolate can absorb moisture, dissolve, migrate to the surface and re-crystallize to form a dry, gritty film

4. Temperature fluctuations: warm temperatures cause cocoa butter to melt and re-crystallize upon cooling at the surface in an uncontrolled manner, favouring the most stable yet unappealing Form VI polymorphs. Store your chocolate at a constant 63°F (17°C) to preserve it.

HOW TO TEMPER CHOCOLATE:

Learning to achieve Form V through tempering techniques is an art. Most chocolate shops have machines that do it for them through a series of heating and cooling stages. Frankly, I don't blame them since it is very difficult to accomplish a perfect temper under sometimes unpredictable ambient conditions. Nevertheless, it can absolutely be achieved at home. First, you need to know that the melting point of each cocoa butter crystal form is different, with form I being the lowest and Form VI being the highest. The most unstable cocoa butter crystals (Forms I, II, III and IV) have relatively low melting temperatures so they melt easily at cooler temperatures.

In the first stage of tempering, chocolate is heated to a relatively high temperature (above the melting point of the most heat-resistant fat crystal, Form VI) to melt all the fat crystals. Then, the chocolate is cooled down below the melting point of Forms IV, V and VI so that these crystals get the chance to form, and the unstable Forms I, II and III remain melted.

Finally, the chocolate is reheated very slightly to melt the unstable Form IV crystals and leave you with the stable Forms V and VI. At this stage, the temperature is above the melting point of the most unstable crystals but below the melting point of the most stable crystals, meaning that the stable forms will predominate and act as a sort of template for the remaining melted crystals. Holding the chocolate at this temperature while stirring will allow a bunch of these stable crystals to form so that it hardens with a slight sheen. Tempering manually can be quite tedious and usually requires you to work with large batches in order to be successful. Pastry chefs have the luxury of large work spaces with stainless steel surfaces on which they can spread and temper their chocolate. At home you can use a marble slab or your granite counter top. But for those that prefer to keep their work contained, there are more simple ways.

There are two forms of tempering chocolate. The "from scratch" method involves a series of heating and cooling stages, and the "seeding" method involves adding a small amount of tempered chocolate to feed the melted chocolate with stable crystals. Whichever method you use, you absolutely need an accurate digital instant-read thermometer.

From scratch:

For dark chocolate, you first heat it to 118-120°F (48-49°C) over gentle heat in a double boiler to melt all crystals. Then cool rapidly to 80-82°F (27-28°C) with constant stirring until it thickens considerably. This can also be achieved by pouring about half of the chocolate onto a cold surface like a marble slab or counter top and spreading it out thinly with a palette knife or large offset spatula before scraping it back into your bowl and stirring it into the warm reserved melted chocolate. This increases the surface area of the chocolate and encourages rapid cooling to eventually bring down the temperature of the entire batch. Finally, reheat to 88-90°F (31-32°C) to melt out the unstable crystals.

Seeding:

In order to ensure that Form V crystals are present in the highest quantity in tempered chocolate, very small pieces of chopped or grated solid tempered chocolate is added to melted chocolate during the cooling process to convince Form V to form. This is called seeding, because these pieces act as seeds or nuclei on which the melted chocolate will conform. To do this, first heat the chocolate to 118-120°F over gentle heat in a double boiler to melt all crystals. Then add small pieces of solid tempered chocolate (one tablespoon at a time) to cool down the melted chocolate to the tempering range, 88-90°F. This provides stable crystal seeds and encourage the growth of beta crystals. You can also add a piece of solid, unmelted tempered chocolate to provide seed crystals. In either case, constant stirring is a must!

The easiest way to get perfect chocolate for dipping and decorating is to not temper it at all. I know, why didn't I just tell you that in the first place? Well that wouldn't be very scientific of me, would it? Majority of chocolate is already sold in tempered form, allowing you to melt it while still maintaining its temper. The easiest way is to never heat chocolate over 90°F so that you never lose all of the prized stable crystals and your melted chocolate remains tempered. The key is to chop or grate it very finely so that it melts quickly and evenly. Constantly stir the chocolate as it melts very gently and slowly over very low, indirect heat only until it reaches the tempering range, 88-90°F.

HOW TO CHECK YOUR TEMPER:

For either method, the chocolate must be kept within its tempering range before use or it will lose its temper and you will have to repeat the full tempering process. Yikes! To see if your chocolate is tempered, smear a bit onto a piece of waxed paper – if it dries shiny and hard within 5 minutes, then you're right on track.

Chocolate Ganache:

Ganache is a wonder in a baker's world. It can be used in many ways:

- While slightly warm, it can be used as a glaze.

- Let it cool to room temperature with occasional stirring and it can be used as a creamy dense frosting.

- Bring on the beaters at room temperature and it transforms into a light, whipped frosting or filling.

- Or, chill until firm without agitation and form blissful, silky smooth balls to make decadent chocolate truffles.

Ganache is an oil-in-water emulsion of heavy whipping cream and chocolate. The continuous phase is composed mostly of water from the cream and the oil phase is composed of both milkfat globules from the cream and cocoa butter fat droplets from the chocolate. Cocoa particles are also suspended in the water phase and some of their components can bind water. Ganache can be made from anywhere between a 1:1 ratio of cream to chocolate to a 1:2 ratio. The latter ratio will produce a firmer texture, and the extent of firmness depends on the cocoa content of the chocolate.

There are few basic yet important steps for making ganache:

1. Finely chop the chocolate and place it in a heatproof bowl.

2. Heat cream in a small saucepan over gentle heat until bubbles begin to form around the edges and it just about comes to a boil. Some recipes may instruct you to simmer the cream to increase the shelf life of the truffles.

3. Pour the hot cream over chopped chocolate.

4. Let mixture stand without stirring for 3-5 minutes.

5. Gently stir mixture in a circular motion, starting from the center and working your way out to the sides like a spiral until it is smooth and glossy. Begin using a whisk with brisk strokes, making small circles in the center. Once you see the glossy ganache forming in the middle, stir gently using a rubber spatula, making big circles as you extend to the sides of the bowl until completely blended.

6. Pour mixture into a shallow glass baking dish and let cool at room temperature for 1-2 hours, or use it in any way described above.

Although this process seems fairly simple and straightforward, there are some technical points to remember:

SMALL PIECES: Finely chopping the chocolate allows for rapid and even melting. Letting the mixture stand for a few minutes untouched allows the hot cream to slowly and gently melt the chocolate. It also gives time for the mixture to cool down, preferably to about 110°F, before stirring. This helps to form a homogeneous, smooth ganache as it lets the chocolate and cream come to the same temperature, making it easier for the two phases to form an emulsion. A proper emulsion will prevent separation of the oil phase once the mixture is set. If the cream boils too vigorously and gets too hot, it can cause the emulsion to break and appear greasy. If this happens, you can try to revive it by pulsing the warm ganache in a food processor until smooth.

It is as important not to chop the chocolate too fine as it is to not chop it too chunky. In other words, the chocolate should be in small pieces but not fine crumbs. If the pieces are too large, the hot cream won't be enough to heat the chocolate through all the way. But, if the chocolate is chopped too fine, it will rest very compactly in the bowl so that the cream can't get all around the pieces. Instead, the heat will melt the pieces at the surface and cause the chocolate fines to clump without penetrating efficiently.

GOOD RATIO: The ability of cocoa particle components to bind water can play a role in causing warm stirred ganache to turn into a greasy mess. It can also cause a smooth, glossy ganache to set up with a grainy texture. This is an issue when ganache is made with a high ratio of chocolate to cream, especially when using bittersweet chocolate. Although cocoa is mainly considered insoluble in water, starch components in cocoa particles can absorb moisture from the water phase of the emulsion and swell up as the mixture rests. This gives less room in the water phase for milkfat globules and cocoa butter droplets to remain individually suspended, causing them to coalesce or merge together to form a single droplet. These larger fat droplets cannot sustain their suspension, so they separate from the mixture and eventually form clumps that translate to a coarse mouth-feel.

GENTLE STIRRING: Chocolate is very high-maintenance and requires gradual heating and cooling. Over-mixing can bring about a rapid decrease in temperature, which causes the fat to separate upon cooling and results in a less refined texture. Gentle stirring is all it takes to reduce the fat to tiny droplets suspended within the water phase to form an emulsion. Too much agitation can also introduce air, which will make the ganache stiff and grainy. To avoid this, use a rubber spatula or a wooden spoon to bring the hot cream/chocolate mixture together and never *beat* with a whisk.

Pouring the stirred ganache into a shallow dish exposes the mixture to a larger surface area and helps it to mature evenly at room temperature. Maturing refers to the gradual and complete crystallization of cocoa butter, which creates a sinfully smooth, melt-in-your mouth texture. I do not recommend immediate refrigeration of ganache because it can develop an oily or greasy consistency as it warms back to room temperature. The delicate emulsion can break and cause some milkfat to separate upon rapid cooling.

PS: a perfectly round truffle bugs me. I like them to be rough and rugged-looking because they're supposed to resemble truffles (the fungus) from the ground. So go ahead, be rustic.

"If you say you don't like chocolate, I won't believe you"

Dark Chocolate-Covered
Coconut Candy Bars

Candy-Making:

Making candy isn't as hard as it sounds. Just do it on a dry (not humid) day and you'll be thankful. A candy thermometer is an essential tool for these recipes, whether it is a traditional alcohol thermometer or the digital instant-read type.

CARAMEL:

Caramel never ceases to amaze me because it is so simple, yet so complex. It is essentially made from one ingredient: table sugar. Through the simple action of applying heat, it transforms into the most complex and flavourful substance.

Caramel is a sweet, brown, aromatic syrup produced by the process of caramelization. It involves heating plain white sugar until it breaks down at the molecular level and forms an array of new flavour compounds that are bitter, sour, roasted, buttery and fruity. I think a lot of people are intimidated by the idea of making caramel at home because most recipes are subjective and the method involves plain old judgment on your end. The secret to great-tasting caramel is having the confidence to let it get nice and dark but not burnt. Undercooked caramel just tastes sweet and weak, while burnt caramel tastes terribly sour and bitter. For a simple quick caramel, as for crème caramel or a caramel sauce, you don't need a thermometer and its doneness can be determined by a change in colour. It is best just to learn to rely on your nose and your eyes.

CARAMEL SAUCE:

Although caramel gets some of its flavour from caramelized sugar, it is also a product of Maillard browning from cooked dairy products. When cream is added to hot sugar syrup, its sugars (lactose), as well as the simple sugars in the caramel (glucose and fructose), react with milk proteins to produce more complex and delicious flavour compounds.

The first step in making caramel sauce is to pour sugar in an even layer in a heavy gauge deep metal saucepan and heat it with a splash of water without stirring until it transforms into a dark amber syrup. The water dissolves some of the sugar to help get the caramelization reaction started and promotes even cooking. This water will evaporate as the sugar cooks. It is important to avoid stirring liquid caramel because dissolved sugar molecules will bump into one another and re-join, creating a clumpy mess. Gently swirling and tilting the pan ensures even cooking/colouring and avoids hot spots.

You can brush the sides of the pan with water using a pastry brush to wash down sugar crystals that collect along the sides if necessary, but I rarely find the need to do this as swirling the pan usually catches any stray crystals.

The addition of cream and/or butter once the sugar develops into caramel actually lowers the temperature of the sugar and brings the reaction to a halt to prevent burning. The result is a smooth, creamy, rich and complex sauce.

CARAMEL CANDY:

Candy recipes are generally very simple, requiring you to combine all or most of the ingredients in a pot and apply heat. The tricky part is that it is very sensitive to moisture because the final texture depends on how much water is left in the boiling sugar mixture. Less water results in harder candy, whereas a higher water content creates softer candy, like chewy caramels. Too much water, though, and the candy will not set, making it almost impossible to cut into neat little squares. Too little water and your teeth will break, although this isn't so bad if your intention is to make hard candy. Dissolved solids, such as sugar, increase the boiling point of a solution and the temperature to which the mixture boils is directly proportional to its sugar concentration. The less water there is, the more concentrated the sugar solution, and so the hotter it will boil. That's why candy requires constant attention and an accurate thermometer. You need to halt the cooking process at precisely the temperature stated in the recipe to achieve the desired texture. A narrow range of one or two degrees F is acceptable for most recipes since it is very difficult to gauge a specific temperature when using alcohol thermometers.

The most daunting part for most people is the journey from raw sugar to caramelized sugar.

If there are impurities or debris in the pan you could end up with a chunky sugary mess. So, it is important to start with a clean pan and make it on a dry (not humid) day. I like to make caramel in a small saucier, or rounded saucepan with soft rounded edges so that nothing gets stuck in the bottom edges. I do not prefer to make it in a frying pan because the surface is often too large, making it difficult to achieve even caramelization.

At first you will notice that the sugar and water will turn into a simple clear syrup. As it bubbles away, it will change to a golden colour and may appear quite granular. The liquid film between the fairly large bubbles might even appear chunky and you might panic in belief that you've totally ruined it, but don't! If the temperature is hot enough, these grainy sugar crystals will break down or melt and you will be left with a smooth, nearly transparent liquid. I have rescued ghastly looking chunky caramel by simply cranking up the heat to essentially melt it and convert it into a syrup.

Once you see it turn golden, stay very close because it will caramelize very quickly at this point. Many people stop cooking caramel too soon because there is a fine line between not enough colour and burnt sugar, but you'll get the hang of it. You are looking for a reddish-brown colour. You'll notice that the bubbles will subside and the foam at the surface will become more dense, fine and golden-coloured as the last drops of water try to squeeze through the surface and evaporate. This is your cue to remove it from the heat and proceed with the recipe, whether it is to add cream and make a sauce or pour it out onto a silicone mat and make hard candy decorations.

Be careful as you add the cream, however, because it will bubble up violently as its water content boils off (wearing an oven mitt for protection is a good idea). Do not try any tasting experiments because sugar reaches temperatures in excess of 300°F. It may take practice but it is worth it.

Corn Syrup:

The addition of corn syrup helps to soften the texture of candy and maintain fluidity of sugar syrups by preventing crystallization. It provides an assortment of glucose mole-cules and long glucose chains which interfere with sucrose mobility by getting in between these simple sugar molecules to prevent their re-crystallization. Without corn syrup you can run the risk of having a grainy caramel. The addition of certain acids, such as cream of tartar, vinegar or lemon juice, promotes the breakdown of sugar by increasing the rate of reaction (it helps to cleave the bonds that hold glucose molecules together).

FUDGE:

It's one of my favourite treats and one of the first things I ever learned to make – I guess I was a pretty ambitious kid. Like most candy recipes, fudge is made with a whole pile of sugar, some cream and chocolate. This is the real stuff I'm talking about, and not that '5-minute' version made from sweetened condensed milk. What a cheat.

The chemistry behind making fudge follows the same principles as caramel candy in that it needs to be cooked to a specific temperature (soft ball stage) in order for it have the right sugar concentration to produce that velvety texture. However, just cooking it is not enough. If it is left to set completely at this point, you will be left with a thick chocolate syrup.

The unique step in fudge-making is the application of mechanical beating or strenuous man power (to the point where you will wear your arm out) in order to initialize crystallization. Once the mixture cools to 110°F, you must beat the mixture very vigorously until it begins to lose its sheen and turn matte. This can take nearly 10 minutes by hand, and obviously less if using a mixer. What this does is it encourages the formation of millions of very tiny sugar crystals that dissolve instantly on your tongue so that the fudge has a melt-in-your-mouth texture. Patiently waiting until the mixture reaches precisely 110°F ensures that the sugar molecules have cooled enough so that they are less mobile than they would be at higher temperatures, making them less likely to bump into other crystals to form larger, coarse ones. Beating it simply exposes the mixture to air and allows it to cool and set very quickly so that the crystals don't have time to build mansions upon themselves. If the mixture is over-cooked, the fudge will have a dull appearance and a dry, crumbly texture, whereas under-cooking will make it soft and a bit runny with a glossy sheen.

The addition of butter at the very end helps to lubricate the sugar particles during mixing to create an especially creamy texture.

Jamming it up:

Jam is a type of spreadable fruit gel. It acts as a preservation method due to added sugar which tightly binds water released from the fruit during cooking and thus decreases the water activity (i.e. the amount of water available for microbial growth).

The beauty of jam is that it can be made with only 3 simple ingredients:

1. FRUIT 2. SUGAR 3. ACID

Jam without pectin? That's right. No *added* pectin. There's plenty of pectin in the cell walls of the berries themselves, so why not extract it and do things the old-fashioned way?

Although some may be tempted to skimp on the large quantity of sugar used in a jam recipe in an attempt to save calories, I strongly advise against it! The added sugar not only serves to increase the product's shelf life, but it is vital in the development of a gel structure. It must be present at a very specific concentration in order to produce the right consistency. I guess you can say that jam is serious business.

The crystal clarity and firm structure of fruit gels is due to a compound called pectin which is naturally present in the cell walls of most fruits. A "gel" refers to a network of cross-linked molecules that entrap an aqueous solution, such as water and its solutes.

Pectin, a long-chain molecule composed of sugar subunits, will only form this network in the presence of acidity and a high concentration of sugar. Furthermore, it is very particular. The pH or acidity level must be around 3.0 (or 0.5% acid by weight), while the final sugar concentration must be between 55 and 65%.

HOW TO MAKE JAM:

To make jam, pectin must first be extracted from the fruit's cell walls by cutting it into small pieces and heating it slowly in a saucepan. Pectin molecules gradually dissolve into water that is released from the fruit during heating.

To re-build the pectin structure, a large proportion of sugar is added (45 to 50% by weight) to bind water between pectin molecules, thus bringing them closer to one another for optimal interaction. The mixture is then brought to a boil to evaporate some of the moisture and concentrate pectin.

When pectin molecules are initially extracted from fruit cell walls, they adopt a negative charge which causes them to repel one another, making it impossible for them to come close enough to form a gel. Adding an acid solution, such as lemon juice, neutralizes or removes the negative electrical charges of pectin molecules so that they can unite at specific sites and create a gel.

Boiling the mixture to 220°F indicates that the sugar concentration has reached 65%. This is the same concept that applies to making fudge. The boiling point of a sugar solution increases proportionally to its sugar concentration. If you don't have an instant-read thermometer or a candy thermometer, you can still make jam by monitoring the rate of drip of a dab of jam down a tilted cold plate. It is ready when it drips very slowly and doesn't spread.

Silky Dark Chocolate Honey Truffles

Makes about 45 truffles

For the ganache:

6 oz/170 g bittersweet chocolate (72% cocoa), chopped into very small pieces

2 oz/56 g semisweet chocolate (54% cocoa), chopped into very small pieces

¾ cup 35% whipping cream

2 tbsp golden honey

pinch of salt

For the coating:

⅔ cup unsweetened cocoa powder

4 oz/113 g bittersweet chocolate (72% cocoa), very finely chopped

Place 6 ounces of chopped bittersweet chocolate and 2 ounces of chopped dark chocolate in a medium heatproof bowl and set aside.

In a small saucepan over medium-low heat, combine cream, honey and salt. Bring the mixture to a very gentle boil, reduce heat and simmer for 30 seconds (simmering the cream will help to extend the shelf life of the truffles). Watch carefully so that the mixture doesn't foam up or boil over. Remove from heat and set it aside for 30-40 seconds to let the bubbles settle before pouring it over the chopped chocolate. This resting time is crucial as it lets the cream cool slightly so that its heat intensity isn't so high that the shock of the temperature difference causes the fat in the chocolate to separate. Let stand without stirring for 5 minutes to allow the heat from the cream to gently melt the chocolate.

Using a wooden spoon or rubber spatula, gently stir mixture in one direction starting from the center and working your way toward the edges until it is smooth and glossy. Pour into a shallow 8 x 8-inch glass baking dish and let cool to room temperature, about 1 to 2 hours. Refrigerate until firm, at least 3 hours.

Line a baking sheet with parchment or wax paper. Use a melon baller or small spoon to scoop teaspoons of ganache, quickly form them with your fingers to round off the edges and then roll them between your palms to form roughly-shaped balls. Place balls on prepared baking sheet and freeze until very firm, about 15 minutes.

Place cocoa powder in a small bowl and set aside.

Place 4 ounces of chopped bittersweet chocolate in a medium heatproof bowl set over a pot with ½-inch of barely simmering water. Stir constantly with a rubber spatula until two-thirds of the chocolate is melted and there are still some solid pieces left. Remove from heat and continue stirring – the residual heat will continue to melt the solid pieces. Return bowl to the pot briefly to melt any stubborn pieces if necessary. The key here is to not let the temperature of the chocolate rise above 90°F or else it will lose its temper and won't set up with a crisp snap.

Now, be prepared to get messy. This is the best way to make truffles and by the end you will probably be covered in chocolate (do a little happy dance!). Spread some melted bittersweet chocolate on your clean left hand and quickly roll a chilled truffle in it, turning it to coat using your right index finger and thumb (the idea is to create a thin coating of chocolate). Immediately place it in the bowl with cocoa powder and roll it around until evenly coated. Repeat with remaining truffles.

Store truffles in an airtight container and refrigerate until ready to serve. Leave them at room temperature for about 10 minutes before serving to let the ganache become silky smooth.

Homemade Dark Chocolate Almond Granola

Makes about 5 cups

Ingredients:

3 cups large flake old-fashioned rolled oats

½ cup whole almonds, coarsely chopped

⅓ cup sweetened flaked coconut

⅓ cup sunflower seeds

2 large egg whites

1 tsp ground cinnamon

¼ tsp fine sea salt

4 tbsp packed dark brown sugar

⅓ cup amber honey

1 tbsp extra virgin olive oil

½ cup sultana raisins

3 oz/85 g bittersweet chocolate (72% cocoa), coarsely chopped

Preheat your oven to 300°F. Line a large baking sheet with parchment paper and set aside.

In a medium bowl, stir together oats, chopped almonds, coconut and sunflower seeds; set aside.

In a large bowl, whisk together egg whites, cinnamon, salt and brown sugar just until sugar is dissolved. Whisk in honey and olive oil until well blended. Add oat mixture and stir until well combined and the oats are completely coated with egg white mixture.

Spread granola in an even layer on the prepared baking sheet and bake until golden, 25-30 minutes, stirring with a wooden spoon every 5-7 minutes to ensure that it bakes evenly and does not burn around the edges.

Transfer pan to a wire rack and let cool completely. Transfer granola to a large bowl and stir in raisins and chocolate. Store in an air tight container or in mason jars.

Enjoy this as a snack at any time of day on its own or with plain yogurt or milk!

Zesty Lemon Curd

Makes about 1 cup

Ingredients:

⅓ cup granulated sugar

1 ½ tsp finely grated lemon zest

2 large eggs

1 large egg yolk

pinch of salt

⅓ cup freshly squeezed lemon juice

2 tbsp unsalted butter

Combine sugar and lemon zest in a mortar and pound with a pestle until the sugar is fragrant and slightly yellow in colour. You can also pile it onto a clean cutting board or in a small bowl and use the back of a spoon or your fingertips to rub the zest into the sugar. This will coat the sugar crystals with fragrant oils from the lemon peel, adding a whole new dimension of intense lemon flavour to this curd. The sugar also acts as an abrasive to help break down the zest so that you don't end up with large pieces of it that would distract from the silky smooth texture of this curd.

In a medium heatproof bowl, whisk together eggs, egg yolk, lemon sugar, salt and lemon juice until smooth. Set the bowl over a pot with ½-inch of simmering water (or use a double boiler). Whisk gently over the heat for 2 minutes.

Switch to a silicone spatula and stir constantly until thick enough to coat the back of a spoon (using a spatula prevents the incorporation of many tiny air bubbles that whisking would otherwise cause). This takes another 5-10 minutes. The mixture will begin to smell very citrusy and the consistency should be similar to low-fat yogurt or pudding.

Remove lemon curd from heat and pass through a fine mesh sieve and into a medium bowl to remove any pieces of cooked egg (this happens to the best of us). Immediately stir in butter until completely melted and smooth.

Transfer curd to a small jar or airtight container, place a piece of plastic wrap directly in contact with the surface, and refrigerate until thoroughly chilled. This curd will last for about a week in the refrigerator.

✪ The Power of Eggs:

Lemon curd is a type of stirred custard made from a cooked, thickened egg mixture. In the presence of heat and acid, egg proteins begin to bond to one another, transforming the liquid mixture into a smooth thick mass. In order to do this, gentle cooking is necessary to minimize the possibility of curdling. The acid from lemon juice helps to transform the ultimate structure of proteins (a process called denaturation) which unravels their natural folded structure so that their side chains are exposed to react with the surrounding environment. When this happens, the proteins begin to form bonds with each other (coagulate) in a gentle way to form a continuous network of proteins with water held between them. This is what creates the thick and silky texture of citrus curd. Over-cooking will cause proteins to bond too tightly, squeezing water out from between them and giving them a rubbery, lumpy texture. For insurance, indirect heat via steam is used to moderate the cooking temperature since boiling water cannot exceed 100°C. This recipe uses whole eggs to add firmness for a thick, spoonable texture, while the extra yolk adds creaminess and tenderness.

Classic Homemade Strawberry Jam

Makes about 1 ¼ cups

Before you start this recipe, I have to warn you about skimping on the sugar – don't do it! Added sugar not only serves to preserve the jam and provide you with lovely toast for the next few weeks, but it is crucial to help the pectin molecules rearrange themselves into a gel structure. It must be present at a specific concentration in order to produce the right consistency. The recipe is short and simple, and the results will be sweet as long as you follow these basic principles. So, please don't try to test the limits of this recipe. If not for me, do it for your peanut butter.

Ingredients:

1 lb (16 oz/454 g) rinsed, hulled and quartered strawberries

6 oz/170 g granulated sugar (about ¾ cup)

1 oz/30 ml freshly squeezed lemon juice (about 2 tbsp)

To make jam, pectin must first be extracted from the fruit's cell walls. So, place cut strawberries in a large 4-quart saucepan over medium-low heat. Cover and cook gently until they begin to release their juices and look soupy, about 5-7 minutes. This will extract pectin from the fruit into the juices released during heating.

Uncover the pot and stir in sugar. This re-builds the pectin structure to bind water between pectin molecules in order to bring them closer to one another.

Increase heat to medium and bring mixture to a boil. Reduce heat to medium-low and simmer until thickened, 10-15 minutes.

Use a potato masher to break down the large pieces of fruit, leaving it a bit chunky. Stir in lemon juice and continue to boil gently, stirring often, until very thick and syrupy, about 15-20 minutes. This evaporates some of the moisture and concentrates pectin.

The mixture is thick enough when you are able to see the bottom of the pan as you stir and it sets up quickly when dripped onto a very cold plate (i.e. a plate that has been left in the freezer for 5 minutes). Alternatively, the jam is ready once the boiling temperature registers 215-220°F on a candy thermometer.

Pour it out into a sterilized mason jar, seal it and let cool at room temperature before refrigerating. This jam must be stored in the fridge but it lasts for weeks, if you can manage to keep it that long.

✪ Vanilla Sugar:

To add a subtle vanilla flavour to this jam, use vanilla sugar in place of the regular granulated sugar in the recipe. To make it, start with about 3 cups of sugar. Slice down the length of a vanilla bean using a sharp paring knife, scrape out the seeds and place them into an airtight container with the sugar. Bury scraped bean in the sugar and seal tightly. Let sit for 1-2 weeks. Use in recipes as desired in place of regular, granulated sugar. Continue to add your spent vanilla beans to the container.

Gingerbread Truffles

Makes about 36 truffles

For the ganache:

7 oz/200 g bittersweet chocolate (72% cocoa), chopped into very small pieces

⅔ cup 35% whipping cream

10 whole cloves

1 tsp finely grated fresh ginger

3-inch piece cinnamon stick, broken into pieces

⅛ tsp freshly grated nutmeg

pinch of salt

1 tbsp fancy molasses ❷

For coating:

8 oz/227 g pure white chocolate, very finely chopped

1 oz/28 g pure milk chocolate

To make the ganache, place chopped bittersweet chocolate in a medium heatproof bowl and set aside.

In a small saucepan over medium-low heat, combine cream, cloves, ginger, cinnamon, nutmeg and salt and bring it to a simmer. Remove from heat, cover and let steep for 20 minutes.

Stir molasses into cream mixture and reheat it over medium heat until it just about comes to a boil. Immediately pour it through a sieve and over chopped chocolate. Press against the sieve to squeeze all the cream through the ginger fibers. Move the chocolate around gently with a spatula just to bring majority of the pieces in contact with the hot cream. Let stand without stirring for 3 minutes. Use a whisk to gently stir the mixture from the center until it begins to look glossy.

Finish stirring with a rubber spatula until evenly blended and smooth. If not all of the chocolate has melted, you can heat the ganache gently by placing the bowl over a pot with ½-inch of barely simmering water. Stir occasionally until there are no lumps. Let cool for 1-2 hours at room temperature and then refrigerate until firm, at least 3 hours.

Line two baking sheets with parchment or wax paper. Use a melon baller or spoon to scoop teaspoons of ganache and roll between palms to form roughly-shaped balls. Place balls on one of the prepared trays and freeze until firm, about 20 minutes.

Place white chocolate in a heatproof bowl set over a pot with ½-inch of barely simmering water. Stir constantly until almost completely melted (some small pieces of solid chocolate should remain). Remove bowl from over pot and stir until smooth, allowing the residual heat to melt the rest of the chocolate. Do not over-heat the chocolate (it should not reach over 88°F).

To begin dipping, retrieve ganache balls from freezer. Balance one on a fork and submerge in melted chocolate, letting excess drip off and scraping the bottom of the fork against the rim of the bowl if necessary. Gently slide the truffle off of fork and onto the second lined baking tray using a toothpick. Continue like so, coating remaining balls, and re-warming chocolate periodically for a few seconds over hot water as necessary if chocolate becomes too thick. Let truffles set at room temperature until hardened, about 1 hour. I like to work in 3 batches, freezing the ganache balls for about 5 minutes and reheating the chocolate just barely between batches.

Let truffles stand until chocolate coating has set. If your kitchen is warm, you can place them in the fridge. Once hardened, gently melt milk chocolate in a small bowl set over a pot with ½-inch of simmering water (or do it very carefully in the microwave, stopping to stir every 15 seconds). Fill a small resealable plastic bag with melted chocolate and push it into one of the corners. Snip the tip off of that corner and drizzle a thin stream of chocolate over each truffle in a zig-zag pattern.

Once set, store truffles in an airtight container in the fridge but serve at room temperature.

❷ For a stronger and more robust gingerbread flavour, substitute the fancy molasses with 2 teaspoons of dark cooking molasses, which is less sweet and has a more pronounced bitter licorice taste. Cooking molasses is essentially a blend of fancy and blackstrap molasses.

Toffee Sauce

Makes about 2 cups

Ingredients:

1 cup turbinado sugar

4 tbsp light corn syrup

6 tbsp unsalted butter

1 ½ cups 35% whipping cream, divided

¼ tsp salt

In a heavy-bottomed 2-quart saucepan with high sides, combine sugar, corn syrup, butter and half of the cream over medium-low heat. Stir constantly until sugar is dissolved and mixture is smooth.

Increase heat to medium, bring mixture to a boil and cook until it reaches 275°F (135°C), stirring very frequently. Remove pan from heat and very carefully and gradually stir in remaining cream until well incorporated and smooth. The mixture will bubble up violently, so wear an oven mitt to protect your hand from the steam.

Immediately pour toffee sauce into a heat-proof bowl and let cool completely at room temperature. Store in the refrigerator in an airtight container or mason jar. Re-warm in a hot water bath or in the microwave on 50% power before serving over ice cream or drizzling over apple pie.

Salted Caramel Sauce

Makes about 1 cup

TIP: if your boiling sugar looks chunky and granular, crank up the heat to break it down, but keep a close eye on it. It will liquify quickly and change from clear and colourless to dark amber in seconds.

Ingredients:

1 cup granulated sugar

1 tbsp light corn syrup

3 tbsp water

½ cup 35% whipping cream

½ tsp pure vanilla extract

½ tsp fine sea salt

In a small 1 or 2-quart saucepan, pour sugar in a single layer. Add corn syrup and drizzle water around the inside edges of the pan. Bring this mixture to a boil over medium heat without stirring. Continue to cook until caramel is a rich dark amber color, 15-20 minutes, swirling pan to colour evenly. The mixture will change from granular-looking to a liquid syrup. Wash down the sides of pan with a pastry brush dipped in water to dissolve any crystals that may form.

When caramel is almost ready, the large bubbles will subside and a golden foam will appear at the surface around the edges. Remove caramel from heat and very carefully stir in cream until smooth. Be cautious as the caramel will bubble up violently and create lots of steam. Pour caramel into a heat-proof bowl or volumetric measuring cup and stir in vanilla extract and salt. Allow to cool to room temperature before storing in the refrigerator in an airtight container.

Mexican Hot Chocolate Truffles

Makes about 30 truffles

For the ganache:

6 oz/170 g dark chocolate (64% cocoa), chopped into very small pieces

½ cup plus 2 tbsp 35% whipping cream

1 tsp light corn syrup

¼ tsp ground cinnamon

5 whole allspice

5 whole cloves

1 small "bird's eye" or Thai chili,❷ seeds removed

½ tsp pure Mexican vanilla extract

For the coating:

6 oz/170 g dark couverture chocolate (64% cocoa), very finely chopped

To make the ganache, place 6 ounces of dark chocolate in a medium heatproof bowl and set aside.

In a small saucepan over medium-low heat, combine cream, corn syrup, cinnamon, allspice, cloves and seeded chili. Heat the mixture gently, stirring frequently, until it just about comes to a boil and bubbles begin to form at the surface. Remove from heat and immediately pour it through a very fine mesh sieve and over chopped chocolate. A very fine mesh will strain out most of the cinnamon particles. Discard chili and spices. Shake the bowl gently to let all of the chocolate pieces come in contact with hot cream. Let stand undisturbed for 4-5 minutes at room temperature.

Gently stir the mixture in one direction starting from the center and working your way toward the edges until smooth and glossy. Start with a whisk and finish stirring with a spatula. Stir in vanilla extract until combined. Let cool at room temperature for 1-2 hours and then refrigerate until firm, about 3 hours.

Line two baking sheets with parchment or wax paper and set one aside. Using a melon baller or small spoon, scoop teaspoons of ganache and roll between palms to form roughly-shaped balls. Place balls on one of the prepared baking sheets and freeze until firm, about 20 minutes.

Place 5 oz of finely chopped couverture chocolate in a heat-proof bowl set over a pot with ½-inch of barely simmering water. Stir constantly until almost completely melted (some small pieces of solid chocolate should remain). Remove bowl from over pot and stir until smooth, allowing the residual heat to melt the rest of the chocolate. Add remaining ounce of chopped chocolate and stir until smooth and melted, placing bowl over hot water for a few seconds if necessary. Do not over-heat the chocolate (it should not exceed 90°F).

To begin dipping, retrieve ganache balls from freezer. Balance one on a fork and submerge in melted chocolate, letting excess drip off and scraping the bottom of the fork against rim of bowl if necessary. Gently slide the truffle off of fork and onto the clean lined baking tray using a toothpick. Continue like so, coating ganache balls and re-warming chocolate periodically for a few seconds over hot water as necessary if chocolate becomes too thick. Let truffles set at room temperature until hardened, about 1 hour. I like to work in 3 batches, freezing the ganache balls for about 5 minutes and reheating the chocolate just barely between batches.

Store these truffles in an airtight container in the refrigerator. They are incredibly smooth at room temperature but still soft straight from the fridge.

❷ You can find bird's eye chilis at Asian grocery stores, but if you still have no luck then you can substitute with a generous ⅛ tsp of dried red chili flakes. To prepare the chili, wear rubber gloves and slice it in half lengthwise with a paring knife. Scrape down the length of each half to remove seeds. If you don't have rubber gloves, be sure to wash your hands thoroughly after handling the chili.

✪ NOTE: If you haven't got time for dipping and chocolate-coating, another lovely option is to coat these truffles in a spiced cocoa mixture. Sift together ⅓ cup of unsweetened cocoa powder with ½ teaspoon of ground cinnamon in a medium bowl and roll each ball of ganache into it until evenly coated. In this case, omit the corn syrup in the recipe to create a firmer ganache.

Creamy Old-Fashioned Chocolate Fudge

Makes about 60 pieces

Ingredients:

1 ½ cups granulated sugar

½ cup packed light brown sugar

3 oz/85 g bittersweet chocolate (72% cocoa), very finely chopped

1 tbsp light corn syrup

¼ tsp salt

¾ cup 10% half & half cream

2 tbsp unsalted butter, cut into pieces and at room temperature

½ tsp pure vanilla extract

Line an 8 x 8-inch baking pan with aluminum foil leaving a 1-inch overhang on all sides and lightly grease it with butter.

Combine both sugars, chopped chocolate, corn syrup, salt and cream in a heavy-bottomed 2-quart saucepan with high sides over low heat and cook, stirring constantly, until sugar dissolves and chocolate is completely melted, about 5 minutes. Increase heat to medium and bring mixture to a boil. Attach a candy thermometer to the side of the pan and continue to cook, without stirring, until mixture registers 234°F, washing down sides of pan with a wet pastry brush to prevent sugar crystals from forming as necessary. The total cooking time will be about 15 minutes.

Immediately remove pot from heat, transfer the thermometer to the heatproof bowl of a stand mixer and pour the hot fudge mixture into the bowl without scraping the bottom of the pot. Add butter and vanilla extract. Do not stir. Let mixture cool in bowl, undisturbed, until it registers 110°F, about 2 hours.

Once cool, remove candy thermometer, attach bowl to the mixer fitted with the flat beater/paddle attachment and beat on medium speed, stopping occasionally, until fudge begins to hold its shape when dropped from a spoon and starts to lose its sheen, about 5 minutes. The mixture will continue to appear glossy as it is beating, so make sure to stop the mixture and check for doneness after the first 3 minutes.

Quickly turn out fudge into prepared pan and spread and press it into the corners before it sets completely. Let stand until firm, about 1 hour before cutting into 1-inch squares.

Alternatively, you can make this by hand with a lot of elbow grease. To do this, once the mixture reaches 234°F, remove from heat, let mixture settle until bubbles subside and then add butter and vanilla extract. Do not stir. Let mixture cool in pot, undisturbed, until the temperature registers 110°F, about 2 hours. Once fudge is cooled, quickly remove the candy thermometer and beat vigorously (nonstop!) with a wooden spoon until fudge becomes very viscous and begins to lose its sheen or turn matte, about 5-10 minutes. Quickly turn out fudge into prepared pan and spread it into the corners. Let cool completely until firm, about 1 hour before cutting into 1-inch squares.

Pumpkin Spice Caramels

Makes about 90 caramels

Ingredients:

½ tsp ground cinnamon

¼ tsp ground ginger

⅛ tsp ground nutmeg

⅛ tsp ground clove

heaped ¼ tsp salt

1 cup 35% whipping cream

1 cup granulated sugar

½ cup golden corn syrup

2 tsp dark cooking molasses

2 tbsp unsalted butter, cut into small pieces

¼ tsp pure vanilla extract

Line an 8 x 8-inch baking pan with parchment paper, leaving a 2-inch overhang on all sides and very lightly butter the parchment; set aside.

In a very small bowl, combine ground cinnamon, ground ginger, ground nutmeg, ground clove and salt; set aside.

In a deep, heavy-bottomed 2-quart saucepan with high sides, combine cream, sugar, corn syrup and molasses over low heat and stir with a silicone spatula or wooden spoon until sugar is dissolved, about 2 minutes. Clip a candy thermometer to the side of the pan. Increase heat to medium and bring the mixture to a boil, stirring constantly. Continue to cook, stirring frequently, until mixture reaches 235°F. Reduce heat to medium-low and cook until mixture reaches 245°F (firm-ball stage), about 20 minutes total cooking time.

Remove pan from heat and quickly stir in butter, vanilla extract and spice mixture. Immediately pour into prepared pan, without scraping bottom of pot, and gently spread it into the corners if necessary.

Let stand at room temperature, undisturbed and uncovered, until completely cooled, about 4 hours.

Very lightly grease a large cutting board with butter (make sure it's one that you haven't cut meat, fish or onions on – you get my point). Pull up parchment to unmold caramel, and invert onto the cutting board. Peel off parchment. Using a lightly greased sharp knife, cut caramel into ½-inch strips. Cut strips into 1-inch pieces and immediately wrap each caramel in little squares of cellophane or waxed paper.

Caramels can be stored in an airtight container in a cool, dry place for up to 1 month.

Caramel Crème Caramel

Makes 6 servings

For the caramel:

⅔ cup granulated sugar

2 tbsp water

½ tsp distilled white vinegar

For the custard:

⅓ cup plus 1 tbsp granulated sugar, divided

1 tbsp water

½ cup 35% whipping cream

1 ½ cups 2% milk

3 large eggs

1 large egg yolk

½ tsp pure vanilla extract

Preheat your oven to 325°F. Have ready six 3-inch round (½ cup capacity) ramekins.

To make the caramel, pour sugar in an even layer in the bottom of a small 1-quart saucepan. Drizzle water and vinegar around the inner edges of the pan. Place pot over medium heat and cook until sugar is dissolved and mixture changes into clear syrup. Decrease heat to medium and continue to cook until mixture turns golden amber, swirling pan periodically for even colouring. Do not stir the mixture or the sugar will crystallize. Immediately and carefully pour liquid caramel into the bottom of ramekins, dividing it equally and swirling ramekins to coat the bottoms evenly; set aside until the caramel has cooled and hardened completely.

To make the custard, first make caramel again by pouring ⅓ cup of sugar in an even layer in the bottom of a 2-quart metal saucepan and drizzle water over top. Place pot over medium-high heat and cook until sugar is dissolved and the mixture changes into clear syrup. Reduce heat slightly and continue to cook until mixture turns amber, swirling pan periodically for even colouring. Remove pot from heat and carefully and gradually pour in heavy cream while whisking constantly until smooth. Stir in milk and return pot to stove over medium-low heat, stirring constantly, until it begins to steam and small bubbles form around the edges; set aside.

Meanwhile, in a medium bowl, whisk together eggs, egg yolk and remaining 1 tablespoon of sugar until well blended. Add ¼ cup of hot milk mixture and whisk until smooth. Gradually add another ¼ cup while whisking constantly. This slow addition of hot milk to cool eggs is called "tempering" as it brings the egg temperature up slowly to prevent curdling the proteins. Switch to a rubber spatula (to prevent foaming through excessive air incorporation) and add remaining milk while stirring constantly. Stir in vanilla extract. Pour the mixture through a fine mesh sieve and into a large measuring cup or clean bowl and pour or ladle it into caramel-lined ramekins.

Transfer ramekins to a deep glass baking dish. Add enough hot water to come halfway up the sides of the ramekins. Bake until the edges are set and the center is just slightly wobbly, 25-30 minutes. A knife should come out clean when inserted into the centers. Transfer baking dish to a wire rack and let ramekins cool completely in the water bath. Once cooled, refrigerate until completely set, about 2 hours. To serve, run a sharp knife around the outside edges of the crème caramel. Place a plate serving-side-down over the ramekin and invert so that the bottom of the ramekin is facing up. Gently remove the ramekin, giggling it slightly if necessary to let the custard come loose.

✿ WATER BATHS: An important aspect about making custard is to maintain a steady, even cooking environment to prevent the delicate egg proteins from cooking too quickly and curdling. Baking crème caramel in a water bath prevents the custard from drying out, keeps the temperature around the ramekins uniform and also moderates the heat intensity since the temperature of water cannot exceed its boiling point (212°F).

✿ SPUN BURNT SUGAR GARNISH: To create the burnt sugar garnish, make the same caramel that you used for the hard candy layer that forms the top of the crème caramel. When ready, use a spoon to drizzle the amber liquid syrup, swirling it around in mounds over a silicone baking mat to form little nests. Let them cool completely until hardened and transfer to crème caramels immediately before serving.

Salted Honey Butter Caramels

Makes about 90 caramels

....

These caramels are soft, chewy, sweet and salty, and they melt in your mouth like nobody's business. They won't stick to the roof of your mouth, glue your gums together or pull out any fillings, and they are not at all cloying thanks to the nice balance of butter and salt that coats the palate so gently. They definitely taste like caramel but also distinctively like honey, which makes them feel particularly homemade.

....

Ingredients:

1 cup 35% whipping cream

⅓ cup golden honey

2 tbsp light corn syrup

1 cup granulated sugar

2 ½ tbsp unsalted butter, divided

½ tsp pure vanilla extract

heaped ¼ tsp table salt

1 tsp flaked sea salt (such as Maldon)

Line an 8 x 8-inch metal baking pan with parchment paper, leaving a 2-inch overhang on each side and very lightly butter the parchment; set aside.

Combine cream, honey, corn syrup, sugar and 1 tablespoon of butter in a heavy-bottomed 2 or 3-quart saucepan with high sides over medium-low heat. Stir constantly until sugar is dissolved. Increase heat slightly, bring the mixture to a boil and clip a candy thermometer to side of pan. Continue to cook over medium to medium-low heat, stirring very frequently, until mixture reaches 235°F. Reduce heat slightly and continue to cook while stirring constantly until it reaches 246-248°F, about 15-20 minutes total cooking time. Stay close as the syrup will cook very quickly at this point – if the phone rings, don't answer it!

Remove pan from heat, and quickly stir in remaining 1 ½ tablespoons of butter, vanilla extract and table salt until melted and smooth. Immediately pour into prepared pan, without scraping the bottom of the pot. Let stand at room temperature without moving until completely cooled and set, about 3-4 hours. After 10 minutes of cooling, sprinkle sea salt evenly over the top.

Pull up parchment to unmold cooled caramel, and invert onto a clean work surface. Peel off parchment. Use kitchen shears to cut the slab into ½-inch strips and then cut each strip into 1-inch pieces. The caramel should be nice and soft, and somewhat pliable so that it is easy to cut. Wrap each one in a little square of cellophane or waxed paper – you need to wrap them as soon as you cut them because they will begin to spread and lose their shape.

Caramels can be stored in an airtight container, in a cool dry place for up to 3 weeks. Or, store them in the fridge to keep them even longer.

Cool Peppermint Patties

Makes 25-30 patties

Ingredients:

12 oz/340 g sifted icing sugar (about 3 cups), plus extra for dusting

¼ tsp salt

2 tbsp light corn syrup

1 tbsp unsalted butter, at room temperature

1 ½ tbsp cold water

½ tsp pure peppermint extract

10 oz/284 g dark couverture chocolate (64% cocoa), very finely chopped

In a large bowl, combine icing sugar, salt, corn syrup, butter, water and peppermint extract. Beat on low speed using an electric hand mixer until it resembles a coarse crumbly mixture. Increase speed to medium and beat until mixture comes together to form a mass.

Knead the mixture a few times in the bowl until it is smooth, soft and pliable but not sticky. Add additional water, drops at a time, if necessary to form a pliable dough but be very cautious as it can become sticky very quickly. You know it is the right consistency when it feels dry but is still soft and has a life of its own when left to rest (it moves and spreads slightly when left on the countertop) – this means it will have a silky and creamy texture. It should not be too dry or cracked. Turn it out onto a work surface dusted lightly with icing sugar and roll the dough into a 9-inch long log. Wrap it well in plastic wrap and then in parchment or wax paper, place it on a flat baking tray and refrigerate until firm, about 2 hours. Rotate it every 10 minutes for the first hour so that it keeps its rounded shape.

Line two large baking trays with parchment or wax paper. Using your palms, roll the chilled log on your work surface to round off the edges and slice it into about ¼-inch-thick coins and lay them flat on one of the prepared trays. Place tray in the freezer while you melt the chocolate (at least 15 minutes).

Place 8 oz of finely chopped chocolate in a heatproof bowl set over a pot with ½-inch of barely simmering water. Stir chocolate constantly until almost all melted but some pieces of solid chocolate remain. Remove bowl from heat and stir until chocolate is completely melted and smooth. Add remaining chocolate and stir constantly until it is melts completely, placing the bowl over simmering water for a few seconds if necessary. Do not over-heat the chocolate (it should not exceed 90°F).

To begin dipping, retrieve peppermint disks from freezer. Balance one on a fork and submerge in melted chocolate, letting excess drip off and scraping the bottom of the fork against rim of bowl if necessary. Gently slide the patty off of the fork and onto the clean lined baking tray using a toothpick. Continue like so, coating remaining discs, and re-warming chocolate periodically for a few seconds over hot water as necessary if chocolate becomes too thick.

Let chocolate set at room temperature until hardened, about 1 hour. I like to work in 3 batches, freezing the patties for about 5 minutes and reheating the chocolate just barely between batches.

Sweet & Salty Trail Mix Granola Bars

Makes 24 bars

Ingredients:

1 tsp unsalted butter for greasing pan

1 ½ cups puffed rice cereal

1 ½ cups old-fashioned large flake rolled oats

¾ cup toasted almonds

½ cup unsalted roasted peanuts

½ cup dried cranberries

½ cup sultana raisins

¼ cup sunflower seeds

¼ cup roasted pumpkin seeds

½ cup smooth peanut butter

⅓ cup golden corn syrup

¼ cup amber honey

¼ cup packed light brown sugar

1 tsp water

2 tbsp flax seeds

½ tsp fine sea salt

½ cup best quality semisweet chocolate chips, plus extra for topping

Line a 12x9-inch baking sheet with aluminum foil and butter it lightly. I know, 12x9 is an odd size, but I find that these granola bars are the perfect thickness in this size pan. You can use a 13x9-inch pan, but leave 1-inch of empty space along the length when pressing the mixture into it.

In a large bowl, gently toss together puffed rice cereal, rolled oats, toasted almonds, roasted peanuts, dried cranberries, raisins, sunflower seeds and pumpkin seeds; set aside.

In a small 1-quart saucepan, combine peanut butter, corn syrup, honey, brown sugar and water over medium-low heat. Stir constantly until the sugar is completely dissolved and the mixture is smooth and pourable, about 5 minutes. Increase heat to medium and bring the mixture to a boil, stirring constantly as it can burn easily. Cook at a boil for 15 seconds. Remove pan from heat and set aside to cool slightly for 30 seconds before pouring it into the large bowl with the oat/nut mixture.

Working quickly, fold all of the ingredients together using a wide silicone spatula until it forms a sticky mass (be careful because it will be hot). All of the ingredients should be coated with the peanut butter mixture.

Sprinkle in flax seeds and sea salt and fold it in until evenly incorporated. Let mixture cool for a minute or two before folding in chocolate chips, which will melt slightly with the heat of the peanut butter mixture so that chocolate coats the entire batch (amazing!).

Turn the mixture out into the foil-lined pan. Press it down evenly and push it into the corners. Sprinkle extra chocolate chips over top, if desired, and press them in gently.

Place pan in the fridge until the granola slab is completely set, about 1 hour. Cut into 24 (1 ½ x 3-inch) bars. Store them in the refrigerator in an airtight container between pieces of parchment or waxed paper.

Soft & Chewy Cocoa Caramels

Makes about 90 caramels

Ingredients:

1 ½ cups granulated sugar

1 ½ oz/42 g unsweetened cocoa powder (about ½ cup)

1 ½ cups evaporated milk

¾ cup golden corn syrup

3 tbsp cold unsalted butter, cut into pieces

½ tsp pure vanilla extract

¼ tsp salt

fine sea salt for sprinkling

Line an 8 x 8-inch baking pan with parchment paper, leaving a 2-inch overhang on each side and very lightly butter the parchment; set aside.

In a heavy-bottomed 5-quart metal saucepan with high sides, whisk together sugar and cocoa powder until there are no lumps. Whisk in evaporated milk and corn syrup until well combined. Place pan over low heat and cook until sugar dissolves, whisking constantly.

Add 1 tablespoon of butter, increase heat to medium-low and gently bring mixture to a boil, stirring constantly with a silicone spatula. Be very patient because once the mixture boils, it will boil vigorously and it will bubble up all the way to the rim of the pan. Be sure to maintain a medium-low heat or it will boil over and it can be dangerous. Since the final volume of syrup is much lower than the initial mixture, using a larger pan would mean that the candy syrup would be too shallow and the bulb of the thermometer would not be fully submerged, giving you an inaccurate reading. So, let your patience shine and work carefully.

Continue to cook, stirring frequently, until the mixture reaches 230°F. Reduce heat to low and cook until mixture registers 244°F (firm-ball stage). If using an alcohol thermometer, the glass bulb should not be in direct contact with the bottom of the saucepan. Be sure to stir constantly as this mixture tends to burn easily at this point. This will require 25-30 minutes total cooking time.

Remove pan from heat and quickly stir in remaining 2 tablespoons of butter, vanilla extract and salt until well blended. Immediately pour into your prepared pan, without scraping the bottom of the pot. Let stand at room temperature, undisturbed and uncovered, until completely cooled, about 4 hours.

Pull up parchment to unmold caramel and invert onto a clean cutting board. Peel off parchment. Lightly butter the blades of a pair of kitchen shears and cut caramel into ½-inch strips. Snip strips into 1-inch pieces and sprinkle each with sea salt. Wrap each caramel in a little square of waxed paper (this takes forever, but it's worth it for the candy!).

Caramels can be stored in an airtight container in a cool, dry place for up to 1 month.

....

✪ Taking Temperature Readings:

As more water evaporates and the mixture thickens, it reduces quite a bit to the point where the bulb of your candy thermometer is no longer submerged, giving you an inaccurate reading. Mine sometimes registers 10 degrees lower than it actually is if the volume in the pan is too little. Because of this, you can easily burn or overcook your candy, leaving you with hard crunchy bits of crystallized sugar in your caramels. To prevent this I like to use a digital instant read thermometer, which you can find at your local hardware store. They are inexpensive, but just be careful because your hand will have to be rather close to the mixture as you take readings.

Also, when working in small batches like this, it is common to get hotspots as some areas may be more concentrated than others (i.e. are hotter than others), so make sure you stir the mixture constantly and efficiently, getting into all of the corners and crevices of the pan. Keep the thermometer moving as well so that you get an average temperature of the whole batch.

Deep Dark
Hot Fudge Sauce

Makes about 1 cup

Ingredients:

½ cup 35% whipping cream

2 tbsp water

3 tbsp golden corn syrup

2 tbsp packed dark brown sugar

⅛ tsp salt

4 oz/113 g bittersweet chocolate (72% cocoa), finely chopped

½ tsp pure vanilla extract

In a 1-quart heavy-bottomed metal saucepan, combine cream, water, corn syrup, brown sugar and salt over medium-low heat. Bring it to a simmer, stirring frequently, until sugar is dissolved. Remove pan from heat and add chopped chocolate. Let mixture stand, undisturbed, for 2 minutes and then stir until chocolate is completely melted and the mixture is smooth.

Return pan to the stove and bring the chocolate sauce to a gentle boil over medium-low heat, stirring constantly. When it reaches a boil, continue to cook for 3 minutes. Make sure to stir constantly and get into the bottom edges of the pan as the chocolate can burn easily. The mixture will be thick and luscious. You'll notice that the bitter, roasted notes will become more pronounced after the sauce has cooked, making it taste even more chocolatey.

Remove pan from heat and stir in vanilla extract. Let cool about 15 minutes and serve warm or pour it immediately into a sterilized heatproof mason jar, seal tightly and let it cool completely at room temperature. Store it in the refrigerator for up to 2 weeks. Reheat very, very gently in a hot water bath before serving over your favourite vanilla ice cream.

Dark Chocolate-Covered Coconut Candy Bars

Makes about 20 small bars

Ingredients:

8 oz/227 g sweetened shredded coconut
(about 2 ¼ cups), divided

2 oz/56 g pure white chocolate, finely chopped

⅔ cup sweetened condensed milk

2 tsp light corn syrup

½ tsp pure vanilla extract

hefty pinch of salt

8 oz/227 g dark couverture chocolate (64% cocoa),
very finely chopped

Place 7 ounces of sweetened shredded coconut in a food processor and pulse just enough to break it down slightly. It should resemble coarse crumbs. Do not over-process because the mixture will become too fine and the fat in the coconut can cause it to clump up. Combine this coconut with the remaining 1 ounce of shredded coconut in a small bowl and set it aside. This will provide some texture contrast.

In a small saucepan over low heat, stir together chopped white chocolate, sweetened condensed milk, corn syrup, vanilla and salt until chocolate is completely melted and the mixture is smooth, about 5 minutes. Stir in coconut until well combined. Cover with plastic wrap and refrigerate mixture until rather firm, at least 2 hours or overnight.

Line two baking sheets with parchment paper and set one aside for later. Remove the coconut mixture from the fridge and use clean hands to shape tablespoons of this mixture into 1 to 1 ½-inch cylinders or logs. It will be sticky but still manageable. Resist the urge to add more coconut because it will dry out the filling and make it crumbly over time. Flatten each log slightly and place them on prepared baking sheet. Continue with remaining coconut mixture. Place baking sheet in the fridge or freezer until coconut candies are very firm. This will help the tempered chocolate coating set almost instantly after dipping.

Place 6 oz of dark couverture chocolate in a heatproof bowl set over a pot with ½-inch of barely simmering water. Stir constantly until almost completely melted (some small pieces of solid chocolate should remain). Remove bowl from over pot and stir until completely melted. Add remaining chocolate and stir until smooth and melted, placing bowl over hot water for a few seconds if necessary. Do not let the chocolate temperature rise above 90°F, or else it will lose its temper and won't set up with a shiny finish and crisp snap.

Remove coconut candies from the freezer and dip each one in melted chocolate, using a fork to roll it until completely coated. Use the fork to lift the coated candy out of the chocolate and scrape the bottom of the fork against the side of the bowl to remove excess chocolate. Use a toothpick to help slide dipped candy off of the fork and onto the other clean lined baking sheet to set. Continue like so with remaining candies. If chocolate becomes too thick, heat it gently over the pot of hot water while stirring until it becomes easier to work with. Let finished candies cool at room temperature until chocolate hardens. Store in an airtight container at room temperature.

INDEX

Made in United States
North Haven, CT
11 May 2024